Trespassing in the Garden of Eden

20 Memories

By Ed Ifkovic

Text copyright © 2013 Ed Ifkovic

All rights reserved.

ISBN 13: 9781491266083
ISBN: 1491266082

Contents

There Must Have Been Some Magic	1
Trespassing in the Garden of Eden	15
The Body of Christ	29
Are You Now Or Have You Ever Been?	41
The Starving Children of China	53
Mouth Noises	63
Cider Apples	75
The King of Junior High	87
And God Created Woman	99
Road Kill	113
"Yes, But—"	125
Piece Work	139
Dante's Hell	153
Zeke	167
Gym Dandy	183
Ghosts of North Carolina	195
The Summer Games	209
The National Press Club	221
The Missionary Position	233
Where Did Our Love Go?	245

There are all true stories, although I've changed most names and other details. It's not my intention to startle or, I suppose, infuriate souls whose lives connected with mine at some moment in time. At times I've also altered time or shifted events in the name of a different veracity. Over the years I've told and retold these stories to anyone who would listen.

There Must Have Been Some Magic

I'm not sure why it's so, but the subject of my birth used to come up at family functions. Actually I do know why—I brought it up. The reason is simple. Decades later, I still find my birth one of the great moments of mankind's history. But my ego-mad account of *what* happened that day (you'll soon see—it was wonderful, trust me) was always subverted by my mother, who changed the subject.

"Did you hear what your cousin Maria said to the grocery clerk?"

"Ma, you told us that yesterday."

"It bears repeating—"

"Ma."

Other times, she simply handed cake around. "Eat, eat. Don't listen to Eddie. You know how he is."

I didn't care—I always persisted.

Because, you see, my otherwise unremarkable birth on June 16, 1943—while bombs were falling across war-torn Europe and at home sugar was being guardedly rationed and my family huddled in the cellar during mandated blackouts—is surrounded by baffling, if a little annoying, family folklore. A hot, blistering day, my father repeatedly said when I asked him about it. So hot you didn't want to move out of the shade—or, I suppose, go into labor or go off to buy cigars. I always felt I was somehow to blame for the meteorological tenor of that day. But Dad answered most questions with dire weather recollections or forecasts, usually storm-of-the-century hurricanes breaking off Long Island or hail the size of the gallstone once removed from (and preserved in a Mason jar by) Aunt Stacia.

("Did you go to Fenway Park to see Ted Williams that year?"
"Yeah, but I think it rained all day.")

There is no definitive record of that day's events, other than the scrap of paper that notes my birth. There never will be. But according to family legend—which my mother insisted was gospel, she'd swear on a Bible—at the awesome moment in the delivery room I did something that so astounded the doctors and nurses that, in the matter of an hour, the entire maternity wing of Grace-New Haven Hospital was wildly buzzing with slack-jawed wonder and audible gasping. Little baby Eddie, much talked about. Talk about your child stars.

"What?" I begged for years.

A shrug of the shoulders. "I can't remember," my mother said. "I was drugged."

"What?" I asked my father.

He'd look up from watching the Red Sox on TV. "I wasn't paying that much attention."

How such a precipitous moment could go unrecorded (or at least gossiped about) I have no idea. Didn't they have newspapers back then? I know radio was definitely invented then. Didn't they have them in New Haven? Suffice it to say, I've since entertained every possibility. Okay—what can newborn babies do at such times? There aren't many options, truth to tell. Scream, vomit, hiccough, belch, relieve oneself ingloriously. Or: laugh hysterically (is this what I left the womb for?), grimace (same question), or give the doctor the finger? Spit into the face of the universe? Yawn, the onset of the ennui that stuck around for the rest of my life. One of my friends once noted I probably had an erection. "You always have been an exhibitionist. I still can't forget that incident in the frozen food section of Foodmart." Though another friend added: "Then, as now, who'd ever notice—or care?" But that priapic moment seems an impossibility, although more plausible *then* than these days, I must admit. I like to believe I spoke a few lines of Shakespeare, or, perhaps, a homiletic ode of my own creative composition. Something a little sardonic and world weary. After all, I was breathing for what? — less than a minute.

Perhaps I slapped the doctor after he slapped me. I'm not one to entertain such abuse easily. Nor one to suffer fools.

So I don't know. Either my mother was hiding some absurdly awful secret—a blot on the family escutcheon—or, as she said, she just couldn't remember.

So I entered life in a burst of question and unsettled dust.

But there's more to the story. The wondrous part mentioned earlier. As chance would have it, I was one of those rare creatures born with a caul, that strange membrane or fragile tissue that shrouds the baby's tender face, removed immediately to prevent smothering. I'm not sure of the statistics (I got the exquisite datum from my mother), but it's something like one in a million. And, of course, its presence is rife with old wives' blather, wide-eyed superstition, and medieval wonder. Such coveted membranes symbolized a life that was to be special, that squawking newborn singled out for something rare and outstanding in life—some mark to be made on this dismal planet. To be sure, after six decades I'm still waiting, rushing to my mailbox daily— and, these days, to download my spam-loaded email—to find out what special treat the Fates have in store for me. A suburban fortune-teller with corkscrew blue-rinse tresses once told me I would be rich and famous "in later life." Well, it was "later life" a decade or so back, and I'm still waiting for the knock on the door from Dame Fortune.

This mythical caul has yet another added bonus. Such a soul as I cannot drown. Never ever. For that reason ancient sailors bought the caul from avaricious midwives, encasing the precious substance in a locket worn about the neck, insurance against death by drowning. I say "ancient" because I can't imagine Johnny Reynolds, the boy down the street who enlisted in the U. S. Navy, probably with visions of heroic battle in some new American war we haven't heard of yet, would be willing to trade his vintage G.I. Joe doll for some shriveled membrane.

I hate water, so the odds that I will have to test this theory or superstition are minimal. I don't swim or even wade—some days I don't even shower. I almost drowned once (in my college gym class of all places, how ignominious and pathetic!), but I didn't. So perhaps it does work after all. Over the years, I've had friends who wanted to hold my head under a filled bath or even in a garden pail, something of a scientific experiment, or so they claimed. I never thought it a good idea. Land is the proper element of mankind, as all Elizabethan travelers knew—not water. Why tempt fate? I don't like messing with the universal order of things.

So getting born was turbulent enough, but a new dilemma immediately presented itself. My parents had chosen names in anticipation of the glorious birth: Linda, if a girl, Kevin, if a boy. In some recollections my mother says it was Kenneth, not Kevin. No matter: according to my mother, when the little pink, wailing creature, *sans* caul, was tucked into her waiting arms, she looked at its cherubic face and announced: "Edward." Now I know I wasn't born a hermaphrodite—maybe *that* was what startled the entire medical profession?—but somehow, I gather, at that moment I did not look like a Linda or a Kevin/Kenneth. But—Edward? Where did that awful name come from? No one in my huge Croatian/Hungarian family sported such august British appellation, such royal signature. "It just popped into our heads," my mother once said. Popped? What was I? An exploding buttery corn kernel?

I never liked the name. All of my life I wanted to be Joseph, my grandfather's name, and my given middle name.

So little Edward was brought back to North Branford, a lazy farm town outside New Haven, and immediately dubbed "Eddie," a name I didn't like but, to this very day, is still used by my family and chummy insurance and vinyl-siding salesmen knocking at my door. In school I was "little Eddie," because I was always the smallest boy in class, life's token runt, and, for a time, "Whiskey," not because I raided the family liquor cabinet with precocious and drunken regularity, but because my last name was a tongue twister: Ifkovic, Ifkie, Iskie, Whiskey. You get the picture? I was the junior-high poster boy for Four Roses.

I remember that the first word I learned to read was "moon," taught to me by my Aunt Helen as I sat on her ample lap, pouring over a little reader she bought for me. I don't know why I remember this but I've been told she read stories to me, pointing to each word that corresponded to a glossy picture. She'd taken elocution lessons, I've been told, so she was the designated driver. I'd been a dull little *lumpen* (another family legend), staring off into space, the dullest of children, mooncalf eyes glazed over from sugar doughnuts, when the juxtaposition of a big yellow glowing round moon and the word with its two "o's" suddenly made me erupt, wriggle in her generous lap, and sound out the word "moon." My family considered it a breakthrough of sorts. At least I was no longer just staring into space, drooling. Frankly, I think it reminded me of Mom's exquisite custard pie.

We lived out in the country, vast stretches of farmland, with the springtime stink of fresh cow manure punctuating our waking. Polish and Italian truck farms surrounded us, and in the fall hay wagons drawn by sluggish horses lumbered by our house. Some neighbors still had outhouses that the farm boys would tip over on Halloween. Actually most didn't wait for a holiday—any day would do. I still remember Mrs. Armondillo pausing as she entered her outhouse (a roll of toilet paper waved in the air) and smiling at me. "Eddie, some day I want you to marry my Linda. But you gotta eat and get big." I'm sure a Freudian would have a field day dissecting the dreams that this moment engendered in me for the next few years.

My family owned the only liquor store on Route 80, the main road of town, just down the hill from my grandparents' huge farmhouse. My grandmother had gotten tired of carrying heavy bottles of beer and whiskey out of New Haven on the town bus, and Grandpa had destroyed the secret still in the basement that had sustained him and the neighbors through Prohibition. The Italian farmers gave us *grappa* but everyone preferred rye-and-ginger highballs. I'd sit on the floor inside the small white clapboard North Branford Package Store, tucked in near the Coca Cola bin, filled with ice-cold water, from which my Aunt Mary would occasionally extract a freezing bottle of Coke for me, for my older brother Bobby—who, every ten minutes, needed to cast another vote for his favorite model in the Miss Rheingold Beauty Contest, often knocking down the pretty display on the countertop—and for my cousin Jimmy Begosh.

We'd sip our Cokes in the gravel parking lot behind the package store, sitting on the peeling green table-benches Grandpa had built. This was the late 1940s, and sometimes some of the town bums would wander onto the lot. Four or five men, Second World War veterans who'd lost their way, hangers-on, nomads, long-bearded souls who limped and stuttered and slept in decrepit cabins high in the mountain woods and drifted down to the highway where, for nickels and dimes, they'd do odd jobs for farm wives, and then saunter over to the package store to buy cheap wine and booze. They'd sit with the three of us, one day taciturn and moody, another day garrulous and story-filled, talking of South Pacific arenas, of Nazis, of death camps, of victory at sea, of women so beautiful who loved them all night long. We sat, open mouthed, although these redundant tales made more sense to us when we turned eleven or twelve than when we were a lot younger. Jack Mabie had a yellow-white, ill-kept beard down to his waist. McGoogan spat tobacco something like ten yards and always smelled like a manure heap. There was always some scab he was picking at with obvious glee. I tried not to look. My favorite was Sam the Bum—that's what everyone called him—who was so kind and sweet. He found trinkets and doodads on the highway and at the town dump, and bestowed them on us. Our mothers took them away, of course. I assumed Sam the Bum was his given name and once, to my mother's horror, I greeted him with a wide grin: "Hello, Sam the Bum." He just smiled. When Sam the Bum died, the rumor mill buzzed that his cadaver was donated to the Yale Medical School. That news, spread by the children and housewives of the neighborhood one long, hot summer day, chilled my very soul. I have fond memories of him to this day. Once he gave me a switchblade knife, which I owned for perhaps ten seconds: Mom spotted it and said she'd give it to me when I was grown up. Even then I didn't believe her. Carrying it made me feel like a pubescent James Dean in a baggy T-shirt.

So the three of us lingered there on the worn benches—we would linger there through junior high—and the old men regaled us with their exaggerated war stories. Or they ignored us, sipping beer and wine until they staggered back to the mountain cabins. And one day when we were just becoming teenagers I realized that they had all disappeared. Even the benches were gone. Why hadn't I noticed?

I remember family holidays like the Fourth of July. Perhaps I'm around five years old because I can recollect whistling noise and fantastic Technicolor and shimmering streams of dazzling light. The Fourth of July was a big deal in the days when fireworks were legal in Connecticut. On the Fourth there were boisterous picnics and barbecues, neighborhood shindigs, and so the package store did a booming business. Our entrepreneurial family erected a fireworks stand between the package store and the Esso gas station we also operated—Grandpa owned the first car in North Branford, in fact, though he spent most of his time telling folks not to touch it—and nothing gave me more pleasure than hanging out around the stand. Pinwheels, fountains, Roman candles, firecrackers, snails, missiles, all kinds of razzle-dazzle pyrotechnics. We were forbidden to handle anything other than caps for our little toy pistols, but no matter: sometimes we'd get hold of some real fireworks, like cascading fountains—don't ask me how—and we'd rush off to the nearby cornfields to detonate them, scaring the crows and sparrows. Such displays would be better after dark, to be sure, but we were little kids. We had to be in by dark. It was bad enough we had to steal the matches. But most of the time we loitered near the fireworks stand—that was the epicenter of excitement. There was always the possibility of catastrophic disaster, which we anticipated breathlessly. Every year grownups gossiped about newspaper stories of speeding cars of drunken teenaged wiseacres hurling lit matches into fireworks stands, and the whole thing erupting in a ball of deadly fire. Doubtless missing the seriousness of such a conflagration, I waited, red-cheeked boy that I was, eyeing passing cars with suspicion and expectation. Nothing ever happened. Speeding carloads of drunken teenagers did speed by, but the most they did was give me the finger as I waved at them.

And on the night of the Fourth Grandpa would take all the unsold fireworks and would treat the neighborhood to an unrivaled display in his backyard, on the vast stretching lawn behind the large farmhouse on the hill. All night long the Roman candles would send luminous balls into the white-black sky. All night long the streams of brilliant color would rain down on us. Screaming with joy one minute, the next I was snoozing in my mother's arms.

One afternoon, when I was around five or six, I aimlessly wandered down the hill from Grandpa's house and into the liquor store, hoping for a free Coke. I had my little cap gun and was shooting willy-nilly at invisible enemies. Inside, quietly, I stood behind a big man who was just finishing a purchase of a six-pack. He and Aunt Mary were laughing at something. Bravely, I stuck the barrel of my toy pistol into his lower back, pressed the trigger, and fired. More than once, in fact. *Pop pop pop pop.* Deadly assault with a plastic weapon. The man jumped and swung around, wildly. For a moment I saw a flash of anger in the man's face, an emotion I'd come to recognize since I was a constant irritant and pathetic whiner, according to my family. But he looked down at me and obviously saw a pint-sized boy in a white T-shirt with the neck stretched woefully out of shape. It was a fashion look I perfected and displayed for years to come, to my mother's dismay.

"You're dead," I shouted.

He waited, clearly not dead. "You like shooting people?"

I nodded. Who didn't? My aunt said something and he laughed.

"Come with me."

"What?"

"Just follow me."

Nodding, I did. I have no idea why Aunt Mary let me trail after a strange man into the back parking lot, unless she was secretly glad I was being kidnapped and removed from sight and irritation. Be that as I may, stupid kid that I was, I blithely strolled after the towering guy, snapping off rounds of gunfire like a loopy Wyatt Earp. He said nothing as we walked back to the parking lot. Then, near the one car parked there, he paused by the trunk, and I stood there, grinning, not realizing that, indeed, in the next few seconds there was a chance I might be unceremoniously planted inside, smothered inside a burlap sack. Probably still shooting away. *Bang bang bang.*

"You got any caps?" he asked.

I showed him the blue-and-red box and my remaining roll. Five cents a box. Precious ammo.

He popped the trunk and I looked in on case after case of the same brilliant blue-and-red cap boxes, most sealed but one large container wide open.

He grinned. "You can have as many boxes as you can carry."

What? Who said you have to hope for heaven? Intoxicated, I plunged my tiny fingers into the cardboard box and began stuffing my pants pockets. I was a little too timid. Had I been older I would have stuffed them in my shorts, my socks, my ears and nose.

All the while he stood there, grinning, Santa Claus in summer, a six-pack of Budweiser cradled against his chest. I remember dropping a box onto the ground and it slipped into an oil slick. When I bent to retrieve it, he stopped me, a hand on my shoulder. "You don't need that one."

"Okay."

"You like to shoot people?" he asked again.

"Yep."

"Me, too."

My mother wasn't thrilled with me as I strolled into our house minutes later, cap boxes falling out of my pants pockets, fingers grasping enough ammo for days to come. I don't think she believed my story about the generous salesman until Aunt Mary phoned her. But let me tell you, I was the neighborhood hero that following week, dispensing caps to lesser mortal with all the drama of a Pope issuing papal bulls.

But there's always a price for unsolicited manna from heaven. Mom, with her East European dark sensibility, always spoke of "rainy days" and "don't get too happy"—because there was always some darkness seeping unawares onto your pleasant horizon. Get ready. The boom will be lowered. It happened that Christmas. I was in kindergarten, mostly a wasteland in my memory—a blur of someone tying my shoes, someone putting me on a bus, and, oddly, a snapshot of a school bus driver named Mr. Ferguson who dropped me off to a waiting mother, who had steamy Campbell's tomato soup and crackers waiting on the kitchen table. But I can clearly see my teacher Miss Randall, a tower of a woman, or so I recall her. She always stood directly over you, the smell of antiseptic lye soap hitting you hard. That I remember. To this day, she is no blur of memory: she's a vivid snapshot. Stout, with a head of tight gray curls, a severe woman in thick sensible shoes. I was always so afraid of her—unlike Miss Carpet, my first grade teacher the following year, whom I planned on marrying—and I recall Miss Randall yelling at me for something. Actually she yelled at me a lot. She yelled at everyone a lot.

But that Christmas was special, with an orchestrated school pageant, enacted on the little stage in the school auditorium for family and friends and those who had no plausible excuse for escaping the invitation. Miss Randall hurled herself into such pageantry with all the gusto and aplomb of Cecil B. DeMille staging some KKK epic with expansive hand gestures and bombastic marching orders. I was not too keen on participating, preferring to languish in some corner, an undiscovered talent. I liked to sit out life, tucked into a desk seat with a Disney pop-up book. She told my mother that I was a "bump on a log," which didn't bother me at the time because I had no idea it was intended as insult. I liked logs. With my brother I fashioned a log cabin in the woods. I sat on logs all the time. I was a regular Paul Bunyan.

Miss Randall also believed everyone should sing. Loudly. And dance. Gracefully. "Singing and dancing are ways to show you are happy." So was sitting in a corner, I felt. But somehow she'd come to believe I possessed a particularly melodic voice, my cute piping-high soprano boychick voice. Sitting with my mother in front of the Zenith console radio, I admit, I did imitate Vaughn Monroe's crooning, as well as the other Arthur Godfrey warblers. So, for the pageant, Miss Randall commanded me to sing, of all things, "Frosty the Snowman," a solo performance that scared me silly. We rehearsed endlessly, me standing still—actually frozen in place—while my hands methodically dressed Donnie Perillo, a huge sweating mass of baby blubber, who was, I guess, Frosty. More like Melty. I had to put a hat on him, a thick scarf, and God know what else. I was Little Eddie and I had to stand on tiptoe to place the "old silk hat" atop his unwashed and faintly foul hair. We rehearsed and rehearsed, rote gesture, mechanical and robotic, because Miss Randall did not believe in spontaneity and ad-libbing. She didn't allow chance in her universe. She pretty much didn't believe in anything that wasn't memorized. At the end, when poor Frosty melted away after running amuck through the county square—with the barrels of sweat Donnie was literally capable of excreting—I would stand there like a wind-up toy, waving to a departing Frosty, who would, I informed everyone, come again another day. If bad luck prevailed. Then I rehearsed a bow from the waist.

The afternoon of the extravaganza arrived, a day of sleet and rain, my mother recalled, and the auditorium was filled with overeager parents with cheap Kodaks. My mother sat there by herself, with Dad working at the factory and my being unable to hire a rousing claque to support my stage debut. Choirs of older students sang "Silent Night" and "O Come all Ye Faithful," interspersed with a succession of insipid vaudeville routines with a yuletide motif. The other students, up to the fourth grade, did their routines, and when the kindergarten moment arrived, Miss Randall assumed her place on the side of the stage and proceeded to pound the piano keys in the same heavy-handed deliberate way she pounded obedience into her little charges. She obviously believed all music should sound like thunder and doom, very Wagnerian. We were the cute ones—the kindergarteners—and Miss Randall trooped out the cuddly girls who sang "We Wish You a Merry Christmas." At times her piano drowned out the tepid, meager voices.

In the wing I sweated. My bowtie—yes: a bowtie, thanks to Mom—was coming loose. Donnie looked oddly calm with only a reasonable puddle of perspiration around his feet. Then I was announced and Donnie and I mechanically stepped stage center. The beginning strains of "Frosty the Snowman" began and I started to sing, a little nervous, but, I'm certain, beautifully melodious. After all, I was well rehearsed and could do this in my sleep. Donnie, whose only responsibility in his own stage debut was to stand there, dressed in white, looking more like an ungainly pile of shoveled snow than a symmetrically fashioned snowman, was suddenly shaking. His face got beet red. He hiccoughed. I thought he'd cry. I never liked him because he was a loudmouthed bully who used his humongous weight as a threat. Once, coming back from the boys' room, I crossed paths with him. "I don't like you cuz you're a baby," he announced. He pushed me and told me he could beat me up if he so desired. I believed him. I apologized to him and rushed by.

Now I sang in my sweet soprano voice, with Donnie as the "jolly happy soul": "There must have been some magic." I warbled about the old silk hat and all that dancing around. I placed the old derby cap on Donnie's head, jumping up to do it (I'm convinced he'd grown five inches since assuming the part). Luckily he did not dance around. He was merely trembling. I continued my tale of Frosty running around the town with a broomstick, with me theoretically trying to catch him. If I could—Donnie was shaking like a bowl of jelly.

Just as I threw the scarf around his neck, I heard an abrupt, tremendous cacophony of piano keys, like fists pounding madly at the old ivories. I was so startled that I jerked the scarf so tight that Donnie, himself alarmed, let out a fart so seismic had I been directly behind him I'd been thrown against the back wall. Now ordinarily such behavior would have delighted me, but the music came to an emphatic halt.

Glancing to the side, I noticed Miss Randall slip sideways off the piano stool, topple onto the floor, and in seconds she lay there, a mountain of a woman, the soles of her sensible shoes facing me, as well as an indecorous amount of white slip. Pandemonium broke out as men in the audience jumped onto the stage and carried Miss Randall off to a side room. People were frantic and screaming out loud. Donnie, I swear, wet his pants and ran off the stage. Now I had not rehearsed such a coda to my performance. What I did know was the ironclad routine and so, to the horror of some—including my mother—I stood there and quietly sang the end of the song, *a cappella*. I was there waving goodbye and supposedly listening to Frosty telling me not to cry because, well, he'd be back another day.

And I added: *Thumpity thump thump Look at Frosty go.* Neat as a pin in my pressed white shirt, red bowtie, and creased black trousers, I finished with a flourish, bowing deeply from the waist. No one paid any attention to me because people were rushing left and right. I, in the eye of the storm, exited stage right, where someone was trying to revive the sadly dead Miss Randall.

Trespassing in the Garden of Eden

Her name was Eve and she spent her long days toiling in the Garden of Eden. Actually her name was Eva, my Hungarian grandmother, and, well, she did spend her days toiling in the Garden of Eden. That garden was, indeed, that special—nearly a half-acre of manicured stone pathways and circular flowerbeds, with Japanese red maples, lush magnolias, dazzling beds of bleeding hearts and peonies, and stupendous horticultural exotica I believe only she could give names to. We grandchildren were forbidden to enter the winding, pebbly paths unless strapped to the side of a designated adult. That rarely happened. Even the grownups were afraid of paradise. This was *terra incognita* for all but the chosen few.

Of course, my cousin Jimmy and I spent much of our time there. Trespassing.

What made this garden so forbidding—and thus a magnet for boyish invasion—was its legend. Grandma had a green thumb, platinum card level. One family story tells how she walked by an odd-looking tree on the New Haven green, liked the look of it, snapped off a twig, returned home, stuck it dramatically—collective drum roll—into the rocky Connecticut soil, and, lo and behold, a flowering tree sprouted.

At summer's end, sitting on a wooden-stave chair in the backyard, she'd peel open the seed pods of zinnias, marigolds, and other annuals, dispensing the aromatic contents into Maxwell House coffee containers. This was one of her rituals, practiced in solitude. But zinnias and marigolds were the peasants, the plebian upstarts that flowered under her care. I remember once being led in with others to view an oval mound at the intersection of pathways, perhaps fifteen feet across, a rise of earth dense with huge pitch-black tulips. Years later I was told they were really some hothouse hue of darkest indigo, but Grandma labeled them her black tulips. Everyone oohed and aahed, although I remember—I was perhaps thirteen or fourteen—that such a dark display struck me even then as a little macabre. Reading a steady diet of comic books with grotesque, otherworldly imagery, with aliens, gangsters and mischievous gnomes come to life, I found that bed of black tulips entering my nighttime visions.

I suppose it was beautiful. Well, the whole garden was supremely beautiful. People traveled from far and wide, asking to view the precious blossoms. She even ringed part of the Edenic border with southwest cacti—an amazing spectacle, to be sure, in good old New England. Fifty-gallon drums were cut in half, iron handles welded on by my uncle Johnny, and Grandma grew six/seven feet tall cacti, long spiky shafts of pale green, with occasional bursts of Georgia O'Keefe blooms. All of us gasped in wonder. In late fall my Grandpa groaned and cursed as he (and others) had to tote the heavy drums into the dark recesses of the warm cellar to guarantee survival through the icebound winter.

Grandma gave the orders.

Grandma was a woman I never understood. A hard-nosed, often bitter woman, filled with an anger that was sometimes followed by amazing generosity, she had left her native Hungary at thirteen, made her way to America by herself, and lived a hardscrabble life by the time she married my grandfather in New Jersey and then settled on a rural Connecticut farm lot, all scrub oak, swamp maple, and mud flat. Grandpa worked at a nearby trap rock quarry and Grandma helped dig the cellar of a huge ten-room home, backbreaking work, stultifying work. She had, I think, sixteen children, half of whom died as children, a couple of them burned to death in scalding cauldrons during canning season, one hit by a wild out-of-control car. So she came by her bitterness honestly.

When I made her acquaintance, she was a large woman in florid housedresses who liked to do four things, in particular. One was to spend her days at the movies in New Haven. One time, I was told, she sat through *Gone with the Wind* all day long, and the family considered calling the police when she didn't arrive home on schedule on the town bus. Another was her life in the kitchen, for she was a stellar chef. She never measured ingredients, just tossed flour and eggs and butter and sugar and yeast into huge yellow enamel bowls. The result was apple strudel, raised powder doughnuts, poppy-seed bread, walnut *potica*, rum *babka*, and chicken paprikas you could die for. Home fries with paprika, onions, slathered with sour cream. She never made just a dozen raised sugar doughnuts. She made one hundred. She was always cooking for the Tsar's imperial army. She probably expected them to appear on her lawn.

And when she was not cooking, she was in that precious garden, probably her favorite recreation. Most of her children lived nearby on half-acres of land doled out as marriage gifts, parceled lots hewn from the large spread of farmland. She insisted her daughters—usually my own mother—clean her home, tend to household activities, do the laundry, keep the huge house intact, while she hoed and transplanted and weeded in her garden.

But the thing she *really* excelled at—and this was the role she cultivated more than her rows of leafy lettuce—was the dispensing of her peculiar and harsh brand of justice. Or perhaps I should say vengeance, for *justice* seems too civilized a word here. Here was Eve posting rules on the signposts in Eden. No one was free of her censorious eye, especially not her children and all the grandchildren. Especially not the grandchildren she always frowned on. In particular, me, my brother and sister. You see, Grandma played favorites but, worse, she pitted family members against one another, creating spitfire little soap operas she enjoyed watching. She liked to have her grown daughters in a constant state of warfare. She would tell one daughter some skewered tidbit, patently false, but with a modicum of truth, suggesting that another daughter had said such-and-such. The angry phone calls would begin, the snubbing, the battles erupting. Family members fought for years, then fell into cold silence, like tombstones positioned in some tidy rural backyard.

"I no understands what's wrong with my childrens," she would say. "All they's do is fight."

Life in her later years was good for Grandma. At twilight, strolling up the hill from where my own family lived, I'd spot her holding a late September rose up to the fading light, awe in her face, pleasure in her grip. She looked like some ancient East European goddess—admittedly overweight and with an old-lady blue perm—in some fertility ritual. Life, as I said, was good.

With her many daughters and sons, it was inevitable that I had an obscene number of first cousins on my mother's side, especially since one aunt had nearly a dozen offspring. And we all lived in homes surrounding Grandma and Grandpa's massive house on the hill—East European style, where the family lived in a kind of hierarchal compound. Such an arrangement made it easy for Grandma to cultivate her favorites. Some of the first cousins could do no wrong, blessed among mortals. Others, like me and my siblings, were traditional scapegoats, despite my brother Bob being her first grandchild. Not surprisingly, since she used my mother as a drudge, we were the underlings she needed to insult. Each year Grandma and Grandpa vacationed in Florida, came back with tales of waiters and waitresses who doted on them, which, of course, necessitated Grandpa lavishing huge monies on them. For months afterwards, letters arrived, postmarked Florida, with sycophantic rambling and blatant requests for a few bucks. That first night back home, ritualistically, everyone in the family had to be in attendance for the royal gift-giving. Trinkets and baubles—number two pencils stamped with St. Petersburg, seashell necklaces and cheaply-framed pictures—were distributed. T-shirts with clever slogans they themselves didn't understand. "Thank you, Grandpa." "Thank you, Grandma." Later on, through word of mouth and secret phone calls, we learned of the silver platters, gold cuff links, and expensive fountain pens other family members proudly displayed. Grandma's justice? If someone had won her favor, that person was rewarded. If someone had offended her—even if the violation was unintentional or even unnoticed by the offender, who might be three years old—there was a price to be paid.

One time I was moving through her backyard and bumped into her. For some reason she asked that hideous question adults plague children with: "Eddie, what you gonna be when youse grow up?" Of course, I had already decided that troublesome decision. Fervent Catholic that I was, a lover of the incense-laden St. Augustine's Church and now thrilled to be confiding my news, I sang out: "A priest." A long pause from Grandma, then a sardonic (I imagine it now) chuckle. "A priest? I don't thinks so. Someday you gonna burn in hell."

Grandma as theologian.

Christmas especially was payback time, a ceremonial bloodletting that masked itself as family togetherness and bonhomie. It was actually a happy time, of sorts, especially if you were too young to understand the often cruel and deliberate machinations of adults with a cause. Or claws.

But, like all kids, I loved Christmas. My own parents had little money in those days, my father eking out a living on factory wages. We couldn't even afford a car. That was one reason we were *familia non grata*, for Grandma preferred the "richer" relatives, blessing them with expensive gifts and public displays of unconditional love. One winter, I recall, Mom and Dad kept lying to us, saying they'd eaten when we knew they hadn't. Dad had been laid off from his job, and the days were long and cold. We kids were given the cans of beans with slices of Wonder Bread. We recall that we had no refrigerator that winter. But they made

Christmas special for us, with small gifts and an ample dinner. So we decorated the house with red-and-green streamers we made from wrapping paper, as well as a Christmas tree we bought from the country-western crowd that lived in the trailer park a mile or so away. One year, I remember, we spent one dollar for a huge fir. From a guy named Dwayne.

Christmas Eve was mandatory attendance at the grandparents' home. In my memory the day was punctuated by familiar pleasures. In the afternoon *The New Haven Register* arrived with its traditional printing of Clement Moore's *A Visit from St. Nick* on the first page. I waited for it, reveled in it. That, to me, was somehow the start of Christmas. I'd read it out loud to myself. That, and the little sing-along carol books handed out at Catholic Sunday School, issued by John Hancock Insurance, with the chalky blue cover depicting a snowbound village at night. I assumed it was Bethlehem. I still have mine, all these many years later.

In the early evening we'd lock the house and troop up the icy hill, past the dead winter garden, to the huge house ablaze with color and light. Grandpa decorated the fifty-foot spruce on the front lawn with hundreds of strings of outdoor lights, and that magnificent tree, seen for miles by drivers on Route 80, certainly rivaled any tree on any town green. Garlands of evergreens hung off window frames. Candles illuminated countless windows. My family was into show time, big time. Inside the festive rooms the feast began—the traditional Slavic fish, but everything else as well. Homemade dumplings in thick, aromatic gravy. Warm, oozing cottage cheese in every bite of the fluffy dessert rolls. Pots of goulash simmering on the stove. Layer cakes so high they were in danger of toppling. Sugar cookies dripping with colored glaze. My aunt Katie, married to an Italian guy named Joe, always brought a gigantic Italian rum cake, layer upon layer of creamy confection. While the grownups drank beer and wine and told hilarious or melodramatic stories, the one thousand (it seemed) first cousins of all ages whooped and hollered and banged and collided and vomited and gurgled and spat and got in everyone's way. Family hostilities and nagging gripes were forgotten for the occasion, with just a few over-the-top necessary snipes and barbs. You couldn't let your oiled sarcasm get too rusty on a Christian holiday.

Then, the climax. Eva's moment of truth: gonna find out who's naughty and who's nice.

When I was a small boy, I didn't know the ropes as I would later on, when Christmas at Grandma's took on more of an edge. At five I was fresh from killing Miss Randall, one notch already on my boy's belt, but still naïve as can be, an innocent babe idly humming "Silent Night" and praying for (requested from the store Santa at Newberry's in New Haven) a paint-by-numbers set for Christmas. I'd seen one depicting frisky dogs romping around a dog bone. This was real art we were talking about here.

In the huge front porch of the house, against the upright piano, a gigantic tinseled tree towered over mountains of elegantly wrapped presents. This is what we kids waited for—and doubtless the parents dreaded. The dispensing of the royal favors. The true meaning of Christmas. Grandpa shouldered the task, kneeling by the tree and reading out the names while Grandma sat, a bedecked Buddha with a new perm and rhinestone brooch, on a straight-back Windsor chair, a beatific smile on her face.

My cousin Susie got the ten-speed bicycle we'd all been eyeing. Joey got roller skates. Not bad. Henry horseshoes. Mary a frilly dress, with a slightly uneven hem. Lois got a necklace. Linda a toiletry set that clearly did not please her. My grandfather called out the names quickly, as though, I suppose, dreading the inevitable letdowns and flashes of anger that usually ended these evenings.

Susie got a beautiful doll. Her second gift. She must have been especially nice to Grandma that year.

Jack got a collection of fairy tales. Not a reader, he preferred knives and guns. Years later he'd buy his own—but that's a different story.

Some of the grownups received gifts, elaborate coverlets, kitchen knife sets, mirrors, and—well, there was also that tablecloth with the stain on the edges. That went to my mother. That blouse with the unraveled lace around the collar—to my Aunt Sissy. Aunt Maria clicked her tongue when she opened a gift box to discover a paperweight with the paint flaking off the glossy painting inside the translucent plastic. People were frowning.

You see, Grandma liked to buy seconds or "irregulars" as she shopped during the year, amassing her stash in a hallway closet, off limits to all. No inferior product was left behind, no sale left unattended, and often her shopping bags spilled over, if the price was right. So by Christmastime, what with her steady ritual of shopping for bargains, the hall closet was filled to brimming with the detritus of year-end white sales and mid-summer clearance racks. She liked to haggle over prices, even in stores where prices were established, like Sears Roebuck or Shartenberg's, a prominent department store in New Haven. She'd badger and whine and plead until, a smile on her face and the huge cloth hat slightly askew on her head, she walked out of the store with her booty. She was notorious for taking the early bus to New Haven, waiting outside a particular store, intent on being the first customer of the day. These were Jewish storekeeps, some of whom, at least back then, held the superstition that to lose the first customer of the day was to insure financial ruin for the remainder of that day. Grandma would present a routinely low price, they'd squabble back and forth, both she and the store-owner getting into it, and eventually she would get most of what she wanted. It was an elaborate game she and owners played, I guess, probably reminding both of the Old Country market-places in Russian or Austro-Hungarian Empires, where such salesmanship was commonplace and expected. Oddly, many of these Jewish men and women became fast friends, and on weekends carloads of Goldfarbs and Rabinoviches partied all night long at the house. In fact, Grandma hinted, more than once, that her family had been Jewish in an earlier century, hence her maiden name Wise or Wize. Of course, other times she whispered about the gypsy blood she'd inherited. None of this made much sense then—except to make Grandma mysterious. All I knew was that she'd mastered the art of converting a Christian holiday into a fearsome weapon against her family.

Grandpa droned on. Jill got a jump rope and didn't look happy. Donny got a shiny tricycle—and did. My brother Bobby got another number-two pencil set. My sister Geraldine got a hanky set. When my cousin Steve, who was inclined to bite me for no good reason, discovered an A.C. Gilbert Erector Set as his gift, he leaned over and bit his brother.

A half-hour into the orgy of giving and I hadn't received a thing—nothing, nada. Zippo. Nothing. Five years old and toyless in the land of Oz.

So I did what any self-respecting five-year-old would do. I wailed so loudly and thrashed about so fitfully I seemed in possession by demonic spirits. What snake was lurking near that Garden of Eden? I lay on my back and had a tantrum. The celebration came to a crashing halt. Doubtless heads shook. Of course, it was that little Eddie again, that whiny brat who always wanted his own way.

"Pa," one of the aunts said, "find Eddie his gift."

Grandpa, always the family peacekeeper, started sifting through the piles, squinting at the nametags. He pushed his way beneath the tree, glass balls banging and tinsel shimmering. He reemerged empty handed. "Eva," he said to my Grandma, "help me." She shrugged. "What does it look like?" he asked. He looked back to the stacks, boxes spread out like the aftermath of a Macy's bargain basement sale.

"I no buy him gift this year."

Had I heard that right? Yep: that thick Hungarian accent, laced with homemade sweet wine and powered sugar doughnuts. "I no buy him gift this year."

Now this was crossing some unspoken line, it seemed, even among the anti-Eddie contingent. Even the blue-blood cousins who often gloated over my family's leprosy muttered surprise. I, of course, heard this news without much grace. I ratcheted up my wailing, rolling on the lovely carpet and into, of all thing, the ribbons and torn gift wrappings left behind by luckier cousins—and discovered the awesome power of a full-blown tantrum.

"What?" From Grandpa.

"What?" From Mom.

"What?" From Dad.

"At least I got number two pencils," my brother Bobby declared.

My mother's face, usually so soft and inviting, now hardened into something I didn't like. "Okay," she mumbled, "we're leaving." She deftly grabbed my siblings, nudged Dad who lifted me off the floor, and we headed for the winter coats in the hallway. Scared now, I stopped crying.

What I most remember from that moment is my Grandpa. During the entire hubbub, he turned to my grandmother and said in a strangely hollow voice I'll never forget: "Why you do that, Eva? Why you do that to the baby?"

She didn't answer.

As we rushed past my Grandpa, he reached into his pocket and extracted two one-dollar bills, then tucked them into the breast pocket of my blue dress shirt. He was shaking his head.

So my family, with Mom dragging us away, her face tight with anger, stumbled into the winter night, rushing past the Garden of Eva—a barren wasteland now of plant stumps and ice-caked evergreens—down the hill to our home. We'd spend Christmas morning alone, away from the family.

I didn't plan revenge, of course. I was five or so, remember? And revenge was not a concept I'd even heard of. I was more concerned with tying my shoes and slapping around my little sister. You need a few more years under your belt before that wonderful concoction of revenge and justice comes naturally to you. But it comes anyway, as it sometimes does, without planning, but oddly on schedule. And, as the saying goes, it's best served cold.

A couple summers later my cousin Jimmy and I were heading to the vast forest of nearby Totoket Mountain, where we searched for lost Indian burial grounds (we found them) and valuable

Indian relics (not found, save for a few random arrowheads), as well as the ramshackle mountain cabins of the old bearded men who hung out at the package store. We took a shortcut through Grandma's inviolable garden. It was spring, and the air was redolent with the fetid smell of cow manure, upturned dark earth, and the scent of new-chopped weeds. We thought Grandma might be hoeing in one of the beds near the house, and so we skirted left and right, walking on the pebbly paths but trying to remain sheltered by some boxwood hedges.

"She'll kill us," Jimmy said.

"Nah, we can hide."

He shook his head. "Last time she almost hit us with a rake."

I shrugged. I was seven or eight now, cocky in paradise.

But we ended up in one of the distant corners of the garden, surreptitiously maneuvering through the serpentine paths. And suddenly there it was: a lofty Japanese red maple, resplendent in burgundy leaf and delicate bough. There was nothing around it except a carefully raked and weeded plot of ground. No bushes, no hyacinths, no spring tulips. But nestled under its feathery boughs was a forest of miniature red maples, three or four inches high, hundreds of them, diminutive reflections of the mother lode above. Hundreds of the tiny scarlet sprigs. Jimmy and I stared, dumbfounded.

"Ain't they something?" I said.

We'd never seen anything like it, and we stopped in our tracks. "Wonder if Grandma knows there're here," he said.

Now, of course, that was a dumb notion. This was her garden, and she was Eva in the garden.

For some reason, in some peculiar drift of thought, we wanted to *please* our grandmother. So we knelt on the smooth, manicured black earth, and began pulling up the fragile plants, amassing big clumps in our skinny little hands. It was thrilling—and wonderful.

Proudly, triumphantly, we marched to Grandma's back porch, climbed the stairs, and pounded on the screen door, which was latched. In a few seconds we heard Grandma coming out of the kitchen, wiping flour off her hands onto a dishrag, frowning as she saw the two of us standing there. "Youse botherin' me today?"

"Look," we said in unison as she neared. Jimmy and I thrust our hands out toward her, displaying hundreds of soon-to-be-dead sprigs of what we later learned was a rare type of Japanese maple that germinated every seven years (I think) and were now in their fifth (and obviously final) year.

Now Grandma was a large woman. A big woman. A hefty woman. Let me repeat: a big woman. A woman who loved her cheese and homemade bread. And she obviously seemed much bigger because we were tiny little boys. She stared, open mouthed, at the clumps of wilting seedlings in our hands, and from the back of her throat came a dry, screeching sound, echoey and fierce, that rose in awful crescendo until, I swear, the barnyard dog tied up by the garage started to howl.

Jimmy and I stepped back. "Here," I said. "For you." I actually thought I was pleasing her.

The screaming stopped. But this was not good news.

Did I say that Grandma was a big, big woman? Suddenly, before our eyes, her body swayed like a top at the end of its spinning, her eyes seemed to roll back into her skull, her knees buckled, and she slipped to the linoleum floor. A heap of a woman. Out cold.

Now I had already been through this with the death of my kindergarten teacher, the late and lamented Miss Randall, so I knew the signs.

Well, Jimmy and I had killed Grandma.

In a panic we beat it out of there, headed back through the garden and into the farm fields beyond, panting, sweating, confused, hiding all afternoon in the rows of newly planted pig corn.

We had killed Grandma and there was nothing to do but wait for the town constable to find us and send us to the New Haven lock-up where we would be cellmates of the knife-wielding Negroes from Dixwell Avenue. Of course, we had a few hours before incarceration. The constable, we all knew, got filthy drunk at lunchtime and would sleep it off on the side of the road until late afternoon. We wouldn't be handcuffed and hauled in until suppertime.

But eventually we had to return home, unable to squat in the cornfields until the plants grew high enough to shield us. I arrived home to find my mother preparing supper, putting scalloped potatoes into the oven and calmly asking me if I was hungry. Sort of a strange act for someone whose mother has just been murdered, I thought. What was going on? Soon Dad returned from the factory, sat at the table talking to my mother while nursing a shot and a beer, and then my mother called us to supper. I'd been lingering in the hallway, eavesdropping. Were they going to hand me over to the drunken constable? So I sat at the table, quiet. She obviously didn't know I'd killed her mother. Or did she? Was this some elaborate ruse enacted by the entire family to get me to break down, to confess?

"You're awfully quiet," she said.

I nodded.

What was there to say?

By the way, Grandma's dead and gone, covered with little red maple seedlings, looking like she's a mound of dirt overrun with swarms of red ants. Or: Ma, have you checked the hallway of her house yet?

"What did you do today?" she asked me.

Killed Grandma. And you?

"Nothing," I sputtered.

The telephone rang.

All right—here it is. Hands up. I won't go peacefully.

My mother answered the phone, and to my surprise I could hear my grandmother screaming on the other end. Not only was she was alive, but she'd been trying to call all afternoon. Some fool tied up the party line. My mother listened quietly, interjecting an occasional *ah* or *oh* or—worse! —*ooooh?*—then replaced the receiver. She returned to the table and sat down, all the time staring at me with an odd look on her face.

"What was that all about?" Dad said. "Sounds like she's going off again."

My mother looked at me. "You and Jimmy pulled up all the red maples she's been growing for over five years?"

I nodded. "We didn't know—"

"He did what?" Dad said.

"You know those maples she's always talking about?"

"They pulled them up?"

"Yes."

I thought I saw Dad smile.

"Mom—" I started. She cut me off.

"Eat your supper, Eddie." Then, looking not at me but at Dad, she said, "She spends way too much time in that garden." She sighed. "Way too much time."

The Body of Christ

When I was a small boy, Grandpa sat me on his knee and gave me advice to last a lifetime. "Always stay a Catholic," he said, "and always vote Democrat." I suppose such sentiment bridged both his Old and New worlds. He'd been a young man who'd fled the abuses of the old Austro-Hungarian Empire and then struggled through the gritty and grueling underworld of American sweatshops of the Midwest and New Jersey. His religion helped him survive the fatalism of his Hungarian boyhood in a village called Rezovac in what later became Yugoslavia. And in America the Democratic working-class machine gave him a voice and a place in the vast Republic. Here was a man who, at five, sat on his father's shoulders in a square in Zagreb (then called Agram) and watched Franz Josef ride by on a high white horse. Here was a man who saluted FDR's caravan as it passed by on a campaign spin through Connecticut in the late 1930s.

"What?" I asked.

"You can't go wrong," he said simply.

I promised him I would remain loyal to the Pope and to the party of FDR.

Well, it was certainly easy to remain a Democrat in the successive generations that involved Nixon and the vaudeville act called the Bush family dynasty. But Catholic? Roman Catholic?

I stopped attending Mass when I was in college—courageously eating forbidden meat one Friday in the college cafeteria and not seeing the earth divide and continents collide.

I had started out wanting—fully expecting—to become a priest, although for a nanosecond, I admit, I thought I'd be a florist. With my family, I'd visited a friend's greenhouse in mid-winter, and I liked the lush green and pungent warm soil, the overbearing red flowers—and contrasted it with the icy landscape outside. And I thought: hey, warmth all winter. I hadn't yet heard of Florida. But most times I wanted to be a priest, and it had little to do with the clergy I encountered. The old Irish priests who ran the small parish were bumbling and sometimes uproariously drunk men—in particular, Father O'Brien, a kindly sort often happily slumped on a kitchen chair at Grandpa's on a Saturday night, head resting on his chest, mumbling something about the saints preserving him. An occasional young assistant priest was sometimes part of the local clerical mix, but they always moved on. And the good sisters who taught us Sunday School—always on Saturday, my first unanswerable paradox—were not the happiest crowd at the ecclesiastical party. My deeply religious mother was largely anticlerical, with little use for them. Once, picking up my brother at Sunday School, she arrived in time to see Sister Mary McGee hurl Bobby against a wall for some trivial misdeed. She said nothing, raised as she was to be in awe of religion. But that year, at Thanksgiving, when we were told to donate canned goods for the good sisters, my mother made us deliver paper bags of canned sauerkraut.

It took me years to understand her wonderful statement.

One afternoon, watching my cousin's TV—we did not have one until was I was around ten, when the family preferred Bishop Fulton Sheen to Uncle Miltie—I sat through a story of a shopkeeper who was mysteriously murdered. It turned out that a small boy, finding the man's hidden gun, accidentally discharged it, killing the old soul. The next day at Sunday School I raised my hand, which I did all the time to the consternation of the nuns who liked more compliant, obedient kids, ones who couldn't challenge the high-school education they barely had.

Trespassing in the Garden of Eden

We had been discussing eternal damnation and the wrath of God—always a pressing topic with little boys and girls—and the nun wanted us to imagine burning horribly for ever and ever and ever and *ever*—just for missing *one* Mass on Sunday. Well, I'd often sweated over that scenario, thought it unfair because anyone could have one bad day, but still I believed in eternal damnation. Fire that went on and on and on. There were nights I'd wake up covered in sweat. I was probably six years old. So when I described the story I'd seen on TV to the nun and added, "Will that boy go to hell?" she blithely announced, "Of course." I remember I jumped back, alarmed. *Of course.* Only six years old, and the game was over for the little boy. If he lived to be ninety, he'd still burn in hell, cellmate to mass murderers, pickpockets, and bunko artists. My my my.

No matter: I still relished the idea of being a priest, I suppose, because of the pageantry, the association with holidays like Easter and Christmas, and the mystery of the incense-laden church. Priests seemed to have answers to questions—they never let doubt creep into their conversations. My brother Bobby, an altar boy, never took it as seriously as I did, maybe because he saw things close up. Kneeling in the pew one Sunday morning, I heard him intone: *Hail Mary, full of grapes* . . . Followed by a barely stifled giggle.

Not me: at six or so I'd go into a rage when the family skipped Sunday Mass, demanding to be allowed to walk the few miles there, although my mother shook her head at that threat and went about her business.

I looked forward to First Communion as though it were a carnival setting up shop on a Sears Roebuck parking lot, with clowns and whistles, with Necco wafers and JuJu beads. Oddly, I can't remember anything about that august day, and for some reason there are no family photos. In general, we were not a Kodak moment family. I probably did something questionable, but who knows? But what I do remember vividly is the week *after* my First Communion. Filled with spiritual bliss and a beautiful intoxication as though I were Jonathan Edwards condemning sinners in the hands of an angry God, I went to St. Augustine's hell bent—maybe that's the wrong word here—on spiritual nourishment. A babe in the ecclesiastical woods.

Having received First Communion and experienced the body of Christ—that thin tasteless wafer that you couldn't chew or swallow but had to let melt in your mouth, a God-blessed M&M that oozed blessedness into my body by osmosis—I wanted more. Who wouldn't? I'd made myself a vow to get communion *every* week. There was only one wrinkle: no one in my family had gone to Saturday afternoon confession. I deemed them infidels, covered as I was with the purity of the previous week, so no one in the family could receive communion that morning. But that would not deter me from my personal Holy Grail, even though I was timid in public, afraid to approach the altar railing unless surrounded by family members.

I did, anyway. After all the ringing of the bells and the mystical genuflecting, the crowd surged forward. I hesitated, but, determined, followed. By the time I arrived, the railing before the altar was packed shoulder-to-shoulder, farmers in Sunday best and women with showy hats and black veils. But skinny little me, I managed to edge myself in between two redeemed souls. I was a tiny speck, shoulders scrunched up, my electric cowlick standing on end, and my little fingers gripping the railing.

Father O'Brien was then nearing a transparent dotage, having started on that path as a young man, doubtless. He often stammered, lost his train of thought, started over. But a good man, to be sure. But now he meandered through his senior years, a situation aggravated by a frequent tipping of the elbow, usually, as I've said, at my grandfather's house on a long Saturday night. Sometimes at 7:00 Mass, which was when my family attended, usually arriving at six a.m.—to get a good seat? —he would be a little wobbly on his feet.

I wasn't paying any attention to his movements as he ambled down the line, intoning "Body of Christ," followed by whatever we were supposed to reply. I don't think it was "Thank you." I was just afraid I'd forget to open my mouth or, on opening it, my teeth would clamp down unexpectedly on the wafer, thus embarrassing God and me.

Father O'Brien stood before me, resplendent in robes and God's special aura. For a moment he seemed startled to see me, snuggled in between two oversized citizens of the Church, this little peanut squished in like a sausage in an Italian hero. There I was, dressed in my starched, ironed white dress shirt, my black trousers with the sharp crease, a neat black suit jacket, my polished black tie shoes, and a red bow tie, angelic to a fault.

Pausing just a few seconds, Father O'Brien started to bend down toward me, shifting his weight to reach the little bugger at the railing. But he was a little disoriented—I hesitate to use the word tipsy here—and, in the act of bending over, the gold chalice in his unsteady hands jerked forward, spreading its blessed contents on my suit jacket. I was covered with thin white wafers.

I looked like a domino.

Frightened, I gasped and panicked. The good sisters had stressed that the wafer was, in fact, the very precious Body of Christ, each one a real manifestation of God's giving of His son for our salvation and hope of heaven. This was God we were receiving.

I wasn't thinking along such theological lines at the moment, I must admit. Here I was, not with one Body of Christ—which should have been dissolving, spiritually, against the roof of my mouth—but a host of Christs, a host of hosts, a smorgasbord, an all-you-can-eat Home Town Buffet of blessed delicacies.

Without thinking, I grabbed a bunch of them off my chest, and they squished into some flaky confetti in my grip, like the feeling I'd get snapping dried insects between thumb and forefinger.

Father O'Brien looked from my chest to my little fist. Now, as most Catholics know, in those days no one mortal could *touch* the wafer, for only a priest-as-servant-of-God was allowed to touch the Body of Christ.

Not only had I touched Christ, but, well, I'd shredded Him. You'll never get to Heaven if you tear Him to shreds! That's pretty obvious. At that moment I wasn't thinking clearly, to be sure. Flecks of Christ broke free of my fingers. My mind was aflutter. At that same instant Father O'Brien decided to wax theological, his rheumy eyes widening at the ecclesiastical offense. This violation of dogma was more than he could bear. Stepping back a bit, righting the gold chalice and clutching it to his chest, he thundered down at me:

"Don't touch the Body of Christ!"

The words sailed across the vaulted church, ricocheted back from the lofty stained glass windows, and the congregation—not that I was actually aware of the people behind me—must have wondered what in Heaven's name was occurring at stage left. The usually quiet, meek priest suddenly becoming Cotton Mather.

Don't touch the Body of Christ!

Well, frankly, it was a little too late for that. Blindly, frantically, I brushed Christ (Christs!) off my chest and hands, realizing in some odd way that I was certainly destined for the fires of Hell. This was way up there with murder and mayhem. People often told me I was a fresh-mouthed, whiny child, destined for an unhappy life, and now this: the bolt of lightning had come to send little Eddie into the burning cauldron.

In my ears, the echo: *Body of Christ Body of Christ Body of Christ . . .*

I started to scream, my solution to everything then (and now), falling back on the carpet, legs and arms twitching like a chicken on an electric fence. I just screamed and screamed, unabated. My poor mother, that shy unassuming woman, had to leave the back pew and walk down the long aisle. She picked up the blubbering mess that was her shameful offspring and cradled me against her chest, carrying me back up the aisle and out the front door, where I eventually calmed down.

I only came out of my room that afternoon when I was promised a trip to New Haven for a pizza at Pepe's on Wooster Square.

A week later I noticed my suit in the closet, freshly laundered and free of Christ. I had already moved onto other crises.

By the time I was ten or eleven, however, I no longer wanted to be a priest but I had also, I believed, finally mastered the dark mysteries of the Roman Catholic Church, in particular, the scary confessional, that dark black box where I had to kneel and reveal the (increasingly larger and more interesting) dark side to my character. One time, still a small boy, in a burst of fear and reprisal, I finished my litany of sin by posing what I considered a very strong fear: the threat of eternal damnation. Lying in bed one night I came to the conclusion that I had not mentioned some of the many sins along the way, and that God, in His ledger up there, would hold these transgressions—committed at five or six years of age—against me. So, taking a deep breath, I mumbled to Father O'Brien:

"I think that I forgot to tell you—"

"You're speaking to God."

"—To tell God about something I did that I forgot to tell you—Him—about that maybe I should have remembered before because God—You—Him—doesn't forget and I forgot and maybe that wasn't a good idea because you gotta tell it all in here, the nuns said, and if you don't it's like a mental sin and you—not You, I mean, Me—go to Hell where I don't want to go, of course, and so I'm mentioning this now because I'd like to know what to do about it because I *forgot* the sins I should have told You about and so I can't confess what I can't remember, and—" I paused, delirious.

Father O'Brien mumbled something.

"What?"

"Ten Hail Marys and Five Our Fathers."

"That'll do it?"

"Do what?"

It was all so easy.

So, by the time I was around ten or eleven I thought I'd mastered the art of the confessional, creating a failsafe process that ensured passage to heaven.

"I hit my sister."

"How many times?"

"I dunno."

"How many?"

"Ten."

"All right."

"I yelled at my mother—ten times I'm sure—ten times."

Ten seemed to be a magical number in that environment, and I used it over and over again, and Father O'Brien never seemed to question the fact that I stopped all sinning at that magical number. I suppose now and then I threw in a "fifteen" or a "twenty" but those were used for the hardcore transgressions—like stealing or letting my thoughts wander in Sunday School or at Sunday Mass.

But I always saved *lying* to the very end. "I lied eleven times," I always told Father O'Brien, taking a deep sigh. Ten admitted lies (more or less)—and the eleventh for the very confession I was now delivering. Just in case I had lied to God. I figured I covered all the bases that way.

Now I suppose God saw through this charade—a ten-year-old boy was no match for 2,000 years of Christianity and floods and locusts and people being turned to salt—and other such epic drama. But at the time I believed I was inordinately clever. A bright little fellow one step ahead of dogma and perdition.

In Sunday School the nuns gave us the formula for salvation: stay in the confessional, yapping up a storm of erring-do, while at the same time imagining a black, black cloud floating above you. Keep confessing until that pitch-black cloud turns pure white. Simple, huh? I tell you, had I followed that dictum I'd still be in there, sore knees and parched throat.

But I suppose my sassy attitude, a flippancy that alternated with sheer terror and bumbling confessions, came to a head one Saturday afternoon in late fall. Maybe I was eleven, maybe twelve. I can't remember. I was in a rush for something, headed somewhere, and moved through my catchall of sin at breakneck speak—ten mentions of profanity, ten abuses against siblings, this, that, and the other, waiting for the expected ten Hail Marys and Five Our Fathers which I would say at the altar—also at breakneck speed, a kind of *Reader's Digest* penance. I had a shorthand way of doing penance, eliding all words together into a kind of spiritual stream of consciousness. *Our father who art in the name of the father son the kingdom will be done as it is in heaven world without end* . . . God could fill in the blanks. For God's sake, he must have heard it a thousand times. I wasn't that good at improvising. I could add nothing new.

I was just shuffling my body, preparing to say an Act of Contrition and thus be absolved of my horrible sins when Father O'Brien stopped me. He started to ask questions. I wasn't ready for this. He must have been sober.

Now I must have sounded older than was, with all of my bravado and glibness, because all of a sudden, out of the blue, he said into the dark, ill-lighted screen:

"My son, do you have any impure thoughts?"

"What?"

Louder: "My son, do you have any impure thoughts?"

I must confess—and I don't mean confess in the Biblical sense—that, for all my self-important worldliness, I was in the dark on the subject of a lot of things, and sex was right at the top of that list. In fact, the subject of sex occupied virtually all the slots on that list of things I was ignorant of. But, I confess again—once you start, you can't stop, it's like eating potato chips—I didn't associate "impure thoughts" with sex. Keep in mind I was just a little farm-town boy, and this was before the age of cable and the Free Love movements. I'd never *heard* of impure thoughts. But the sheer weight of Father O'Brien's pronouncement—with deliberate enunciation of the awful words—suggested to me that this was some weighty sin. And since my parents constantly told me I was a troublemaker and a creature of errant behavior—well, I assumed this new, unknown sin was something I had already committed.

"Yes, Father," I said slowly. "I have impure thoughts." Can I leave now?

I heard a sudden intake of breath. "You do?"

"Yes, all the time." Getting into it.

"All the time?"

"Constantly."

"Constantly?"

Was there an echo in here? I was weakening. "Yeah, I guess so."

And then, out of nowhere, probably reading from a manual with one of those small flashlights, Father O'Brien began a mournful lecture that probably was ten or fifteen minutes long but seemed an eternity. I don't remember much of it because none of it made any sense—all this talk of carnality, the passion of the flesh, the hot blood of desire, the risk of injury to the soul, the violation of the marriage contract, the possibility of disabled children, the loss of hair, imbecility, the weakening of the blood, the loss of sanity, the death of innocence and the birth of corruption. Hair on the back of knuckles and its relationship to the awfulness of self-abuse. Okay, I'm making all of this up, but that was certainly the tenor of his pep talk. I got weaker and weaker in the knees, faltering, hungry to be free of the wooden cage.

But I do remember his final remarks. He talked of my healthy future, a life lived in the spirit of God and His Kingdom, and then added: "How are you getting home?"

Was he going to provide transportation, a chariot of fire, now that all the enemies had left my corporal being?

"Walk, Father."

"Do me one favor, son."

"What's that, Father?"

"When you walk home, keep your hands out of your pants pockets."

"What?"

He repeated himself. "Keep your *hands* out of your *pockets*." I agreed to his bizarre condition for early release, but this last remark floored me. What would happen if I put my hands into my pockets? What was there? A mandatory handkerchief—Mom wouldn't let me leave the house without it. Some chewing gum, some marbles, some change. Not much.

Yet I walked Route 80 back home with my hands extended like I was balancing a pole on a high wire.

Obviously I'd committed some particularly pernicious sin, though unknown to me. Depression overwhelmed me, made me feel tight inside, and I moped around the house until suppertime, wandering from room to room, listless and damned from here to eternity. At the table I had no appetite as Mom dished on our usual Saturday night fare—pork and beans, hotdogs and one of her out-of-this-world mile-high chocolate cakes. Devil's food, no less. Of course. God, I'd learned, thrives on obvious irony. I picked at my food, desultorily, and Mom stared across the table at me.

"What's the matter with you?"

"Nothing."

"Eat."

"I'm not hungry."

"Eat."

I shook my head.

She clicked her tongue. "What happened today?" How did she know? Was I the last in on the secret?

"Nothing."

"You go to confession?"

"Yes."

"Something happened?"

I took a deep breath. "I think I'm in trouble."

The whole table waited, expectant.

"And?"

"The priest yelled at me."

Startled: "Why?"

"I got problems."

She waited. Then: "Tell me."

I breathed in. "Mom, I can't stop having impure thoughts."

The family acted accordingly. My father suddenly had to go to the bathroom. My older teenaged brother groaned at my hapless stupidity. My little sister didn't have a clue.

"What?" asked my mother.

"The priest told me to stop having them."

"Impure thoughts?"

"Yes." I was near tears now.

My mother stared long and hard at me until I felt I'd wither under her gaze. And then, a half smile appearing, the mother-instinct kicking in, she said quietly: "Eddie, tell me, just what is an impure thought?"

Helpless, I said, "Mom, I don't know."

She sat back. "Let me tell you something," she said. "Someday you'll have an impure thought, and you'll know exactly what it is. You hear me. So till then I don't want you worrying about it. You hear me, Eddie? Someday—not now."

It was like a ton of bricks had been lifted from my skinny ribcage. Suddenly my appetite returned—and so did Dad from the bathroom—and I attacked my food with gusto. Damnation—for the moment—was not imminent.

One week later, of course, I had my first impure thought, coming in the middle of the night like a gift. And it was a real good one, I must admit. I smiled a lot then—and the next day. But I never told Father O'Brien about it. Nor, of course, my Mom.

Some things are best kept to oneself.

Are You Now or Have Ever Been?

In the 1960s I taught English at a high school on the Connecticut shoreline. I was a young guy, imbued with liberal politics and counterculture zeal, and, I admit, my classes often took on a freewheeling, love-in tone, all tempered by my own innate puritanical sensibility, to be sure. But some of the old-guard teachers held me suspect. One of them was across the hall from my classroom. Mr. Grenwald was a small, chubby man who taught civics and driver-education, a man so hopelessly inept and stupid I'd actually seen whole rows of students soundly asleep while he sat at his desk and read the sports page to himself, moving his lips in the process. No matter: he barely spoke to me, and I knew he wasn't happy with the 1960s, the anti-war protests, feminism, black power, and the downward thrust of contemporary education. One day, called to the main office for an outside phone call, I left my classroom. When I returned, my class was all a-titter, some laughing, some edgy. It seems that Mr. Grenwald had noticed my leaving—it must have been during one of the few moments he wasn't focused on ballpark statistics—and scurried across the hall, into my room, and yelled: "Tell me, is Mr. Ifkovic a Communist?"

When the startled class didn't answer, he fled. That afternoon, when I went to see him after school was out, he turned away, refusing to face me. I let it drop.

Well, if he only knew the half of it—if he only knew all about my better-red-than-dead childhood, my vision of life in a Soviet cooperative, and my years dreaming about Joe McCarthy.

In the mid-1950s I was around ten years old and not really wasn't up to speed on national politics. During the 1952 election I'd watched the Republican Convention on someone's TV, got momentarily excited about Eisenhower, and made myself a shabby cardboard placard that announced to the neighborhood *I Like Ike*—until I remembered we were Democrats. Ike was incinerated in the backyard trash barrel. Nobody in the world, it seemed, was for Adlai E. Stevenson except for Mom and Dad. In school the shop teacher—not, mind you, civics, not American history—polled the class during a wood-sawing break—we were assembling our one-hundredth set of bookends—and I was the only student out of thirty or so who announced I was for Stevenson. I remember his damning words: "Being the only one should tell you something, right?" What it told me was that I was in the presence of fools.

But I'd already learned the dangers of being the solitary voice in the small-town wilderness. In the third grade, at the end of the year, the class discussed where to go for our spring field trip. Happily, I raised my hand and suggested Ocean Beach in New London, where there were not only dizzying amusement rides but also a sandy beach. Everyone thought that idea was inspired until some dipstick kid suggested somewhere else. To this day, I can't remember where he suggested we go, so effectively have I repressed the suggestion. But the popular currents shifted, as they are wont to do, and his idea gained momentum. When we voted it was something like twenty-nine to one, with my being loyal to a better idea—mine. We broke for recess and, on the cold hard cruel asphalt of the school playground, I was jumped by five or six classmates who pummeled me until teachers rescued me.

So early on I learned the price you pay for being different in the country that was supposed to applaud it.

I was to learn that lesson again during the Joe McCarthy hearings.

I'd paid scant attention to Mr. McCarthy and his nefarious Commie witch-hunt. It had nothing to do with me. I was an unconcerned kid playing baseball with my brother, weeding the huge family vegetable garden until darkness fell, and building military forts in the deep woods next to our home. But slowly, quietly, I began to be aware of something happening in the household—Mom and Dad whispering at the late-night kitchen table, sudden panicked or excited looks, hunched over shoulders, glances backwards—all of which stopped when I waltzed into the room. Late at night, sleeping in the bedroom upstairs, directly over my parents' bedroom, I'd hear the same whispering, but sometimes there was a raising of voices, a spurt of wildfire anger, and once, I swear, I thought I heard sobbing. That scared me to death.

Slowly, eavesdropper that I was, I learned the reason: Joseph McCarthy.

Mom and Dad were decent, hard-working Americans, the children of immigrants from the old Austro-Hungarian Empire, from villages outside Budapest, from the villages of Croatia in what was to become Yugoslavia. Farmers, factory workers, quarry workers, homemakers, they voted faithfully, raised their kids to be good and ethical citizens, and paid off mortgages and instilled in us a love for refrigerators and hi-fis. We lived in a world of immigrants who loved America and sent their sons to the Second World War—an Italian and Polish neighborhood of small truck farms, but a world where Grandma and Grandpa in that house on the hill hosted huge parties of drinking and eating—an eternal celebration. Every weekend. I was used to heavily accented story telling, with outbursts in a Babel of foreign languages—German, Polish, Slavic, Hungarian, Italian, Yiddish, others. As a boy, I stared in amazement at the crowds of old timers gathered in that old-style kitchen, the beer and wine flowing, the cheesecake disappearing.

There was Mrs. Kube, from somewhere in Eastern Europe, a scattered, bustling woman in a ratty Persian lamb coat, chasing my father around the yard to exact a kiss from him on her withered cheek. Mrs. Nagy, who claimed to have been Miss Budapest, but Mom said no: that was one of the Gabor sisters. Mr. Meyers, a rotund and overly loud German who would clap his beefy hands so loudly birds in the nearby hills would screech. He'd been arrested during the Second World War as he ran up and down the West Haven beach with a swaying lantern, believing he was signaling in his beloved Nazi submarines. Tolerated because of his wife and not his insane political views, Mr. Meyers was a butcher whose wife had had an affair with another butcher. People felt sorry for her. She was a woman who would eat no food the color of yellow or orange. Carloads of distant cousins from Bethlehem, Pennsylvania, would arrive in the summer and never wanted to leave. One girl, I remember, had had scarlet fever—the name intrigued me, as I looked for redness in her skin—so we had to all talk in whispers. I don't know why. Now and then people would look at her and mumble: "Her heart, you know." She, however, boomed in a loud voice about the joys of shoplifting panties from the local Woolworth's. So the kitchen was a mélange of voices and cultures and, often, arguments about the politics of the homelands. The post-Second World War world of Russian occupation only fueled the fires, and people talked of visiting relatives in Yugoslavia, people they had to meet in public squares, not private homes, talking in whispers, followed by Soviet and Tito's agents.

But somehow I knew my parents' whispering was different from these Old World conversations about earlier wars. I learned it had to do with Joseph McCarthy going on national TV and listing various Slavic-American organizations as Communist fronts. Admittedly there were Slavic congresses that indeed promulgated Soviet doctrine, fifth-column organizations decidedly anti-American, but most such organizations were feel-good immigrant benevolent societies that fostered a better life for the immigrants and their children. But Slavic was Slavic, it seemed, and McCarthy, descending towards madness, was xenophobic in a big way. He denounced virtually all Slavic or East European organizations as treasonous, and one of them was our beloved Croatian Fraternal Union, a Pittsburgh-based benevolent society that began as a traditional burial society at the end of the nineteenth century. As American as could be, loyal to a fault, the CFU found itself labeled subversive, Commie-dealing, part of the Red Menace McCarthy creamed his pants over. It was nothing of the sort. What I remember is the Junior Lodge of the CFU, which sent us children's storybooks, with pictures of Lincoln and George Washington to color in. Simplistic jokes and pleasant little serials about American kids just like us. I looked forward to those magazines. Everyone we knew in the Croatian community of Branford was a member of that insurance lodge, and various cousins of mine helped run the local, which ironically held its monthly meetings in the tiny colonial building where Yale University was first established.

But suddenly there was trouble.

I heard bits and pieces of my parents' conversations, but what I did hear scared me. Because *they* were frightened out of their wits. Here they were, stalwart citizens of the glorious Republic, and daily they read of people called before the HUAC—the dreaded House Un-American Activities Committee— lives ruined, jobs lost, families torn asunder, and, worse, raids by the Immigration Bureau in the night, and deportation to the Soviet Union. Of course, they had little to fear—though maybe I'm wrong here— but these were harrowing times. The newspapers and radio were filled with story after story of people found in contempt of the Congress, big-name people, Hollywood celebrities, Broadway luminaries, university professors, of people "squealing." Of people betraying brothers. The haunting specter of fifth-column infiltration was everywhere. In school one teacher read us a story of how a young boy turned his Commie parents in, and they were arrested by the FBI. The boy was a hero, the teacher said. Was she looking at me?

My folks were afraid. Once I heard Mom: "What are we gonna do?" Another time: "How could we know?"

When I watched Joe McCarthy on TV, an ugly man with dark jowls, sallow skin, and seeping venom, I hated him—feared him. Somehow he was responsible for my parents' sadness and anger and fear.

"Where did we go wrong?"

"What shall we do?"

When I walked into the kitchen or living room, the chatter would stop, but not the fear in the eyes, the twitching of the lips. "What about the children?" In short order McCarthy quietly removed the CFU and a few other organizations from his black list, and, at least on paper, life returned to normal. We went back to watching the Reverend Fulton J. Sheen's *Life is Worth Living* on our new Admiral TV. But that was too easy a conclusion. For, in the middle of the McCarthy hearings, as night after night my parents whispered in the hallways, I began to have the nightmare that was to plague me, uncontrolled, for years to come. And it was always the same feverish nightmare, two or three times a week, coming at me full-force until I woke up screaming in the upstairs bed.

The scenario was always the same: in the long dark night I am suddenly awakened from a blissful sleep by the sound of strident voices outside the house. In my pajamas I crawl to the window that overlooked the deep woods abutting our property, and I realize that Mom is talking to someone through the open window in their bedroom, directly below my brother's and my room. Sequestered in the night shadows and hidden under the wind-driven foliage of the maple trees are two people, a man and a woman, both dressed—this is etched on my mind—in khaki-colored raincoats with lots of buckles and buttons. They are wearing hats that cover their foreheads. I never really hear their words but the voices are insistent, deliberate. They sound like Mr. Meyers when he got mad. What I hear is Mom pleading with them: no no no no. Not my Eddie. For they have come to the edge of the forest in North Branford, Connecticut, population

1,000, to take me—me! —back to the Soviet Union with them. And they're not leaving without me.

Now why the Politburo cannot do with the services of an enslaved ten-year-old boy who occasionally wet his bed—with nightmares like this, are you surprised? —I had no idea.

At those times I would wake up, screaming, and hear my mother rouse herself to come upstairs to comfort me.

I suffered through this awful dream for years. Each time it seemed more real, the two Soviet agents becoming characters I felt I knew. Sometimes—but rarely—I dreamed of Joe McCarthy but he was always encased in a twelve-inch Admiral black-and-white TV and for some reason he was yelling, not at me, but at Miss Connecticut, a local woman who held that honor years before and visited my Grandma on occasion, a plump, heavily-made-up blonde I used to stare at, not believing she could ever have held that coveted title. What she was doing with Joe McCarthy I'll never know. She wasn't even Slavic. But years later he did strike me as the kind of man who might hang out with cheap barfly whores. Not that I would know.

Those were bad times, I recall. My father fell off our roof doing some repairs, and was out of work for six months. I have images of him stooped over, in pain, making his way to the bathroom, a shadowy presence in the hallway. With my mother I'd watch the McCarthy-Army hearings on TV, when she was not watching *Queen for a Day*. We never spoke, the two of us, sitting there watching the beginning of the end for good old Joe. But we didn't know that then. It seemed the nightmare would go on forever. But I know I lived in a state of continual fear, fed by fifth column TV shows and John Cameron Swayze's ponderous nightly newscasts.

The next spring, I think, it all hit home. I was home from school because of the flu, alone in the house because my brother and sister were at school and Dad was back at work and Mom was also working at the factory now. I slept in my parents' bed downstairs, just sleeping all day, battling a fever. The radio was on for company, and, too tired to change the station, I listened to McCarthy's voice droning on and on. Later in the afternoon I went to the bathroom, and, returning to bed, dizziness swept over me and I fell, hitting my head on the doorjamb. I must have been unconscious and, in that state, I remember sounds: soft buzzing noises, humming that sounded close to my ears but then swept away, tantalizing me. And then there was light, that shaft of compelling light that we would all be reading about years later, that warm, intense light that beckoned me, drew me, enticed me. The sweet humming, the aroma of dying flowers, and the comforting light: I followed them up to a brick wall in which there was a miniscule hole. The ray of light ended there, and I started to move through that narrow opening. Suddenly, almost to the other side, I came face to face with a world of screaming demonic faces, shrill and awful, grotesque beings piled atop one another, flowing, pushing, and shoving. Venomous gargoyles, spitting and vomiting. So horrific was the vision that I was startled awake, and I found myself lying in a sweaty heap on the hall floor. I was alive. I was panting. I was insensible. But I believe at that moment when I entered that opening I had been close to death: had I gone through I would be dead. I wasn't ready. When I woke up on that cold linoleum floor, my fever had broken.

Somehow, irrationally perhaps, I blamed it all on Joe McCarthy. I still do.

But I end this story of Joe McCarthy with a coda: the tale of Mr. Leon Epstein. A few years after my McCarthy wars, I was in the seventh grade in the town's new junior high school, and our algebra teacher that year was Mr. Epstein, a man that even to my untrained eye was out of place in the sleepy, rural town of North Branford. Something about the man said bright lights, big city. Something about him also said displaced person. Lost soul. He always looked uncertain in his rumpled suit and tie—and I mean that literally. He wore suits that reminded me of something—I wasn't sure what—and it wasn't until years later than I realized they looked like Hollywood costumes of the 1930s and 1940s black and white films. The kind John Gilbert wore, with a fedora atop his head. Always solid colors, like deep brown or dark mustard. Or a dark blue, but dull and metallic. Or funereal black. With wide, billowing pants and Sam Spade lapels. What I'm saying is that the colors were somehow *wrong*.

The suits were *wrong*. But he was a wonderful teacher, although I admit he struck me as too bright for our annoying, lazy class. Quietly he'd explain some algebraic equation to the masses, speaking logically and slowly, and I, for one, started to understand math for the first time in my life. Always a reader, always an excellent student in English and History—high placed on those brutal aptitude tests we were subjected to—I couldn't fathom math at all. Algebra was, frankly, runic mystery. Mr. Epstein somehow got through to me. He'd explain some fact or equation and I'd sit there, saying to myself: yeah, sure, that makes sense. But he was also a very kind man, especially to the eager, talkative kids. Like me. When he asked about your family and picnics and jobs, it didn't sound phony. Once, when Jimmy Fournier was clowning before class and his T-shirt rode up his back, we all witnessed the long horizontal welts across his back. We all knew his dad whipped him all the time, usually for no reason. In those days no one did anything about such blatant abuse, but well I remember the look on Mr. Epstein's mobile face: I'd never seen a face cave in like that, such raw horror and concern, such—well—real pain. I never forgot it.

When someone asked him if he went to the local church, he said no: he lived in New Haven and was Jewish. That frightened some of the kids.

But I admit he tried too hard to befriend us sometimes. Certain subjects were out of his league. "How about that World Series?" He tried talking about baseball to some of the boys, stiff, formal remarks about the Yankees and the Red Sox—I didn't follow sports so such attempts were wasted on me. Nobody reacted because it just didn't ring true. He looked tremendously uncomfortable. I felt sorry for him. When he was just himself, he did all right.

But I liked him a lot, and he sent home notes to my Mom about my wonderful progress.

But November was election time in the small town, and suddenly, out of nowhere, he became the big campaign issue. You see, back in his early days in New York City, the son of left-wing Jewish intellectuals and schoolteachers, he'd been enrolled as a member of some Communist Youth group. In the post-Stalinist era he'd recanted his youthful indiscretion, and when he was hired by my happy little town to teach us urchins algebra, he fully informed the Board of Education of his shadowy past. No one had a problem with it. But in the Republican-controlled town, the Democrats, I guess, thought they'd make an issue of it all, and, in short order, it was nasty business all around.

The quiet, unassuming man was the center of debate and firebrand politics, caught in a vicious eddy of attack-and-accusation. This was, after all, the immediate afterglow of McCarthy years and that cancerous witch-hunt, and the nation was still taking prisoners out in the provinces. Mr. Epstein said nothing, but the local politicos—who never had a real issue outside of zoning referendums and manure pollution—suddenly made him the scapegoat for Communist scares and the brainwashing of their children. So now the Red Menace had a face. Commie, Jew, New York City, intelligentsia, the Rosenbergs—a ready-made package for all our fuzzy fears. Mr. Epstein submitted his resignation, bowing out, and one Monday morning he did not show up in the classroom. I remember he'd filled the blackboard with algebraic definitions we were always to consult. On Monday morning the board had been eerily erased. For the rest of the year the town hired substitutes—mostly blue-haired old ladies who knew nothing about algebra. Or children, for that matter. Which is why I never learned algebra, and in successive years, including college, barely squeaked by.

Filled with heat and wonder, the students started a petition to reinstate him, with most of us signing the document. But when parents got wind of it, students suddenly started crossing their names off the wrinkled sheet. My mother—who had already been through the McCarthy wars—talked of him constantly, filled with melancholy and sadness. After all, he'd sent notes home about how wonderful I was.

My signature stayed on the useless petition. I think it was one of a handful.

Frowning, without comment, the principal threw it into the wastebasket when I handed it over.

Mr. Epstein disappeared, we learned, into a life in New Haven. Years later I was happy to learn that he had become a successful independent publisher of specialized books on modern art and classical music, and I often noticed his name on the spines of elegant books I spotted in bookstores. I wondered if he remembered his little venture into rural Connecticut and the bitterness his presence engendered.

But a couple of years after he left the school, my mother read in *The New Haven Register* that his daughter had graduated with honors from some prestigious private school. I noticed how happy it made her as she clipped the item from the paper. That night she wrote a letter to him, commenting on his daughter's success. She spent most of one night writing and rewriting, looking for the exact words. I read all the drafts, but she never asked for my opinion. Mr. Epstein never wrote back. But I do remember a couple of lines from her letter to him:

"You were a kind man in an unkind time," she wrote. "You were an honest man in a world of liars."

The Starving Children
of China

The first day of fifth grade Miss Hubner gathered the class in front of the pegboard hanging behind her desk. Pressed in between classmates who smelled of starched shirts and chocolate milk and peanut butter cookies, I stared at the blank board. She waited for silence. She didn't have to wait long: she was a gigantic woman, nearly six feet tall, with clunky, heavy-soled shoes that made banging noises as she walked the aisles. Her eyes peered out through thick rhinestone-studded eyeglasses, the lenses magnifying her pupils so they looked like glassy agates. All she had to do was glare at you and you shut up. But she smiled a lot that first day, and that was good.

"This is important," she said. "Very important." I listened, but only a little: all teachers said everything was important. This was one of the life lessons I'd already learned. In the third grade when we had to take mandatory tap dance lessons from a visiting dancer with a spangled, sequined outfit that exposed the fattest thighs I'd ever seen, well, I rebelled, always forgetting to leave recess in the yard to be on time in the school basement for the shuffle, glide, whatever routine. When my repeated absences were noted, the teacher called me to her desk. "This is important," she said. "Dancing is important."

"This is important." From Miss Huge. I mean Miss Hubner. It had taken the class barely a half-second to give her the appropriate nickname.

She held up a photograph clipped from *Life* magazine, moving it slowly left to right—like show and tell, with her doing the entire showing and certainly the telling. I leaned forward. It was a grainy black-and-white snapshot, perhaps eight by ten or so, depicting some war-ravaged landscape in China. In the background you saw burned-out or bombed-out huts and an overturned cart—which Miss Hubner pointed out, *tsking* as she did so. But in the foreground was an emaciated child, mouth open in a silent scream, eyes wide with terror. The face dominated the landscape.

"The starving children of China," Miss Hubner intoned, and waited.

We waited. This *was* important.

"Do you understand?" she asked.

We obviously didn't and she knew it because she didn't pause. "All over the world children are starving, all over the world there is war and destruction. Do you know how lucky you are to be in this country, in the United States, where children do not starve and we don't lived in burned-out buildings?" She caught her breath. "Do you understand now?'

We all nodded insanely. "Every day you should thank God you're in America."

As we watched, she carefully—dare I say ritualistically—thumbtacked the photo to the center of the pegboard. She turned back to us.

"This is my *most* important photograph," she said, soberly. "I keep it as a reminder to me and my students of how the world can be a cruel place."

We nodded, acolytes in the new world order, 1953 style.

"All year long I want you to look at it, especially when you're ready to do something you shouldn't. Think before you act. The

Chinese baby is watching you. He is saying: look what you have. I have nothing."

We went back to our seats, without genuflecting.

All day long I couldn't take my eyes off the suffering child. At lunchtime, sitting with my peanut-butter-and-jelly-on-rye sandwich, with institutional milk, I had trouble eating. I was thinking of China. Now I knew that if you dug a hole straight down through the earth you'd reach China. All kids knew that, and there was one time my cousin Jimmy Begosh and I started the Big Dig in his parents' backyard, not getting very far on a swimming pool. It was August and we were in need of a swim. When his father came home from lunch, he chased Jimmy into the house with a switch to his bottom and sent me home.

So now I would have the miserable face of China staring at me all through the year.

So I began the fifth grade.

Miss Hubner was too much of a giant for me to love, though I usually adored my teachers. In the first grade I became obsessed with Miss Carpet, a severe spinster the kids didn't like, but I loved her. Timidly I asked her for a photograph and she seemed genuinely stunned by the request. A month later she quietly handed me a headshot that, she later told my mother, she'd had specially taken at a local photographer's. Strangely, she said, she had no pictures of herself available. (I still have that photograph.) It was a wonderful gesture. I followed her around like the proverbial puppy dog, but I was probably more an irritant than a pleasure. At night, my whole family would sit in front of the console Zenith radio, with me right up against the speakers, and listen to *Sergeant Preston of the Yukon* and *The Fat Man* and other radio-days melodramas, and my mind would wander to Miss Carpet. Was she at home listening to Sgt. Preston yelling "Mush!" at his large husky King? At night, in bed, I dreamed of the Arctic tundra, of places like Nome and Juneau, and of Miss Carpet.

When I was in junior high school I worked for one week one summer at a local Catholic carnival on a field owned by the Doody Farm, selling hamburgers and hotdogs. One Friday night there was a long line of pushing people, but I noticed two old, old women standing at the far end of the counter, just waiting, so I went to talk to them. "Are you Eddie Ifkovic?" one asked. "Do you remember Miss Carpet?" the other said. That shocked me. "Yes," I said. The woman smiled. "She often talks of you. She said you had the sweetest voice as a boy." I was rushed, a little confused, a fairly callous adolescent, and I had a job to get back to. "Hey, tell her I said hello," I said, a little too glibly, turning back to my hot dogs. I've always regretted my abrupt turning away, chalking it up to teenage rudeness. Minutes later I noticed the two women standing at a distance, staring at me, just staring. Over the years I've come to believe that one of the women was, indeed, Miss Carpet, whom I didn't recognize. They were tiny woman, skinny and shriveled, and in my recollections Miss Carpet was tall, regal, statuesque. How did they know who I was? And why was Miss Carpet still thinking about me—then a fifteen- or sixteen-year-old boorish teenager? I didn't know. Well, frankly, I *was* the one who asked her for her photograph. Which, as I've said, I still own.

I never asked Miss Hubner for her snapshot. That would have been a pretty ugly scene, especially if my fellow classmates overheard. Frankly, it just never entered my mind.

I hung out with a group of kids who didn't fit in with the elite of town. In North Branford then there were two groups of kids, although the lines often blurred. On our side of town, metaphorically speaking, were mostly Italian and Polish folks, immigrants and their children. A smattering of Irish and Germans. And the other side of town, again metaphorically speaking, was the world of the old Yankees or Anglo-Saxons, the polished kids who talked breezily of skiing weekends and snow lodges up north. My own friends resorted to building igloos out of ice-hard snow and, if we wanted to go downhill on the snowy banks, we slid on our asses. Life was simple.

One of my casual friends was Annie Porsini, a chunky girl who was very Catholic and very loud. I vaguely remember her coming to school one day with a book titled something like *Facts of Life and Love for Teenagers*, which she'd stolen from her older sister's bureau, but she herself clearly didn't have a clue what it was about. No one listened to her as she waved it in our faces. We were ten years old. We had other things to worry about. She wore her hair in a frizzled little Orphan Annie style and someone suggested she stick quarters in her eyes during recess. She didn't think that was funny. A few years later she screamed at me because I used the expression, "That shook me up," which, she claimed, was offensive sexual language. I ignored her. She'd tell everyone off in a clipped, precise voice, but if we shot a barb in her direction, her mother would phone our homes with threats of million-dollar lawsuits. It was mind-boggling. Her mother was the arch-villain of our simple days, a skinny, angry woman with huge unblinking eyes and a hawk nose that always seemed to be dripping something unpleasant onto her chest. She didn't seem to like anyone, and, in particular, she liked to pass judgment on hapless young people. Sometimes she'd drive us somewhere—to a park or school outing—and there was always some disaster waiting. You could count on it. She looked forward to it. She also never used the directional signals on the car, preferring to extend her arms and indicate left, right, u-turn, God knows what else. But her hand maneuvers were so idiosyncratic and labor-intensive that cars screeched to a halt behind us, some veered onto sidewalks and into hedges. Horns blared. Strips of rubber tire across two lanes. She'd look surprised. One time a friend named Joey commented on her signaling, saying, "Are you drying your nails, Mrs. P.?" Mrs. P. glared into the rearview mirror, the car veered over the line, and we were almost hit head on by a dump truck carrying manure for the Morello farm.

Joey was never allowed in her car again. Banished.

One time we picked up Freddie Trunski, walking along Route 80, headed home. A sometime friend from class, he was a bland boy, just there, harmless as toast. He sat in the back seat and Mrs. P. kept eyeing him through her rearview mirror, like she knew something we didn't. After greeting us, he'd probably said two words the whole time, those being "Thank you."

We dropped him in front of his driveway. But as Mrs. P. pulled away, she said, in a loud, angry voice, "Just who is he?"

I spoke up. "That's Freddie Trunski. He's—"

She interrupted. "I mean, who IS he?"

"He's Freddie Trunski." Was she deaf?

Impatient: "I mean, who does he think he is?"

"What?"

"I hate people who put on airs."

I started to say something but stopped. I was missing something here. Freddie was maybe eleven years old.

"Somebody should speak to his parents," she said.

Nobody said anything. Mrs. P. continued her harangue. "Some people these days. What's the world coming to?"

I looked at her daughter Annie. She was nodding her head in agreement, obviously horrified at the state of the world.

So I was learning that many grownups were bonkers, off the deep end, but I think I knew that before. What I didn't know was how to deal with death and dying. Now my father's father had died when I was a little boy, and I have only one vague, impressionistic image of Anthony Ifkovic, Sr. as he stood on my parents' front lawn: a distinct sensation of being lifted up and held. Nothing more. When I was in kindergarten the house up the street caught fire, an ill-kept rooming house filled with dirt-poor Italian immigrants, and I stayed home from school because I'd seen a fireman carry out the bundle of blankets holding the body of a little classmate who'd been trapped inside a basement apartment and was dead when they found him. But I was too young to understand what was happening. But one morning in class, Miss Hubner announced that Jamie Peterman would not be returning because his parents had died in a car crash. I'd seen the newspaper article the day before in *The New Haven Register*, a snapshot of his mom and dad in happier days. But Jamie was a loner, his family only recently moved into town from New Haven, so he was a stranger to most of us.

But a month later Miss Hubner announced that Rose Mary DeLucca's mother had died of a sudden heart attack. Now that news hit home: Rose Mary was part of our little group of friends, a giggly, cheery girl who thought everything I said was downright hilarious. And we all knew her mother, who always drove us places, a tiny Italian woman who gave us food and more food. And then more food. I was stunned at the news, coming as it did during school. I did not know how to handle it. Rose Mary dropped out of class for two weeks, and when she returned we all left her alone. I didn't know how to talk to her. She looked so beaten, so sad. We never mentioned her mother, but that's all I thought about. It was bad enough I had to face the starving children of China, but now I was assailed by a new, equally dark story. Her mother: that laughing woman dead in a box.

Which led to my stupid comment.

A month or so later, on a Saturday afternoon, somebody's father was driving a bunch of us somewhere, maybe to get hotdogs at the Branford shore, and we picked up Rose Mary at her home. We hadn't seen much of her since the death, especially outside of school. I was babbling and nervous, and Rose Mary looked back at me. Without thinking—and I don't know where this came from—I blurted out, "Rose Mary, how's your mother?"

She didn't answer me, turning away, but my face burned with shame. The other kids looked at me as if I had lost my mind. I started to say something, then mercifully shut up. That night I lay in bed, my cheeks hot to the touch, beating myself up over and over. What the hell was wrong with me? *"Rose Mary, how's your mother?"*

In school I found myself staring at the photograph of the Chinese child. Those eyes accused me, but of what I wasn't sure. I only knew that I'd violated some code, secret though it was. When Miss Hubner saw me gazing at the photo, she smiled, nodded approvingly. Red-faced, I turned away.

After all, I was a good boy. I harmed no one. In school I was the model of respectable behavior, and, unfortunately, I became in some way the poster boy for The Good Student. And nobody wants to be a poster boy. "Why can't you be more like Eddie?" Of course, these words were the kiss of death: I was insulted, pushed, ostracized, mangled, overturned, suspended by my feet, given the finger, called "sissy boy," "teacher's pet," (to which one of my teachers, overhearing the jibe, said: "not teacher's pet, teacher's helper"—as if that would smooth feathers). Yes, that helped my standing a lot. When I accidentally broke the mirror Miss Hubner had hung over the supply cabinet, she simply smiled and said, "Seven years of bad luck for you, Eddie." Oddly, I considered that omen good news. I believed her. That afternoon, on the bus ride home, my best friend Tony insisted I did it on purpose. "Why?" I asked. "Like I want bad luck?" "So Miss Huge can feel sorry for you."

"No, she doesn't," I yelled.

"You're like her *pet*."

Tony was pissed because, earlier that week, Miss Huge had singled him out for his sloppy work, and used him as an example for the class. For the hundredth time I told myself I needed a new best friend.

Tony, frankly, had only one story—his glorious future. After high school he was going to Hollywood to become an actor. Everyone said he'd make it big. His mother promised to pay for acting lessons in New Haven. He'd be on TV. He'd act with John Wayne. He'd be a matinee idol. The fact that he looked like a chubby Dumbo with an irregular buzz cut and had eyes so close together they were in danger of melding—and that he was afraid to stand and recite before the class—none of that deterred his dreams. He did, in fact, migrate to Hollywood right after high-school graduation, but by then we were no longer friends. Once I thought saw him in a crowd scene on *The Mary Tyler Moore Show* but I couldn't be certain. He still looked like Dumbo but he had psychedelic long hair.

To his credit, Tony initiated me into a life of crime. He and I stole two scratched 45 rpm records. One, I hate to admit now, was by Julius LaRosa, which makes this story all the more lame. The other is best forgotten—whatever it was. Sometimes on rainy days Miss Hubner let us play music on the little RCA player she had, and kids brought in records. Somehow the two 45s were forgotten by the owner—abandoned, I liked to believe—and ended up in a pile of junk in the cloakroom. Tony wanted them desperately, and I agreed it was a great idea. I was suddenly contemplating a career in music. If Dumbo could become a Hollywood matinee idol, all slicked over and glassy eyed on screen, I could be Eddie Fisher, all charm and tuxedo. When I'd asked Mom for voice lessons, she'd stared at me as if I'd asked for extra ammo for the family Lugar. So one afternoon, lingering after school, Tony and I tucked the 45s under our coats and ran out of the building. No one ever was the wiser, and it was never mentioned.

Or so we thought.

Near the end of the school year some kids were talking about something with Miss Hubner out of the room, and all of a sudden someone mentioned the disappearance of two 45s months before. Someone else chimed in, and then it seemed like the whole world knew about it. Had it been on the evening news? Was there an all-points-bulletin out? Was *The New Haven Register* sending out an investigative reporter? The talk went on for a bit, and then, as though rehearsed, five or six kids turned and stared full into my face.

"What?" I said.

"Nothing," one said, and someone else said: "Shhh."

That was the end of it.

Tony and I discussed it that afternoon, hanging out in his backyard. He blamed me for "confessing"—being "a rat." I pleaded innocence. Here was a big unsolved mystery, at least for us. What had we missed? Mystery swirled around us, two neophyte culprits of crime. I remember thinking: there are things I may never understand. One was obviously the popularity of Julius LaRosa, but, more important, there was a world out there that kept its secrets from me. Life suddenly seemed a little more complex.

On the last day of school, a hot June day, I looked forward to summer, but something was wrong. Rose Mary was leaving to live with relatives in New York. Dumbo/Tony was spending the summer with cousin in Providence. My cousin Jimmy Begosh was going to camp. I felt deserted. On that last day we were all commandeered to clean and pack up the classroom, washing down the blackboard (they were black then, not green). taking down the maps, charts and other decorations. It was a frenzy of activity as we filed, stacked, and organized. Miss Hubner led the charge, posting orders, chronicling lapses in work ethic and errant behavior. She stood there with a pointer and directed us as though she were Toscanini leading the NBC Orchestra. At the end of the day, as we gathered our belongings together, she said her goodbye, handed us our report cards. *Do not open. Give them to your parents first. Do not open. Hear me?* And waved us off. She looked exhausted, a survivor of a Russian gulag. Some rhinestones had broken free of her eyeglasses. She waved us off, her job done. We filed out to a waiting bus.

But I'd forgotten something and rushed back to retrieve it. Miss Hubner was clearing the pegboard. As I scooted to the door, I saw her remove the tacks from the cherished picture of that starving child of China. Throughout the year she'd thumped it with her pointer, directing our attention to it. Indeed, I'd memorized its black-and-white starkness. There were now tears on the edges, a rip in one corner. Idly, she looked at it, and then, with an indifferent shrug, she crumpled it up and tossed it into the wastebasket.

Mouth Noises

Mrs. Hartley told us there was only one behavior guaranteed to put her over the edge: Mouth Noises. "I will not tolerate mouth noises," she announced the first day of sixth grade.

I didn't have a clue what she was referring to.

I could see why farting would send her into orbit, or the rubbing noises made with one's arm under an opposing armpit. Or burping one's corned beef hash, cafeteria style. Tricks of the boyhood trade.

Needless to say, I was the first offender—the test case, the sacrificial lamb. During the first week of the school year, on one of those oppressive September days when the classroom was unbearably hot because the windows only opened so much, we were doing an Art Project. That meant cutting up colored construction paper and gluing the pieces onto each other in the hopes that Matisse might not feel threatened. I was always very impressed with my inspired concoctions, convinced that if I couldn't be a singer on *Your Hit Parade* or a priest, I would be, well, Norman Rockwell, whose heart-tugging confections graced *The Saturday Evening Post*, which my family loyally subscribed to.

All of a sudden—I swear I was intentionally bumped by that fat fuck Donnie Perillo who occupied a space and a half of precious earth—I dropped a jar of paste and inadvertently emitted a sound, a high-pitched squeal.

It was, I immediately learned, a Mouth Noise.

Mrs. Hartley seemed old and feeble, but she could move like an Olympic speed racer when wrongdoing was afoot in her fiefdom. Hovering over me, she screamed, in a sound not very much different from my own recent high squeal: "Did you make that mouth noise?"

"I dropped—" I started to explain what had happened, but Mrs. Hartley did not believe in accidents. She once announced that "Accidents don't happen. If you think things through, you'll know what is coming, and then stop it." I didn't subscribe to that philosophy then—and not now, certainly—but Mrs. Hartley put a hand on my bony shoulder and said: "You did that on purpose."

"What?"

"Mouth noises."

"I dropped—"

"I will not tolerate mouth noises."

I guess she'd had a lot of trouble with pre-teen boys who made it a habit to squeak and scream and shriek and sputter, all done purposely in her earshot to drive her to the edge of institutionalization. Suddenly I found myself led—in fact, dragged by the ear (a Victorian gesture that seems to have disappeared from elementary schools in American)—to the principal's office, that forbidden land at the front of the school where no one wanted to go. I was yelled at, given no chance to rebut the accusations, and sentenced to an afternoon sitting outside her office near where the secretaries were stationed, in front of the look-at-me-I'm-guilty glass wall, sitting there without book or appeal, as classes passed by, as other teachers looked at me with squinted eyes, with *tsk tsk* mouth noises of their own, as the long dreary afternoon passed, and my purgatory finally ended. That afternoon I rode home on the school bus a defeated little boy.

Then things got worse. Within days I became not only the Master of the Mischievous and Menacing Mouth Noises but the indifferent Bad Older Brother. While waiting one morning for the school bus with my younger sister Geraldine, I spotted the bus coming down the hill, and my sister saw it too, and, in a panic, ran smack dab into the side of a passing Volkswagen Beetle. The car pulled over, the stunned occupants got out, and my sister lay on the ground like a disheveled doll. The bus pulled up, seemed indifferent to the catastrophe, and I, following suit, blithely got on the bus and nodded good morning to the driver—and off we went.

A couple hours later, as I sat in Mrs. Hartley's classroom during arithmetic, the principal walked in, spoke to Mrs. Hartley, and they called me outside into the hallway. "In case you're interested," the woman said, a little snidely, "your sister is fine. She was only stunned. No injuries."

I'd already figured that out—I don't know how—but she'd looked okay lying on the ground with her books and lunchbox resting on her forehead.

Then the principal shook her head. "Why did you get on the bus?"

What kind of question was this? A trick one? "I had to go to school."

I had to go to school.

Such loyalty to the institution of American education did not impress them. Mrs. Hartley and the principal exchanged chances that clearly indicated I was a hardened, soulless little beast, one already infamous for mouth noises, a killer of his beloved kindergarten teacher during a Christmas pageant, a boy destined to be hanged.

I was glad Mrs. Hartley didn't know the half of it. Indifference to my sister's plight might be one thing—even my Mom commented on my odd behavior as she pampered my sister with some chocolate cake and caresses—but I'd already tried to kill my sister before.

Actually, twice.

Indifference was, I thought, a step up the moral ladder. At a Fourth of July family barbecue the food was prepared on a red-hot cast-iron plate set atop cement blocks. All afternoon my grandparents and others turned hot dogs and hamburgers, steaks, corn, vegetables on that plate. A year back, as maybe twenty-five people sat around it, talking throughout the late afternoon, I'd happily stepped up and hurled a packet of firecrackers onto the hot grill, which, of course, exploded and sailed into the air. The mills of God may grind slowly but they seem to have remarkably good aim: the remaining firecrackers slammed into my face—no one else's! —and I was left with second-degree burns on my face. Not a soul was sympathetic to me.

So a year later, forbidden to handle fireworks because I was still on parole, I fought with Geraldine, as I did throughout the year. In a pique of anger I hurled her onto the hot plate where she burned off the palms of her hands. (In her failed memory she says I hurled her doll on top of the plate and, in trying to retrieve Betsy-Wetsy, she fell onto the blazing iron.) In either case I'm the heavy here, and the sight of my sister walking around with two bandaged hands was ample reminder of my sinning. Of course, every relative I encountered in weeks to come—especially the puritanical aunts—addressed my errant behavior more forcibly.

Then, one afternoon, on a long hot August day, she and I were fighting at the edge of the woods near our home. It had been a dry summer, the stagnant waters of the woods had dried up, and the nights were humid and merciless. We lived at the base of Totoket Mountain, which rose up above the trap rock quarry, and sometimes when my cousin Jimmy and I hiked through the dense undergrowth and stony ravines on that mountain we'd hear the ready rattle of a nearby mountain rattlesnake. That always set us running. But it was also the territory of the venomous and dreaded copperhead, and during the dry season the vipers would slither down the mountain, thirsty and probably looking for revenge. We had an expanse of green lawn stretching out behind our garage, next to the woods, and we were warned not to run in our bare feet on the dewy lawn at night, for the copperheads liked to luxuriate there, mesmerized by moonlight and deer and probably the sound of my singing in the shower. I did not know how much of this was adult story-telling to scare us little buggers, but I believed every word.

So one afternoon, battling with my sister at the edge of the woods, getting frustrated and filled with boyish and brotherly rage, I grabbed her arm and swung her in circles, preparing to hurl her into the undergrowth where the skunk cabbage and Indian pipes hugged the swamp maples and chokecherry bushes. But just at the moment when I started to let go of her arm, I spotted a still copperhead poised in a bed of marsh marigolds, right near us, frozen in place, possibly threatened by our wild and dangerous actions, an old copperhead deliberately coiled and ready to strike. Yes, I said, coiled. I was in the process of hurling my sister—her palms still scarred from our earlier battle at the barbecue—onto the waiting snake. Some odd familial instinct kicked in, and in the act of letting her go, I also reached out and grabbed her, pulling her away, and the two of us toppled onto the lawn. She, of course, was totally baffled by my sudden chivalric behavior, so woefully out of character and expectation, and when I mentioned the copperhead we both looked. It was no longer there, having disappeared into the dense bed of swamp grass. She didn't believe me.

In any event, one way of looking at the story is that I actually saved my sister's life. However, that's not the version most family members recount.

So Mrs. Hartley didn't know of my nefarious track record with my sister's mortality. But no matter: in short order, there was a wonderful metamorphosis in my relationship with Mrs. Hartley. I became her darling, her pet, and all my past transgressions were forgiven. You see, I was an eager student, hungry for knowledge, and Mrs. Hartley was a dedicated teacher who responded well to facile minds she could influence. I was a good student, but not a noteworthy one, a plodding scholar. Books were just there—not entertainment I'd seek out. That would change. Mrs. Hartley kept a wide bookshelf by the front window, and we each had to read one book a week and report on it. So I read and reported, but I was constantly switching books, starting one and then abandoning it, bored unless some bit of adventure caught my eye. Mrs. Hartley wasn't happy. That would change.

One day I chose a book titled *The Door in the Wall* (I recently learned, via Internet, written by Marguerite de Angel), an historical fiction about Robin, a royal lad, who is tutored by a monk named Luke. I read one page, yawned, and put the book back on the shelf. Mrs. Hartley spotted my gesture and made me retrieve the book.

"I can't get into it," I said in defense.

That afternoon, while the others were in the library, she made me stay with her, and I sat next to her. I still remember her reading aloud, her finger touching each word deliberately, emphasizing and coloring the words with a life I certainly didn't know anything about. She kept pausing: "See what's happened? See?" And she looked at me with steely eyes, demanding I comprehend.

I did. After a few pages the story came alive to me. The boy's life caught me. And then she stopped. "Take this home." I did. And I read the whole book that night. Frankly, it was as though I had just learned how to read. Like I'd been doing it all wrong for years. Like my life had entered the pages of that book and I was a part of the action.

From that moment on, I swear to God, I became the inveterate reader I am to this day. I read and read—I couldn't take enough books out of the library—and I read and read. I devoured books like they were the penny candy I bought at Loeber's General Store by the town green. By the time I was in high school, when I took a full course of classes with a host of extracurricular activities, including being editor of the school paper, I read an extra four or five novels a week. My arms sagged under the load as I walked from the library. I'd read so many adult novels that the town librarian, Mrs. Hill, told someone I was taking books home for my mother. No boy my age could read so much, she insisted. I read everything. At home I read the Funk & Wagnall's Encyclopedia my mother had gotten at the supermarket in New Haven, one volume at a time. I read the Farmer's Almanac. I read. And read. Thank you, Mrs. Hartley.

Of course, my mother helped, too. Each year, at the January white sales in New Haven, the department stores filled table after table with old stuff, in particular, I'm assuming, the linens and sheets that gave the sale its name—but stores like Grant's and Shartenburg's also displayed tables of books, doubtless remainders, obscure novels and biographies, histories, and even textbooks. For years my mother carted home shopping bags filled with cheap books, and most languished on the bookshelves of the house. I think that Mom believed that if there were books everywhere, sooner or later someone (besides her) would read them. She'd left school in high school to help support her family, but was always a reader—a book club sent the mysteries of Erle Stanley Gardner into our home. And Edna Ferber, Fannie Hurst, Taylor Caldwell, Thomas Costain, Frank Yerby, A. J. Cronin. Now, influenced by Mrs. Hartley's expert tutelage, I looked around the house, and, lo and behold, there was Mom's ready-made library. I read through everything. I read an absolutely terrifying short story called "The Monkey's Paw," the memory of which still gives me the shivers. But I especially recollect one thick bluecloth volume she brought home that same year. It was a college text, an anthology of American literature, and it was the book that changed my life: Whitman, Cooper, Bryant, Longfellow, Twain, and even Henry James's "The Lesson." But most of all Edgar Allan Poe.

Mrs. Hartley also had another passion: Hawaii. Even though I don't think she'd ever been there, her daughter lived on one of the islands. And periodically she'd bring to class long white boxes filled with exotic tropical blossoms, often lush and delicate leis. Living dangerously, she actually wrote the word *lei* on the board, and Donnie Perelli laughed so loudly I thought he'd pass out. Then she passed around the flowers. I can still recall the brilliant primary colors but, more importantly, the heady scent of decadent bloom. It was all preamble to a class project on the Hawaiian Islands. I did volcanoes, and built one, which erupted thanks to baking soda (supplied by Mom) and water (supplied by the school). We even tasted pineapple for the first time, at least some of us—I didn't like it then, don't like it now. She passed around pictures of the deposed royal family, and I stared into the bitter countenance of Queen Liliokalani as she posed for the impertinent photographer. I learned words like *poi* (and resolved never to try it) and *luau*, which reminded me of how I hurled my sister on the barbecue, and *hula*, which tapped into my bubbling-under-the-surface sexuality. It all seemed so faraway—so wonderful—so exotic—far from the drab little farm town of North Branford where recreation revolved around concerts from the Fife and Drum Corps on the town green, or Saturday night square dances and Grange potluck dinners held in the Town Hall. The only other excitement was when one of the Andrews farm boys, up on Forest Road, went off into a periodic bout of madness and used the tractor to spread manure all over the two-lane road, tears of joy flowing down his unshaven and maddened cheeks.

The burgeoning sexuality of the sixth grade was something Mrs. Hartley knew how to handle. All she needed were repression and Scotch tape. Along with the overblooming *leis,* her daughter sent her a series of heavily illustrated books of the traditions of the Islands. And, Heaven forefend, some of those glossy pages had actual photographs of Polynesian maids swaying (or boating) topless. But Mrs. Hartley had planned ahead. Just as with the walls of mostly untouched *National Geographic*s she displayed, each page had been carefully examined. And a strip of construction paper, covered with tape, hid the offending bosoms. Of course, that taboo drove us all mad. We probably wouldn't have given the pages more than a passing glance—after all, this was school and these were dull photos in texts, not gas-station girlie calendars that were cartoonish in their sexuality—but the bandaged photos drove our budding hormones wild. Some boys—not me—tried to peel of the tape, but Mrs. Hartley must have anticipated that: her tape was some industrial grade she doubtless invented in her basement. The boys tried spit and hot breath, in what was probably their first sexual moment, but to no avail. Sometimes the tape did give a bit, but the page was irreparably ripped, the exposed breasts were smudged and a little bruised, and Mrs. Hartley lowered the boom. The culprit was usually Charlie Davis, a walking pustule with considerable body drainage problems, oversexed at that young age, light years ahead of the rest of us, a boy who stroked an erection which, I gather, was always present, especially when Mrs. Hartley showed us slides of the glistening beauties of Hawaii, as the class sat in the darkened room. Sometimes he'd make mouth noises.

In April of that year, just after spring break, a new student entered class, a tiny shy girl named Franny Corelli, moving out of New Haven's Italian district with her family. Part of the problem was that, even sight unseen, she was thought of as one of the big-city émigrés, strangers who struck us as worldly and odd and distant. But the real problem when she arrived was the color of her skin: she had a swarthy complexion, a hint of mocha. And the rumor began that she was a Negro. In those days we didn't have black folks in the small farming town. On Sundays, driving to the car dealerships on Whalley Avenue in New Haven, to see the new models—a ritual my Uncle Johnny insisted on every fall—we'd see the flashy Cadillacs and Lincolns cruising Dixwell Avenue, with all sort of doodads and doohickeys hanging off the rearview mirrors. We kids knew nothing about black people, to be sure, except that they scared us. Some popular evangelist named Daddy Grace appeared in the news every so often, a compact little man who allegedly never cut his fingernails (which were now in excess of six inches long, rumor had it), as a symbol of his not doing manual labor. Sleek black Cadillacs would cruise by us, with "We are the children of Daddy Grace" emblazoned on the side doors. We believed all blacks didn't work—or worked as domestic help—carried sharp knives to cut one another, and lived ramshackle lives. And, according to one neighborhood farmer, they all wished they'd been born white.

Poor Franny was labeled a Negro, and once that rumor spread through the hallways, Mrs. Hartley had to address it, with Franny out of the room, of course. No, she said, Franny was not a Negro, but of Italian heritage, as were many in the class—all of whom looked somewhat offended. And if we didn't stop this juvenile nonsense, she said, looking at each and every one of us, there would be hell to pay. We stopped. Within weeks, Franny was inducted into one little clique, and in short order she became as obnoxious as the other girls in her group.

When I told my mother about it, she just shook her head. I knew she was sympathetic to the civil rights agitators in Alabama, our family gathered before the TV at night, watching the sit-ins and police dogs and fire hoses turned on Southern blacks. I understood how such a spectacle made her feel. Once, sitting on the cement steps outside the kitchen, I overheard her telling Dad about a news item in which a gang of rednecks had kidnapped a black teenager and cut off his "you know what." There was fury in her voice. "How can people act like animals?" she said.

Blacks were infrequent travelers through rural North Branford. Once, walking near the quarry on an old, mostly-deserted back road that ran parallel to Route 80, I spotted a parked car hidden under low-hanging hemlock boughs, something unusual. When I peaked inside it, nervy kid that I was, I saw a fat black man sound asleep, head back, snoring. I don't know why I was so shocked but, running down to the package store, I told someone. I never expected the hullabaloo my words created. Word spread about the Negro in the woods, and everyone panicked. Cars pulled up to the package store. Men got out. Fear in the eyes. Anger. A wave of hysteria began, luckily aborted by the town constable, all swagger, pistol, and alcohol. He rapped on the guy's window, roused the man, learned he was a salesman who just wanted to nap, and, now terrified himself by the gaggle of white guys stalking his car, gladly allowed himself to be followed to Route 80 and back to New Haven. In another time we would have put him in a stockade on the town green. Or lynched him.

Another time when a black guy stopped at the package store, my cousin Jimmy, just four or five, kept screaming that the man had "chocolate puddy" on his face. Everyone thought it was hilarious, but no one, I'm sure, polled the man. Then there was the time one of my relatives bought a TV in New Haven, and it was delivered to her house by two young black guys. While they knocked on her front door, the huge console TV between them, she was leaning out the upstairs window, shrieking for help. "There's Negroes in the yard. There's Negroes in the yard." I was standing behind them, with my cousins, waiting to plug in the TV to watch *Kukla, Fran and Ollie*. Even we were startled by her hysteria. The men were looking up at her, baffled, their slack-jawed expressions suggesting that the theory that all white people were, indeed, plain cuckoo had just been proven yet again.

On the last day of class Mrs. Hartley asked me to join her in the nearby book room. There, a little fluttery, she asked if I was Roman Catholic, which I guess she already knew, but I nodded: yes, indeed. Then she handed me a brown paper bag. I extracted a round, framed glossy head of Jesus Christ, a benign face, all blond and blessed. Staring at it, I didn't know what to say. Mrs. Hartley was waiting, a thin smile on her face. The fluorescent light above caught the slick surface, and Jesus shone in the shadowy room. I mumbled "Thank you" and she touched the face of Jesus. "This is so you'll always be blessed," she said. "I expect big things of you." That surprised me, and for a minute I was confused: how did this relate to Jesus? Who was then trembling in my tiny hands. Who was looking at me with a bright halo over His head. Who looked amazingly like Sam the Bum, who wandered the town roads, looking for coins and bottles. "Thank you," I said, again. No one else seemed to think I'd amount to much. "Thank you," I mumbled again. "Don't tell the others," she whispered. "Only for you." And in that moment I realized Mrs. Hartley and I were bound together spiritually and conspiratorially, but I had no idea what this was all about. Mrs. Hartley took Jesus from me and stuck Him back into the bag, then giving it to me. She patted me on the wrist. I started to walk away, carrying Jesus like I carried lunch to school.

"Always keep Jesus in sight," she said to my back.

And I did. For years I kept the small glossy picture in the simple aluminum frame. I never hung it up, but it was always packed away somewhere. Whenever I moved, it went with me. But years later, when I went to look for it, it had disappeared. Somehow, along the way, as I moved from place to place, I had tossed Jesus away, but for the life of me I couldn't remember when that was.

Cider Apples

In the fall of my thirteenth year, I raked leaves, buried myself in them, burned them in fifty-gallon drums Dad placed in the backyard, and took hikes over the hills of the town and looked down on a kaleidoscope of red orange yellow and brown. The smell of burning leaves, acrid and thick, was everywhere, and it was a smell I always loved. Fall was my favorite season. To me, it was the moment before winter, nature folding in on itself. I loved the crisp morning air, the pale filmy sunrise, and the hoary frost on the windowpanes. We played basketball in the backyard, we rolled the gigantic pumpkins in from the fields, and we carted baskets of Mackintosh apples down the hill from Grandma's house. But it was also cider apple time. And that meant money in my pocket, loose coins that I'd jingle the way my father did, his hands perpetually jangling the dimes and quarters, a signature mark for the man. It drove others nuts: for me it was a comfort.

Cider apples. Sure, in summer we picked strawberries, blueberries, cucumbers, tomatoes, just as we hoed and weeded row after row of string beans and lettuce and tomatoes on neighboring farms. But that was drudgery. Somehow cider apples were—what?—a special treat. I'm not sure why.

My brother Bobby, my cousin Jimmy, and I would tramp down the road to the Lawler farmhouse where, in the brilliant fall light, we harvested cider apples in the hilly, stony orchard that rose high above the shimmering lake. Cider apples: the apples that fell from the sagging boughs of the trees, loosened by the autumn winds and rains, snapped off by early frosts and scampering squirrels. During the day the most accomplished pickers—the grownups—filled baskets with the Macintosh or Winesap or Baldwin apples, which were then stacked in the back of an old pickup to be taken to early-morning market in New Haven. But the cider apples were bonus money. Gnarled, bruised, somewhat rotten (but not too rotten), brown-speckled, often worm-filled, these apples were thrown into burlap sacks and then carted to the cider mills, where, crushed and squeezed, the precious juices were extracted, boiled, pasteurized and poured into gallon glass containers. Cider apples: the bittersweet smell of slightly decaying apple flesh, pungent, tart—a smell that stays with you for a lifetime.

Mrs. Lawler, the old woman who owned the orchard, was crazy as a loon. We'd learned that last year when she'd hired us late in the season to pick cider apples after other schoolboys, startled by her sudden bursts of madness and even more by her out-of-left-field accusations (like: "Did you fell that fir tree on the town green?" Or: "Did you paint your house that sickly blue ten years ago?") deserted her. After our initial horror, we just settled in: she seemed a harmless lunatic. And sometimes outright hilarious. "I used to be a looker during the war."

"What war?"

"There was only one war. The first one."

"But—"

"And I was a looker. You know what a looker is?"

I certainly did.

She was probably in her late eighties, but she ran the farm with an iron fist and steely resolve. She was a widow with four grown children, who'd left the old misshapen colonial saltbox for other parts of civilization. Mom said one was out West somewhere, while another was in and out of prison. Occasionally one son showed up to work, but always fought with his mother so that the constable had to be called. The youngest son always wanted to sell the place, sometimes drifting back to the household with a slatternly wife and some squawking brats. But then there were the hangers-on, sons of some distant relatives perhaps, odd creatures with chewing tobacco and obvious gastro-intestinal dilemmas, given the cacophony of sounds involuntarily emitted from their ill-kept bodies. The year before we'd had to work with these men, all of whom spent their time burping and farting, and then laughing hysterically. Mrs. Lawler ordered them all about, and they scurried like broom-chased mice to do her bidding. Sometimes, when the school bus went down the town road, I would spot her striding along, a hoe on her shoulder, a man's ancient hat on her head, stooped over, headed to some field. She never looked up, and the bus driver often skirted too close to her—I'm sure on purpose—and the busload of kids howled. "The crazy lady," they yelled. But she never looked up.

She was an old Yankee, everyone told me, a swamp Yankee, they said. Hers was the last of a line that had long been in America, the end of a colonial tradition. In fact, her forebears were part of the wagonloads of founders who ventured off the shores of Branford, into the north of the town, the wilderness of the hilly land, the untamed forests called North Farms, and began the settlements that eventually became incorporated as North Branford. Some people said she was a Mayflower descendant. Maybe so. The early Lawlers were pillars of the First Congregational Church on the town green, the early town magistrates and clergy, people who sent their first and favorite sons to Yale to become doctors and lawyers and ministers. And proud farmers. These were people who armed themselves with rusty muskets during the Revolution and later heralded the Great Awakening, preaching old-time Calvinism to the faithful. They were, in effect, the Founding Fathers (and Mothers).

What remained by the 1950s was rag-tag inbreeding and incipient lunacy. Sons of sons of sons occupied the old saltboxes that had been built in the early 1700s, and as sons became mechanics and factory boys and left the stony, ruined soil behind, the old furniture and pottery and paintings were sold off. They were still the old Yankees, town fathers of sorts, Protestant stalwarts, but, in the case of the Lawlers, the old lady was the last holdout of the intrepid pioneers. After her, the mongrel crew that shuffled in the hallways would settle in for the last blast of mental disintegration.

Of course, I was only vaguely aware of such degeneration then, but it was talked of. "They were the first ones here," Mom would say, "Puritans." She'd shake her head: "Look at her now." One time she pointed out a granite monument on the town green, some chiseled encomium to the Sons of Liberty who'd fallen during the Revolution. One of the entries: Ezekiel Lawler, who'd given his life so that, many years later, the Esso station on the corner could enjoy freedom.

There were other Yankee families in the town but many of them were not kind to the likes of us. By "us" I mean immigrant Roman Catholics—my family was sarcastically called the "Polacks on the hill," even though we were Croatian and Hungarian, but, I guess, that was close enough—and the old Protestant elite of the tight little constipated town looked askance. As a boy I learned all the horror stories from Mom. A Protestant boy fell in love with a gorgeous Italian girl, married her, and was summarily disowned by his family when he converted to Catholicism. On her deathbed his mother cursed him to Catholic (but not Protestant) hell. Another boy married an Irish girl, a stunner, and they produced a "blue baby," a girl so perfect the gods got envious and took her. His family (and hers) believed it divine retribution for misguided love. In my own family I had a charismatic handsome uncle who, as a young man about town, married the Yankee daughter of a New Haven judge, all good Protestants and Republicans, and the awful silences began. It was a doomed marriage. That was the way it was then. It was a time when Italians could marry only Italians, Slavs only Slavs. To enter sacrosanct Protestant territory was to welcome ominous fate, indeed.

But Mrs. Lawler, in her mostly benign dotage, was a bumbling woman, and Mom liked her, which is why we were allowed to work for her. As she rambled up the road, sometimes she wandered into our yard, looking lost, a man's hat on her head and the cow manure on her boots smelling something terrible. Mom would listen to her babbling, her confusion, offer coffee and cake, and then, when Mrs. Lawler drifted off in pursuit of distant demons, Mom would shake her head. Mom had a thing for lost souls.

Once Mom surprised me. Out of the blue she said, "Years back she was a real mean woman."

"Why?"

She didn't answer. But I learned why. We were working in the hilly orchard one afternoon after school, my brother, cousin and I, and Mrs. Lawler walked up to check on us. She was nearly blind as a bat but could spot a gnarly apple I'd somehow missed underfoot. It was a dark afternoon, the light fading, and she just stood here, staring up to another small orchard, one that was no longer productive, the old trees swaying with hurricane winds and hard icy winters, the fruit small and wormy, useless. She spoke out loud, but not to us. "He walked to an oak tree back there with a length of rope and a desire to die."

That stopped us cold. "What?" I said.

She awoke from her trance. "I'm not paying you to be lazy."

Mom told us that her husband, so long abused and henpecked, so beaten down, a sixth cousin of hers with the same last name—husband and wife were surviving Lawlers!—had hanged himself in the upper orchard. She was a different woman after that day, Mom said, a quirky woman who drifted into marrow-deep madness.

One Saturday, late in October, we were picking apples. But the day was different. When we left home that morning. Mom was sitting at the kitchen table, and I knew she'd been crying. Grandma, in failing health, was in the hospital in New Haven, undergoing surgery. The night before Mom and Dad had been there, and Dad said Grandma was cranky and bitter. She blamed her children for her problems. "When I get old," she said, "they are nowhere around. What good's my children?" Dad told me all this. Mom was quiet. Now, in the orchard, I scarcely thought about Grandma as the three of us gathered the fallen apples.

Every few months Grandma was back in the hospital. Every few months the lashing out at errant children played itself out.

The trees were bare of the good fruit now, and as the day got colder, the air filled with the promise of chilly rain. There was warning of an end-of-season hurricane, and already rough breezes swayed the boughs over our heads. We were anxious to fill the burlap bags—they smelled of feed or old hay—and then head home. We finished the job, tossed the bags onto the trailer-hitch near the dirt road, and headed down to the edge of the lake where Mrs. Lawler stood, eyeing a line of five or six old rowboats she kept there. The waters were getting choppy. Mrs. Lawler always kept folded, often soiled, dollar bills in the pockets of her housedress, and would count out our meager pay methodically and soberly. She was always fair.

"They're rotting away," she said to us, pointing out the green-painted old rowboats, crummy looking vessels she once rented to summer day-trippers from New Haven. Now the seat of one was rotting, the oars of another looked ready to crumble. Green deck paint flaked off. "And the hurricane is gonna kill us all. Kill me." They were not in the water, but certainly full gale blasts could knock them about. She looked at us. "I once dreamed I'd die in a hurricane," she said. She kicked a boat. "I should sell them." Then she cackled: "This one's the only good one," pointing to a boat that struck me as decrepit and un-lake-worthy as the others.

I always wanted a boat—even though I couldn't swim and hated water.

"How much?" I asked.

She turned to look at me. "I don't like it when young folk make fun of me."

I stammered.

"Your money is in the house." She turned away. "Come on."

That was strange. We'd never been in the decrepit saltbox, but we'd heard the stories that circulated through town. The home had lopsided shutters, peeling paint, sagging gutters, and a chimney Santa would never come near. The interior, we'd heard from town taxmen and other gabby town officials, was unbelievably filthy, the eighteenth-century hand-hewn floorboards crumbling and termite-ridden. Now we would see for ourselves, but, oddly, I wasn't that keen on it. She seemed too distant, too out of it. What witches brew, a-boiling in a cauldron on some wood stove, awaited us? In a few days, indeed, it would be Halloween, and I already had my costume: I was going as King Midas, gold-shiny robes created from old curtains I found in a box in the backroom.

She led us past the mudroom into the kitchen. We stood there, stunned. Smells—burnt butter, old sweat, stale food, I didn't know what else—assaulted our senses. We stood there, zombies, flap-jawed. "Sit down," she said. I plopped into the chair behind me, an old stuffed armchair, with all of the cloth missing, and, I soon discovered, with mostly jagged springs and twisted twine remaining. Within seconds a huge dog, some mongrel beast, a pasty red-brown color that defied definition, bolted in from another room and hurled itself into my lap. "Not there," she said. "That's his chair." The dog, all rheumy eye and knotted fur, could not be budged.

"Help," I implored my brother and cousin. They looked at me with a you're-on-your-own look, but Mrs. Lawler called the dog—I think his name was something like Bowls or Bolts or Bower, but it sounded like Bowels—and he fell, literally, off me, onto the floor. I stood up, stepped over him, and the dog assumed his rightful place on the springs and webbing, looking a little too triumphant for my taste.

Mrs. Lawler directed us to the hard-backed kitchen chairs, and we sat, in a line, as though expecting execution. She rifled through a battered canister, which seemed to contain buttons, loose change, and yellowed index cards and clippings, and extracted our day's salary. Then she reached behind her and popped off the tops of three bottles of Coca Cola, carefully handing one to each. Room temperature, grossly tepid, each bottle covered with dust, and, I feared, a little indefinable crud. She waited. Gingerly I tasted the warm soda, ready to gag.

We said nothing.

"You're welcome," she said.

Belatedly: "Thank you."

She smiled.

Before us was a sight I couldn't believe. The scattered Mrs. Lawler had obviously been attempting an apple pie when she'd wandered down to survey the condition of her rowboats. On the table was a bowl of peeled apples, now turned dusty brown from moisture. Cups of sugar, a tin of cinnamon and nutmeg, a sieve of flour—all left unattended on the table. But she'd also started rolling out her pie crust, for a large circular sheet of dough, spread thin, with ragged edges and a dusting of pale flour, lay there, the edges hardening into dark brown crustiness.

She saw me looking. "Getting forgetful," she said. She started to roll out another layer as we sat there, taking a round mound of stiff dough from a bowl, spreading flour on the table, and maneuvering the rolling pin defiantly.

But I've left out something from the story. As we watched the pie being assembled—Mrs. Lawler with her dirty hands, dark crusted nails, working on a table littered with empty milk bottles, with cups of stale coffee, with the remnants of a half-eaten sandwich—as we surveyed this deplorable landscape of the grotesque, two or three chickens—fluttering mother hens, all squeak and frenzy—walked across the kitchen table, one stepping through the rolled-out dried-up crust, on her way to some destination on the other side of the table. Feathers flew in the air.

"I'm fond of pie," she said.

I'll bet, I thought. Chicken potpie.

"If you want to stay, you can have hot apple pie."

Okay, a welcome invitation: let me clear my calendar. No, we hurriedly spat out excuses, put down the barely touched Cokes, and fled out the door, across the leaf-strewn lawn and onto the town road.

"Oh, my God," we all yelled. "Oh my fucking God."

But the road was eerily quiet. It was getting dark too early, and the air was chilly. The hurricane would hit during the night, and we watched the sun setting back over the hills, beyond the apple orchard where we'd spent the day, beyond the dead forest where Mr. Lawler so long ago thought death more beautiful than life. We walked home slowly, dragging our feet. We wanted to get home—Mom would have a warm supper ready on the stove and there'd be Sid Caesar and Imogene Coca on the TV—but we didn't want to get there. The darkening sky slowed us down.

Back at my home, my cousin Jimmy took off, and my brother and I went into the house. It was too quiet, but there was food cooking on the stove. I smelled pot roast, carrots, and potatoes. We yelled for anybody, and Mom answered. We followed her voice into the living room, and we were surprised to see my uncle Johnny and one of the neighbors, an old Italian immigrant who now and then stopped in to visit, sitting there talking to Mom and Dad.

"What?" I said. I knew something was wrong. I paused. I looked at the drawn faces.

"Grandma?"

My mother spoke up. "She was operated on this morning. Gangrene. They took off most of her foot."

I squirmed.

"But she's all right," she said. "She came through."

"Then what?" I said. Something was wrong.

Sighing, she explained, although she kept glancing at Dad. It seemed that earlier that afternoon a neighbor and close family friend, a man named Stanley Zuk, a serenely peaceful man given to whistling "Beer Barrel Polka" as he strolled along, had gone berserk and had shot-gunned his wife of thirty years to death. His teenaged son, a boy I knew, had jumped from a second-story window and ran down the road for help, while his father fired at him from the kitchen doorway. Now something like this did not happen in our quaint, bucolic village. And not to this man, this unassuming sort, a helper, a churchgoer, a man who gave no indication of any rage bubbling beneath the surface of his churchgoing placid exterior. I could recall him puttering around his yard, pruning the overgrown boxwood hedges and waving. Always waving. Always whistling polkas. Or singing:

I don't want her
You can have her
She's too fat for me
She's too fat she's too fat
She's too fat for me.

My uncle Johnny spoke for the first time. He worked with Stanley. "When you told a dirty joke, he walked away from you. Angry."

I stared at him. "What?"

He smiled. "That's how he was."

I knew that Stanley was a friend of my Dad's. And I looked at him. He was staring into his lap.

My mother took a deep breath. "The funny thing is, you know, when we were at the hospital with Grandma around noon—well, she came out of her anesthesia, stared into our faces, and said one word: 'Murder.'"

"What?" Again: "What?"

"Grandma, confused, kept saying, 'Murder, murder, murder. Someone is being murdered.'"

I felt a chill up my spine.

Nobody in the room looked surprised.

Grandma and Grandpa both knew Stanley and his wife Stacia well, old friends. They lived at the far end of the town road. Stanley helped around the yard sometimes, helped to pave the asphalt driveway. But I knew why no one was surprised: Grandma *sensed* such things. Her mysterious psychic visions, although we didn't call them that. Her explanation of omens. Her *feelings* of other worlds. She could *see* things. One time she dreamed that a woman entered the wall, positioned herself inside the framed photograph of her long dead husband, the two then staring, vacant-eyed, from the one-dimensional photograph. She died the next afternoon. And when a wild sparrow entered the hallway of the house and thrashed around, up and down the stairs, trying to escape, the family froze, aware of the East European folk belief: a bird in the house spelled disaster for the family. Not long afterwards, my uncle—the one who married the judge's daughter, then a vibrant man in is early thirties, although a drinker—died. No one was surprised.

These were just the facts of life.

When she pointed out how high the squirrels built their nests in the trees, we knew it would be a snowy winter.

So now there was another vision from Grandma: the specter of neighborly murder on the long town road, the touch of blackness that Grandma drew from her deep and tormented subconscious. At one end of the town road, near the quarry, a man decided that he had to kill the people who loved him. At the other end boys were filling burlap sacks with cider apples for a woman with madness in her eye corners.

Mom looked at me. "Is Mrs. Lawler okay?" she asked.

"Why?"

"There's a hurricane coming," she said. "I know that wind and storms get to her."

I looked away. I thought of Mrs. Lawler, standing at the lake, her eyes on the sad rowboats, the wind twisting and turning them, her aged hand unable to steady them. Up in the old orchard the winds toppled the apple tree where, so long ago, her husband also killed the one he loved.

"What'll happen to Mr. Zuk?" my brother asked suddenly.

My father spoke up. "They'll take him to the nut house."

Mom stood up, adjusted her dress, and sighed. "Enough of this dark day. My supper is burnt," she said absently. "Come on, everybody," she said. "We need to eat some food."

The King of Junior High

When I was twenty-one or twenty-two I hung out with friends at a dance club on Sunday nights, and I always enjoyed watching the dancers. I didn't dance. Every Sunday night I fixated on the same dancer: a skinny blonde girl, a graceful dancer who always seemed in her own world as she glided across the floor, her eyes half closed and her head thrown back in some narcotic ecstasy. I knew her name was Cindy, but I'd never said a word to her. "Ask her to dance," one friend said. "No," I said. Cindy was, well, way out of my league, someone who only danced with the good-looking guys. Her clique was the A-team. I was backfield in slow motion. "Ask her to dance," my friend prodded, week after week.

"No."

"What's the worst she can say?"

"No."

"Well, there you go. Get ready for a 'no' and anything else is a surprise."

That made irrational sense. All she could say is no. Of course, she could say it loudly.

So one lazy Sunday night, goaded by guys who called themselves my friends, I watched Cindy stroll off the dance floor after bugalooing furiously to a Beatles song—and nary a drop of sweat on that pristine brow. She paused near me. "Hi," I said, almost out of breath. "You're a great dancer." Then in a rush: "Would you like to dance?"

Her eyes opened wide, then narrowed.

She stared at me as though I were a new form of germ warfare. Now I was ready for a curt—and even a shrill—No! in thunder. Instead she spat out—

"You've got to be kidding."

You've got to be kidding. Did I hear that correctly? She was calling me pond scum. *You've got to be kidding.* A lowly worm. She disappeared into the crowd, brushing past me, and my buddies were convulsed with laughter. Red faced, embarrassed, humiliated, I rushed into the men's room, splashed cold water over my face and stared into the mirror. I saw . . . ugliness, nerd, failure, circus boy. And for some reason I'll never understand, at that moment of horrible self-loathing, I thought back to seventh grade and the story of Agnes. Her face flashed before me for just a second, and then disappeared. But it all came back to me as I headed home from that bar.

Agnes had the surname Janczek, which meant she followed after "Ifkovic" in most class lists. It also meant she occupied the desk just to my right in many of my classes. I was also the only one who ever actually talked to her. You see, Agnes Janczek was the designated class leper. One of a dozen or so children of immigrants from the Soviet Union after the Second World War— my Mom said they were D.P.s, Displaced Persons welcomed into America by Harry Truman—Agnes just didn't fit in. She dressed in what looked like bleached burlap sacks, never combed her rangy dirty-blond hair, and suffered from her parents' public image. They lived in squalor on a once-abandoned farm, the shingles falling off, the windowpanes cracked. They showed up at town hall meetings to scream about one issue: they believed putting chlorine into the public water supply was a Communist plot. People groaned when they spoke in their thick accents, the word *Communist* drawn out and each syllable emphasized: *Com-mun-ist.* Daddy wore hillbilly dungarees and sported a shaggy ill-kept beard that made him look like a fugitive Trotskyite, while Mommy was a squat penguin who laughed at everything you said but clearly had not one bit of a sense of humor.

But Agnes had her own problems. She was, frankly, ugly as sin. Short, dumpy, with a blotched multi-colored face, all zit and disaster, she lumbered through the hallways, some extra from a horror flick, humped over with head tilted to the side, as if she were hearing a voice inside her head. To make matters worse, she talked through her nose, a whiny, nasal country-western voice that had no appeal in that embryonic rock 'n' roll age. Moody, sullen, a loner, she glared out at the world through eyeglasses that were in fashion when Dewey fired on Manila.

We talked quietly—on occasion. Sitting next to her, it was inevitable. And I felt sorry for her, good, old magnanimous me. Seventh-grade welcome wagon, *sans* fruit basket. I'd ask her about her Thanksgiving ("We had a chicken, of course"), about her Christmas ("We had chicken, of course"). She'd answer me, sort of smile, and turn back to her hideous life. The teachers pretty generally despised or ignored her, preferring more attractive, less rotund learners. Agnes was just too oily, too disliked, too—as one ninth-grade student said in my earshot—*idiot* without the *savant*. I had to look that up.

But that wasn't true: I knew she wasn't stupid, and now and then I detected some real juicy spunk. She usually took what was thrown at her—the cruel barbs of other students and even the insensitive teachers—but sometimes she'd answer back. When the teacher was asking Betty Shortel to give an example of a preposition, Betty, the only class peroxide blonde and junior-high party girl with an interesting reputation, faltered. I heard Agnes whisper: "Try the word *under*." It cracked me up. She hated my friend Annie Porsini, whose mother used to drive us around and make all those sarcastic remarks about people, and, one winter, when Annie was suffering from a nose-dripping cold, Agnes actually said to me: "It's odd when the sickness equals the personality." "What?" I said, confused. She smiled: "Snot."

I loved it. So I sort of liked her. And I think she knew it.

About this time my mother received a letter from St. Augustine's Roman Catholic Church concerning my lack of attendance at the CYO—the Catholic Youth Organization, a meeting of teenagers at the church for socializing and religifying. That fall I decided I didn't want to go, probably complained to my mother about it, and thought I was home free. She let me make up my own mind. Until the formal letter arrived, which talked of my adolescent soul being in peril, what with rock 'n' roll, juvenile delinquency, James Dean hairstyles, leather jackets, and Commie antichrists afoot in the land. So my mother sent me. The session was held in the church itself, all of us sitting in the pews before God, a rowdy, happy bunch of kids. None of my friends were there, and I wanted to be home reading A. J. Cronin's *The Spanish Gardener*. I sat in the back and found myself sitting next to Agnes, also apart from the others. We nodded at each other.

"What are you doing here?" she said.

"My mother."

She made a clicking sound. "My mother thinks there is a God."

I thought that remark strange, but said nothing.

The young priest, the assistant pastor, was a guy who liked to joke and be your friend, a backslapping who's-on-first kind of guy, all Red Sox and happy-go-lucky cheer. His name, I swear to God, was Father Lord. He made me nervous. After he settled everyone down, he started his "lesson," discussing the way the Catholic Church had been maligned and misinterpreted throughout Western civilization. I suddenly found his history lesson fascinating. He snickered at the Protestant Reformation, and I was startled to hear him say that Protestants—he said the word with a snarl—had "created" stories about "abuses" of Catholic dogma. "Nobody sold pieces of the cross as a way of getting to heaven," he said. He pooh-poohed the whole idea of indulgences. Veronica's veil, wood from the cross, perhaps even a napkin from the Last Supper. Stupidly, I raised my hand. "In school I learned that the Protestant Reformation was the result of—" And I was off, quoting chapter and verse of Martin Luther, John Wesley, and the other revolutionary naysayers. "My teacher said that the Catholic Church had been corrupted—"

He cut me off. "Let me ask you one thing," he said.

"What?"

"Are you aware that your teachers are Protestant and your textbooks are written by Protestants?"

I stared. I wanted to say my history teacher was a Catholic but I stopped.

"Don't believe the lies the public educators tell you. You should be in parochial school."

Everyone turned to look at me, as though I were the new infidel in town. I shut up, but noticed the good priest glanced at me now and then, and he wasn't happy.

But I'll always remember Agnes' aside to me: "Guess I'll pick me up one of them there Veronica's veils on the way home."

When I told my mother about the priest's words, she asked me: "Are your teachers lying to you?"

I answered: "No."

I never went back to CYO.

Agnes was kind to me earlier that year when Mom almost died. I don't know how she learned about it, but I guess somebody in her family of failed farmers knew my grandfather—I'd seen them talk once on the highway. I'd told no one about my mother's illness because I was scared out of my mind. I had a dumb superstition that if I discussed Mom's worsening condition she would somehow be jinxed, and disaster would follow Like my Grandma, I looked for omens and talismans in my daily life. Surety in low-jumping grasshoppers. Blood on the moon. Flowers turned towards the sun. My mother's illness came out of nowhere, it seemed. For a week or so she'd lain in the dark bedroom, quiet, quiet, while my father bumbled around, uncertain. But I thought little of it—my mother had periods of illness, usually around holidays, times of withdrawal and silence. But one afternoon I spotted a towel covered with dried bloodstains. And I ran outside. Frantic. The family doctor was an old fool, a fat and distracted quack, who, of course, made house calls for $3.00. No one trusted him, but he was the only game in the small rural town. Dr. Chambers, an unmade bed of a man, carrying that weathered, chipped black bag, rolling his bulk out of a sagging DeSoto with the right fender pushed in. His diagnoses were the town joke. He'd examined you, stare at you as though suddenly realizing he wasn't alone in the room, and then, invariably, ask: "Well, what do you think I is?" He'd even ask the question of achy or vomity kids. Once, when I was maybe ten or eleven and in bed with a hacking cough, I said, "I think I got a cold." He agreed. He was always agreeing. Sometimes people ended up in Grace-New Haven Hospital because of the cold that turned out to be pneumonia, or that pulled rib that metamorphosed into a stroke.

So Dr. Chambers came to see my mother, sitting with her in the dark bedroom, and I remained outside sitting in the back seat of the family Plymouth with my sister, the two of us battling over something stupid. Then we heard the shrill siren of an ambulance coming out of New Haven, breaking the silence of the small town, and suddenly, unexpectedly, it pulled into the backyard, stopping next to our car. My heart stopped. Two men jumped out, maneuvered a stretcher, and rushed into the house. I ran after them.

I'll never forget it: my father sat at the kitchen table, weeping. I froze in place, helpless. I remember so little of that awful night, except for the aimless, idle conversation of the two paramedics, tucking my mother under blankets. They were laughing because the previous patient had been a three-hundred pound man who was wearing drop earrings and women's panties. That I remember. And, when my grandparents rushed in, coming down the hill from their house, Grandma mocked my father for sobbing. Men didn't cry in her world.

That began an awful season, with my mother having to have her spleen removed, a tricky operation then. I overheard my Aunt Helen whisper to my uncle: "People die of that." I closed my eyes. *They die of that.* My mother was in the hospital for weeks, even though my grandfather wanted to fly her to Oklahoma to be ministered to by evangelist Oral Roberts, whose TV sermonizing he'd started listening to. There was a big fight over that, my father saying no, no, no. At night my father would cook Kraft macaroni and cheese. Night after night. And then he drove to the hospital in New Haven, sometimes with us, sometimes alone. Eventually Mrs. Camerata, from across the street, an old Italian immigrant who rarely spoke to us, other than to nod a friendly greeting, became our salvation. Once a week, returning from the hospital, we'd find on the back porch a huge white enamel bowl, covered with crisp white linen. Inside was homemade macaroni and pungent garlicky meatballs, enough food to feed Naples. Whenever I returned the empty bowl, she'd get befuddled, shy, turning away from my thanks. I tell you, years later, I can still smell that tangy, hearty, wonderful dish. No Italian food has ever come close to her bountiful gift.

Within months Mom was back home, healthy and safe.

"Sorry about your Ma," Agnes said one afternoon, just after Mom was taken to the hospital. Not *your mother*, but *your Ma*. It seemed so close to my life.

I nodded.

She was looking straight ahead. "She's gonna be okay."

I believed her.

If I talked to Agnes for more than a few sentences, my buddies commented on it: *You're in love with Agnes. You got a thing for Agnes. LaDiDah. Eddie and Agnes sitting in a tree k-i-s-s-i-n-g.* Kindergarten rhymes. I shivered. I didn't mind her, to be sure, but I had to ration my conversation. That sounds cruel, but this was seventh grade. Not that I was a popular kid, just the opposite, but I did have a couple of friends. What skimpy acceptance I did have I wanted to preserve. With my nerdy bookishness, I skated precariously close to dangerous exclusionary waters. I had perfected a curious balancing act that year. I was "in" but probably just sitting inside the door. In a draft, actually. Doing coat check for the beautiful people. I was also very small. Little Eddie. Worse: Li'l Eddie, like I was a cousin of Li'l Abner in Dogpatch.

When I was a little boy, I feared I'd become a midget. I'd see such people on the streets of New Haven, and I was horrified. "Are you ever going to grow?" I'd be asked, as though I held the power in my own hands.

So I was on the fringe of things, always in danger of slipping into leper-land. Talking to Agnes was punching my ticket to that destination. But ironically Agnes was the unwitting instrument of my being king of the seventh grade, which happened near the end of that year.

Suddenly there was talk about an end-of-year "social," a dance on Friday night in the school gymnasium, socks and no shoes. A sock hop. This was a rare event for us all, randy kids on the edge of puberty, and the school was all a-buzz. We could barely focus on our work because we were *going to a dance*. At night. With chaperones. Dropped off by Dad. Like everyone else, I couldn't wait. I'd probably have the chance to dance with Betty Shortel, who'd been sort of teasing me for a month or so. I mean—she was the platinum-blonde with the tight knit sweaters. We talked on the phone. Well, one time. I called her.

Now here comes the sad part of the story. On the day of the dance it was our only topic. In the morning, some nasty kid asked Agnes whether she was going to the dance that night. Of course, she ignored the lout, but, once said, the line became a dreadful mantra, a singsong assault on the dumpy, unloved Agnes. "Are you going to the dance, Aggie?" Over and over, machine-gun fire. Everyone thought it was pretty funny. As we changed classes, as we strolled through the hallways, the line echoed off the cement walls. Sitting next to Agnes, I could detect the effect on her. *Are you going to the dance, Agnes?* As the morning went on, she started to crumble, but quietly. I could see her slump into her seat, her head tucked into her chest, her eyes narrowed. At one point I saw her hands tremble. So the verbal assaults swelled throughout the morning, like a floodtide rising, and the teachers did nothing about it. I think they were amused by it.

But I was bothered. And I wanted to help. I felt sorry for her, not liking what was happening, but I kept my mouth shut, watching, listening. Something was wrong here.

At lunchtime I got my tray of coagulated corned-beef hash, milk, over-boiled string beans and powdered potatoes, with two slices of white buttered bread, with a chunk of rubbery Jello, and I was going to join my friend Tony at his table. Just then, passing by a curiously paralyzed Agnes, who stood a few feet away from the cafeteria line, just standing there, I heard some vacuous jock lean into her and say, "Agnes, are you going to the dance tonight?" followed by a big phony guffaw, as though he'd just invented the world's greatest witticism. I turned to look at Agnes. She just stood there, hands by her side. I swear I thought she was going to cry.

Holding my loaded tray, I walked back to her and stood there confused, a thirteen-year-old boy on a knightly quest he just didn't understand. I was close enough to smell her, and I noticed she was sweating. She looked small, round, and totally lost to the world. "What?" Agnes said, her voice sharp.

I hadn't thought of what to say to her—I frankly didn't know why I was even standing so close—but I had to say something.

So I said the cruelest line possible.

"Agnes, if you go to the dance tonight, well, I'll dance *one* dance with you."

I emphasized the *one*, making it loud and clear. *I'll dance ONE dance with you.*

Her eyes opened. "What did you say?"

"I said, if you go to the dance, I'll dance ONE dance with you." I was proud of myself. I was the American Red Cross, come to rescue the afflicted. I was a St. Bernard with whiskey and wagging tail.

Suddenly a glazed look came over her, the eyes squinted as though she were looking through a tunnel, and, in one graceful, rhythmic swoop, she drew back her hand, swung out her arm, and slapped me on the side of my charitable face. Now Agnes weighed twice what I did, and the impact of her strike—the sound reverberated off the walls—sent me flying across a nearby lunch table, sliding like an ill-thrown bowling ball through startled fine diners. In seconds I was lifted from the table by two teachers, my pristine white shirt and creased trousers covered with hash, ketchup, and the detritus of life in a school cafeteria, and I was carted off the principal's office, like the felon I was. The rest of the afternoon I had to sit in the outer office in front of the glass windows, noticed by those students and teachers who passed by. I stared back, repentant, for I'd already convicted myself of some heinous crime.

But something mystifying happened that day. Those kids who had witnessed the scene were convinced that I'd somehow found the perfect cutting insult to send Agnes off the deep end, some chilly rejoinder that went beyond the redundant line *de jour* —Are you going to the dance, Agnes?— some line that, well, sent her into orbit. Everyone was talking about the Eddie-and-Agnes musical review, it seemed. All that afternoon, as I languished in the penal colony, the toughest students, the hippest crowd, the cool kids who never nodded at me, smiled, waved, and gave me the old thumbs up. I'd become the new hero, though I felt nothing but shame and confusion. After all, I was just trying to be a nice guy. It's just that I didn't know how. I would have danced *one* dance with her, even though it would have jeopardized my feeble connection to the outside world. I would have *sacrificed* my tenuous social position. At one point I saw Agnes leaving school, getting in line for her bus, but she didn't look in my direction.

On my bus ride home—thank God a different bus—kids slapped me on the back.

That night I went to the dance, and, of course, Agnes was not there. I danced once with Betty Shortel, but she refused a second dance. She thought I was cute—but square. I guess I was *her* charity for the night. Then, midway through the evening, the results of the afternoon voting were announced. And I found myself named king of the dance, an unheard of honor for a seventh grader. I guess even some ninth graders voted for me. In my euphoria I forgot all about Agnes. After all, I was the King of Junior High. Glory be to God. I smiled so much the muscles in my jaw ached. But I was surprisingly happy.

I was, well, royalty.

Coda: Many years later, when I was around twenty-five, I was driving through the small town where I grew up. It was a cold winter afternoon, near Christmas, with a hard, bright sun, and I stopped for coffee at a little diner on Route 80. I sat alone at the counter. The young woman who served me coffee and banana cream pie had been staring and finally said to me: "Are you Eddie Ifkovic?" "Yes," I said. "Do you remember me?" she asked. I stared at her. "Sorry," I said. But then she smiled. "I'm Agnes." I simply stared. I couldn't believe my eyes. Agnes was now a beautiful woman, still short, of course, but svelte, her skin clear of blemish, and her face bright. All the ugliness of junior high had reshuffled itself into classic proportions. With makeup and care, she was frankly gorgeous. "Oh my God," I said, stupidly. "It *is* you." It turned out that she and her husband owned the restaurant, they had two small kids, and life was good. She'd left school during high school, moved away, then returned. "I know I look different," she said. "I, well, wanted something—" She didn't finish, just waved her hand. But I kept staring: Agnes had totally transformed herself.

When she refilled my coffee cup, she said, slowly: "Do you remember when I hit you in the cafeteria?" The old Agnes—direct.

"Yes." A vague memory.

"You know, I've told my husband about that a hundred times." She sighed. "You know, Eddie, you were the only kid who was ever kind to me in all those horrible years of school, you were the only one I liked, and I hit you."

What could I say? "Well—"

She shook her head. "Nobody but you—"

"I still have the scars," I joked.

She laughed, then stopped. She said slowly, "No, I still have the scars."

She wouldn't take money for the coffee and pie.

When drove away, I remember thinking how miserable her life had been, and, worse, how that cruel life had pushed her to make such a radical change, a total turnaround, an obsession with reinventing her appearance, even though on some level she probably understood the superficiality of it all. How could pain be so unbearable that you give up one life for another? I realized how little I knew about her. But she'd found a happy life. She had a husband and kids she loved. She found a place to hide. And then I wasn't so happy when I thought of her remark about the scars she carried. She *did* carry scars from those years—she *had to,* those deep soulful bruises that would never leave her. Because this was total transformation—this was coming back from the depths. This was starting over.

Driving away, I said out loud: "Are you going to the dance, Agnes?"

And then I smiled. Just one dance, Agnes. Just one.

And God Created Women

She came out of nowhere, this Bridget Bardot. One day my cousin Jimmy showed me a page torn from one of his mother's *Photoplay* or *Modern Screen* fan magazines—crumpled, ripped, but containing a remarkable shot of a scantily clad, absolutely galvanizing enchantress. "She's French," he said, breathless.

"What's her name?"

"Bridget Bardot." But he pronounced the final *t*, as in *dot*. Which was how we always referred to her. Bridget Bar*dot*, with heavy emphasis on the final syllable. If our adolescent fantasies sprang from assorted glanced-at girlie T & A magazines, we knew exactly where to dot the T.

Be that as it may, I have to admit that the first woman's breasts I ever laid my eyes on were sadly and grotesquely connected to a male.

Donnie Perillo, my long-standing nemesis—he played Frosty during my first murder, and was the redundant bully throughout grammar school—had, at fourteen or fifteen, blossomed into a quintessential fat boy, probably well over two hundred pounds on the scale. Maybe more. Probably more. Definitely more. Now in those days there was little public concern over gross obesity in children, so Donnie was just dismissed as a roly-poly fat boy—albeit not a jolly one—who simply ate and ate and ate. Well, he did eat and eat and eat. He always had food in his pockets, and during class I'd see him suddenly maneuver the elaborate folds of his trousers—made, we learned, by his equally fat mother—and extract candy bars, Oreos, or, worse, Italian salami grinders in crumpled wax paper. Obviously a bitter boy who didn't understand his own anger or his bizarre genetic makeup, he struck out against other weaker forms of life, pummeling other kids, slapping them, even biting them. And that included me. But by junior high school I'd learned to circumvent his fits of abuse. Part of the problem (but also the solution to avoiding him) was that Donnie was woefully dumb, the kind of boy who stared in wonder at the invention of the house key. By then, I'd learned to keep my mouth shut when I was inclined to say provocative or dangerous things—well, at least a good part of the time. But Donnie had no internal mechanisms to stop his bursts of obscene or embarrassing language. He once announced in class that he knew for a fact that people in his family had been decapitated and had had their heads sewn back on at Grace New Haven Hospital.

Frankly, it wouldn't have surprised me.

Once he said that his father—a butcher in Branford—had invented pork chops.

Okay, I had trouble dealing with stupidity, even then, wise-aleck bright boy that I was. But I didn't know how to deal with his nastiness. If I answered a question in class that was not in the Teenage Boys' Acceptable Answer Book, he was ready to attack. Such as when the teacher asked: "Whitman wrote about lilacs. Do you all know what a lilac is?" My hand shot up. After all, I was a émigré from the garden of Eva's Eden, and lilacs graced our front and back lawns. I helped Dad plant a line of them along the border with the woods. Then Donnie would sniggle and guffaw: "What a girl." That was his response for everything. "What a girl." With the word *girl* drawn out and snarled: *gerrull*. He even used it with—well, girls he considered stupid. "What a girl." Once, on a school bus, someone asked me something. "I honestly don't know," I said. Donnie whooped it up: "Honestly, honestly, honestly, sissy boy." His other favored expression surfaced when he thought he'd be caught for doing some insane antic: "They're gonna hang me by the balls." Now that was a photo op we'd best avoid.

Yeah, he'd be a delight at future class reunions.

But I was talking about breasts, wasn't I?

In gym class—that badland of nightmare humiliation for all but a few well-toned and cocky boys, the ones who already had pubic hair by age four—we played shirts-and-skins basketball. One week the regular gym instructor was out sick. He was an all right guy, I suppose, who only made fun of us weaklings now and then. So we had a substitute, a harsh woman from the community who didn't know basketball from banality. She divided us into two groups and told one group to remove their shirts. Unfortunately Donnie was in that group. Now the regular teacher obviously knew something we didn't, because Ronnie *always* wore a shirt, stained and smelly, but still a shirt. This time Donnie just stood there, unmoving, looking frightened. She yelled at him. He didn't budge. Finally, sputtering, she tugged at his shirt, pulling it up his ample back, and he lifted it off his body.

Breasts! Real breasts. Mamma mia hooters. Cups of catastrophic calamity. These were not just generous fat deposits or an old man's sagging dugs. Let me tell you—these were full-bodied, majestic, baby-I've-got-a-life-of-my-own breasts. We teenaged boys stood there, mesmerized. I think most boys in that class probably still date the onset of full-blown puberty from that very moment. It was an awful moment, to be sure, and, although I hated him with every fiber of my being, I felt a little of his unease. He looked so unhappy there, so beaten. He took his flabby right arm and covered these monuments to pancakes and butter, gripping his left side and never letting go. But we knew they were there—we'd *seen* them. Some of us would never, ever forget that moment. I certainly haven't. As so we played, running around the court like scattered and distracted chickens in a hen house. It was like we were witnessing something momentous, an initiation into some forbidden world, some moment dragging us into adulthood.

So I saw my first women's breasts on this fat, oily boy. This could not be a good sign of things to come.

Of course, when we were in science class, we devoted most of our time to sneaking illicit ganders at Mrs. Bowman's available-for-parties cleavage. She was an energetic teacher, always near the brink of absolute hysteria, easily sent off into the outer limits of utter breakdown. In her forties, I guess, divorced (she mentioned that all the time), she sailed around the room, rushing from one scientific experiment to another—"Today we are making water!"—as she began to show us how to create condensed water. "Rocks," she screamed with the ardor of someone warning of an avalanche. She displayed wonderfully-colored minerals that dazzled us all. "Snakes are our friends," she screamed, holding in her hands a baby garden snake. She insisted on passing the junior-grade reptile around the room so we could see it was not scaly or oily or even hostile. The girls squealed, refused to touch it, and the boys tortured it. By the time it got to me, the little creature was so delirious with anger that it bit me on the tip of my forefinger. It had the effect of a pinprick, I admit, but I howled like a window washer plunging twenty stories to his death on a city street. Donnie Perillo mocked: "Baby girl! Baby girl." When he received the snake, I fully expected him to apply mustard and swallow it whole. So Mrs. Bowman entertained us, and she was obviously good at what she did: she always held our attention.

Of course, when she bent over she got *more* attention. You see, Mrs. Bowman, a somewhat bosomy woman with hips that made their own way through life, wore the tightest sweaters to class, ones that were always cut dangerously low. Cleavage was the word of the day. Talking, lecturing, standing upright, all was hunky-dory. But when she leaned forward, the contours of the globes became, well, manifest. It was a lot more than one could bear, those momentary glances at curved and full and rich flesh. She seemed oblivious, so maddened was she with her scientific productions.

Trespassing in the Garden of Eden

Boys dropped pencils to the floor, fell onto the floor, leaned so far left or right in their seats Mrs. Bowman accused them of copying homework from prudish girls. If Donnie Perillo could have crawled on the floor, he'd have done it. He sat in a chair—no desk could accommodate him—and sometimes he dragged the chair across the aisles like a bumper car careening out of control. Blubber undulating, beefy thighs making smacking noises on the hardwood seat, tongue moving over cannoli lips, he sloughed his way to a good titty shot.

Mrs. Bowman never caught on to the fact that she was educating the squirrelly boys of town. Each week there was a new sweater, the vee-line deeper and lower, it seemed. I didn't know what to make of her. On occasion she visited my Grandma's house. which never made me happy. Teachers should stay in schoolhouses. But they were both into growing flowers—Mrs. Bowman had a famous wildflower garden in her backyard, with delicate lady's slippers and Indian pipes—and, I think, they exchanged plants. Whenever she drove into the yard, I immediately left, if I happened to be there. Overflowing with good cheer, a little crazy perhaps, she also brought a daughter with her: the world's premiere outcast. The girl was in our school, but seemed to inhabit a world of her own, rarely speaking to anyone, often out sick with diseases like pneumonia and "exaggerated colic"—her mother's description to my Grandma—a girl avoided in the hallways as though she carried the Bubonic plague. She looked odd: tiny, squat, thick, a head almost square, with two small eyes lost in the rubbery, scarlet flesh, with a mass of uncontrolled curls on her head. She spoke in gasps and whispers when forced to by teachers. And she spent most of her time giggling. Few of the kids knew her name because some boy had long since given her a nickname: Mummychug. I have no idea what that means or why it came to be, but we all called her that. Sometimes she'd get out of control, whirling like a dervish, emitting high frequency sounds probably heard on Mars. Once I heard someone wonder out loud why her mother allowed such undisciplined behavior.

"Can't she be trained?" he asked, then smiled. "After all, you can train circus animals." Everyone laughed.

When Mrs. Bowman (with or without extraterrestrial offspring) pulled into Grandma's backyard, I escaped to the Garden of Eden.

Mrs. Bowman's classes, then, were forays into sex education, albeit not directly mandated by the Board of Education. One time someone left a crude drawing of a naked woman on the floor of the classroom, exaggerated breasts and an erect penis dangerously near them, and Mrs. Bowman, sweeping through on her way to some catastrophe involving a beaker and poisonous gases, stepped on it. She retrieved it, bit her lip, and crumpled it up. She stared at Donnie Perillo who stared her down: yeah, so what. At the moment I wondered who of the two had bigger breasts.

When it came to the subject of sex, I was the last to know anything. When I was a young boy, my cousin Jimmy—always up on these matters, I don't know how—informed me, as I was sitting up in a tree, that babies were born by men inserting their penises into women and pissing. I decided on the spot never to have children. Jimmy spent a lot of time rummaging through his father's secret possessions, hanging out at local garages, and he had all those salacious calendars, he had that picture of Bridget Bardot, he had information worth its weight in gold. Much of it, I later learned, false—or slightly off.

We were conscious of our changing bodies. For a few summers we went skinny-dipping in the irrigation pool behind the Morello farm, a largely muddied, mosquito-infested, leech-packed stagnant body of water, where we waded up to our waists, not daring to swim in that murky territory, the only cool release we had on hot, brutal August days. On weekends our families would drive to Chatfield Hollow to picnic under hemlocks and to swim in the chilly pond. But mid-week my brother, cousin, and I chose to step into that muddy bottom. We were aware that this act was not allowed because there was a sign posted by the Morellos: "No swimming. And that mean you." As I took off my clothes, I always corrected the spelling and agreement of subject and verb.

So one August afternoon, after checking to see if the Morello boys were plowing or weeding in distant fields or taking their long siestas, we undressed and walked into coolness. Dragon flies—we called them sewing beetles, believing they could actually sew our lips shut—and pesky horse flies skimmed the surface of the still water. Leeches waited to attach themselves to our skin, sucking out the blood. We were always very quiet there but that day, for some reason, we whooped it up, splashing, laughing.

"Hey youse," a voice yelled from a slight hill behind some bushes. We stopped, looked up. There was one of the Morello sons, the dim-witted one who eventually would be institutionalized for walking naked up and down Route 80 and singing "Vaya con Dios" at the passing cars. Tony did useless farm chores, not trusted by his family. Now, grinning, he pointed at us. "You can't read," he said, and he went to point to the sign, which was, unfortunately, behind him. So he got confused. "Get out." So the three of us trooped out, buck naked, nervous, expecting the town constable to haul us off, stark naked, to some kangaroo court on the town green. Tony stood before us, a man in his early forties with the mind of a fifth grade boy, wagging his finger. Shaking, chilled, we waited. All of a sudden he pointed downward, his forefinger addressing our respective penises. And he started to laugh, out of control. Pointing, giggling, hysterical—as though such an abysmal deficiency of nature could not be borne. He shook and rolled. He sputtered. "Baby dick, baby dick." I covered myself up, which seemed to set him off into higher realms of hysteria. At that moment we grabbed our shorts and T-shirts, hung on ready branches, and ran off as tree limbs snapped at our naked flesh. My face burned with shame and anger. That night, after a bath, I climbed onto the rim of the tub, trying to get a view of my body in the mirror: skinny boy with—what? —I couldn't see down that far. But I remembered Tony's pointing and laughter.

The next day Jimmy stole a pack of Lucky Strikes from his mother. We'd been itching to smoke since we were kids. My father smoked unfiltered Camels, two packs a day, and that struck me as the stuff of heroism—movie detective or man about town in café society. I knew Jimmy's mother secretly smoked, always hiding behind the garage to do so. Grandma frowned on such unladylike behavior, and there would be hell to pay if she were discovered. But stealing these cigarettes seemed safe enough: she could hardly raise a ruckus. His mother liked to give lectures. She'd once heard Jimmy and me using foul language—she wouldn't tell us what she actually heard but said it was filthy and disgusting and for us to stop—so we had no idea what scatological words she'd eavesdropped on. We were always babbling about something, exploring the language we heard older boys use. Stupidly Jimmy and I decided to reinvent the English language, just in case some Mothers' Tribunal called upon us to explain our wayward linguistic lapses. "Okay," I told Jimmy, "here's what we say. *Tits* is illegal information. *Boner* is thanks for something free. *Jerk off* is running wild, out of control." Actually, now that I think of it, these definitions were sort of on the money. There were six or seven others, all gone from my memory. I don't know why we assumed mothers had never heard these words nor knew the meaning. We were never summoned to testify, so luckily we were spared one more moment of public humiliation.

With a fresh pack of Lucky Strikes we headed to the forest, the woods directly behind the Morello farm, where huge hemlocks grew over mossy ground. I don't know why—a desire for total secrecy? —but Jimmy and I climbed to the upper reaches of the biggest hemlock, a feat we often did anyway, and settled ourselves on a thick bough perhaps thirty feet off the ground. Jimmy extracted a cigarette for each and I produced the (stolen) wooden matches. It was a thrilling moment, a grown-up moment, a coming-of-age gesture that had me trembling. This was, I knew, forbidden. But it was also amazingly cool. James Dean in a white T-shirt, with a pack of Luckies in his rolled-up sleeve. A bicep and a snarl. Manhood.

The cigarette between my lips, the taste of tobacco rich and pungent, I struck a match, lit mine, then Jimmy's. The two of us inhaled as deeply as possible. As they used to say in Victorian novels, at that moment I knew no more. As my head filled up with smoke, an amazing dizziness swept over me, a high tide of utter delirium, light-headedness that took over my entire skull. Suddenly, involuntarily, I let go of the boughs I was holding onto for balance, and I began to slip through the branches of the mighty hemlock, sliding my way down to the hard-packed and unyielding earth. Wildly clutching at branches, I managed to gain some control just as I hit the lower branches and bounced onto the mossy earth. I was all right, I realized, but scratched, bleeding here and there, bruised. I threw up on the soft green moss. Jimmy came tumbling after.

"I fell outa a tree," I explained to Mom, who eyed me suspiciously. She never understood my zest for tree climbing. As a younger boy, I used to hang upside down on the lower limb of a maple tree in the backyard. For long periods of time. Once, I guess, I must have slipped and must have been unconscious, because the next thing I remember is crawling up the cement steps leading into the kitchen, waking up as I rapped on the door. Mom heard me and opened the door. "Just what are you doing?" she yelled, staring down at the heap of son at her feet. "I fell out of the tree." She misunderstood me. "You fell out of the tree and landed forty feet away on the steps?" No one in the family ever believed my the-day-I-was-unconscious story.

"You know you can't believe anything he says," Mom told Dad.

"He takes after your side of the family," Dad said.

I never knew what Jimmy did with the pack of cigarettes. Needless to say, just the idea of a cigarette made me turn green and feel like heaving.

From that familiar hemlock tree we could look out over the back of the Morello farm, beyond the forbidden pond, and one day Mrs. Morello stopped me on the town road. I didn't expect her to point to my penis and giggle, in the tradition of her demented son, but the idea did cross my mind. No, she wanted me and my cousin to help clean out her basement. She'd pay us two dollars and fifty cents for a morning's work. Or course we said yes.

Mrs. Morello was a formidable woman, a chubby woman with a narrow head and eyes the size of peas, a woman who announced to anyone who'd listen that she was a strong woman who took no prisoners. "During the War I had three sons in Europe. Three. You hear me? I had to be strong." She didn't mention the fourth son, the blithering idiot named Tony, my irrigation pond nemesis, who'd obviously spent the war years studying charts of reproductive organs. But in the moist, smelly basement of her farmhouse, she stood with folded arms and barked out orders. Move that box out. Put that crate there. Sweep the corners. Snag those cobwebs up by the rafters. Step on that red ant—now. Drag out that old armchair. It was a walkout basement and so we lugged piles of stuff out, and then, at her direction, hosed down the old cement floor after spraying it with some noxious disinfectant. Rivulets of lemon yellow water streamed out the door, shushed out by our wide brooms, and into the storm drains. "Looks like a giant is pissing in the back room," Jimmy said and then, taken with some frat-house boy idea, unzipped his pants—Mrs. Morello upstairs taking a phone call—and sprayed the back floor. More yellow, more stream. Unbelievably Mrs. Morello returned and wanted to know what that offensive smell was, raising her nose like she was Miss Marple stumbling upon a dead body. I was annoyed—but a little impressed. With all the accumulated odors of old stained junk, decaying rags, boxes of old turpentine cans, with bottles of disinfectant splattered all over the place, with residue from the oil tank, with the hint of old sawdust, with the mildew and mold of the walls—how in God's name did she smell anything else? We played dumb.

"Maybe it's a dead rat," I said.

"We don't have rodents here."

"Mice."

"This is a Catholic household."

Okay.

Trespassing in the Garden of Eden

We ended the long sweltering day by carrying packed boxes of refuse to the steel drums behind the back barn, five or six crates of old magazines, yellowing newspapers, discarded junk mail and catalogues, unusable clothing like broken shoes and paint-smeared dungarees. I stacked up the boxes carefully—her demented son, she said (not using that phrase, of course) would later burn everything in the barrel drums. And, I thought cruelly, probably the barn with it. But one box tied with twine slipped out of our hands, and out fell maybe twenty or thirty girlie magazines, a treasure trove of flesh and desire and strip-club spangle. Jimmy and I went nuts. No other word. Raving, acned boyhood run amok. Jimmy and I greedily leafed through semi-sexual, 1950s soft-core titillation, show girls with huge breasts (but not, I noted sadly, bigger than Donnie Perillo's), each tipped by a little sequined *thing*—I later learned it was called a pasty. Our jaws dropped. All fairly tame by a later decade's values, but deliciously risqué enough for teenaged boys in the Leave-it-to-Beaver age. I'm sorry, Mrs. Cleaver, but we just gotta take a peek. And somehow these pulp magazines were probably more scandalous with all the hinted-at sexuality, the off-hand nuances, the insinuation of naughtiness, the peek-a-boo wink-of-the-eye taboo. There was a pile of such magazines with titles like *Hush* and *Confidential* and *Man Life*, and we wanted them. Every single one of them. They had to be ours. Ours. Me. Possession is nine tenths of a boyhood erection.

"Strippers," Jimmy said, transfixed.

"Strippers," I echoed, a hand trembling.

This was pirates' booty, this was sunken treasure, this was frankincense and myrrh, this was fodder for any masturbatory fantasy any teenage boy could ever concoct. We wanted it all.

Mrs. Morello was calling us. "What's taking you so long?"

Longing, that's what. An itching in the groin. A boiling of the hot blood. That's the long and short of it, Mrs. Morello. Ask Tony, your resident degenerate. We looked at each other. We'd have to devise a plan. So, late that afternoon, after collecting our money and thanking Mrs. Morello, we headed toward home, circled back through the adjacent farm backfields near the forbidden swimming pond, and, hidden by a bank of wild raspberry bushes, we surveyed the backyard. Mrs. Morello sat on her back porch, sipping a drink with Tony and some other woman I didn't recognize. If we approached the barn, we'd be spotted. They chatted. In despair, we went home. But at twilight, as darkness crept along the land, we ran back and did our own creeping. Crawling on our bellies like invading Teddy's Rough Riders going up San Juan Hill, we got to the untouched (and unburned—that lazy Tony!) boxes, found our wealth of girlie magazines, and, hunched over and hidden in the thickening shadows, we ran into the night forest. Success. Mission accomplished.

We hid them in a secluded spot, the backside of a huge granite rock, but first we spread them out, savoring the find, even though we were squinting in the fast-approaching darkness. This was paradise all right. But darkness fell and we had to leave, covering the box with a snapped tree limb.

That night in bed I could barely sleep, the excitement was so great. Eventually I drifted off, dreaming of Las Vegas strip clubs, girls parading down polished bar tops. One magazine had something about someone called Mae West. And Gypsy Rose Lee. I remember another one: a photographic tribute to Miss Nude USA, a glossy issue of blond beauties in g-strings and pasties. That put the Miss Rheingold contest at the package store to shame. I finally fell asleep.

Near dawn I was startled awake, groggy and bothered. Something woke me. Wind and rain pounded the windowpanes, a ferocious nor'easter that came out of nowhere. The clapboards rattled and the gutters spewed water into the driveway. All morning long, driving winds and torrential downpours kept us inside. I walked around like a caged animal. I snapped at my mother who, thinking I was in the grip of cabin fever, suggested playing a word game. How about initials, she said. Male or female? Living or dead? How about GRL? I considered. Gypsy Rose Lee. But I said no to her and hid in my room. When the storm ended and the sun broke through, Jimmy and I ran to our hiding place in a panic, to find our box of earthly delights.

The cardboard sides had caved in, now sticky and clammy, and the cheap pulp magazines were soggy, stuck together, soaked throughout. I picked one up and it fell apart in my hands. They were all ruined. Miss Nude U.S.A. was gone from view, dissolved into mush. A crime against nature, I swear. "Shit," Jimmy said.

I nodded, standing there, my wet and sticky fingers squeezing mushy pulp.

Jimmy and I looked at each other, and I swear there were tears in our eyes.

Road Kill

When the school year ended and I'd settled into my sixteenth summer, I announced to the family that I planned to sit in the shade of the big maples out back and read. All summer long: piles of books. I also had the idea to write a novel. I already had the title: *The Night Will End*, a tragic story of a lonely drunk who sees the light because of his sexual liaison with a remarkably loose woman he meets at a Leggett's Drug Store and a nerdy teenage boy who is on a mission to save the world—one drunk at a time. It was partly autobiographical. Well, at least *one* of the characters was based on real life. I made this announcement at supper one night. No one said anything, my father staring at me with a look that suggested a paternity test might be in order.

The next evening my father had his own announcement. I was to report at 7:30 the following morning at the town garage, where he'd got me a summer job working on the infamous town road crew. He had a different look on his face that night: Welcome to the real world.

The dreaded road crew. I'd heard stories.

Jobs for teenagers were in short supply in a rural town that had no restaurants to speak of, and the farm supply stores, the General Store in the center, and the outlying farms rarely used summer help.

So the town crew was it—ten or so teenaged boys, hired to sweep roads, help with cleaning leaves from drains, assist in the annual tarring of the town roads, clipping overhanging tree limbs, clearing brush. Sounds exciting—the rough outdoors, a perfect summer tan, a flexing of teenage boy muscle. In truth, it was like a Soviet death march to a Siberian labor camp. A season in hell with sand in my eyes and broken fingernails. Worse: passing carloads of kids from school hooting and hollering like you were the newest recruit on a Georgia chain gang. I'm exaggerating here, to be sure, but perhaps only so much. The work itself was often grueling because it was under a hot, unrelenting July and August sun.

My first day on the job I was assigned a solo performance, a trial by fire: to sweep the length of a back road, a treeless plain of hot tar and cars that whipped by so fast my ears flapped like boat sails. Shirtless, with a new crew cut, with new work shoes, and jeans torn appropriately in the knee, I pushed that goddamn broom like I was Sisyphus moving that rock up a ledge. Another extreme figure of speech I won't apologize for. At the end of the day I was exhausted, and no one said thank you. But it was a job, and in a few days I got used to it.

But the job had other—more menacing—aspects that made the summer such an ordeal. But I didn't learn that at first.

I worked with the other boys from school, who were at first wary of me. Most were okay, a couple of gear heads, a couple of school jerk-offs, but most were average Joes who hardly knew I was alive in the school hallways. I was the bookish outsider at school, the one careening corners with an armload of textbooks, dressed in a preppie white shirt, black slacks, and penny loafers with the *de riguer* shiny copper penny inserted. Later on one kid told me they were surprised to see me show up that first morning. But I kept my mouth shut, did my job (which, I later learned, was the thing that got me accepted—they thought I'd loaf around, sneak peeks at paperback copies of *Anna Karenina* or something) and, when we all sat in the shade of a tree on the side of the road for our lunch break, we all shared trash talk—girls and girls and how we hated the bosses. It was labor-camp survival.

So the job was tolerable because we were, after all, adolescents with too much wild energy and spunk. But it was the bosses who made our lives miserable. This was road crew nightmare. You see, in the small insular own, shielded from the big city and hidden by mountains of regret and reprisal, mixed with heavy does of favor and entitlement, town business flourished by the process of who-knows-whom. Who *owes* whom. Whose sister got in trouble with whom. The constable who looked the other way. One hands washes... etcetera. That's how I got the job: Dad knew someone, he made a phone call, the next morning you're in prison stripes. So, too, the hiring of the "bosses"—and we had many. All of them seemed to be drunkards, the only word on their skimpy resumés. Besides the summer boys, the road crew consisted of this band of older guys, and they were mostly loners, outcasts, sots, failures, miscreants, lunatics, wife-beaters, possibly a few felons—the flotsam and jetsam of male adulthood. Worse, half of them chawed away on chewing tobacco, an activity that leaves the practitioner looking like a slobbering farm animal going hell-bent-to-leather on some masticated alfalfa. Since the job paid almost nothing and since it flourished by cronyism, these guys were a kind of *ad hoc* club: lost souls with hip flasks and bile. Most were Second World War veterans who'd somehow slipped a cog, returned to civilization broken men, drifting sorts who could never again pull it together.

Take the boss, our "foreman," a decent-enough guy who ran the operation officially—which was why, I guess, he was "boss." He only drank some days, when he'd disappear until late afternoon, but when he spoke to you he kept flicking his huge, porous, beefy red drunk man's nose with a nervous forefinger. It drove me to distraction. That, and his occasional temper tantrums. He spoke with a gravelly, sandpaper voice, and when he thought we were being unduly lazy—sometimes we'd take longer than our half hour lunch break when no one was around— when the real men were drinking their lunch at Woody's Tavern across town—he'd let go with a hail of *fucks* and *shitheads* and *asswipers* and *pussies* and *scum* and— On and on, a delicious run of verbal diarrhea, so out of control, so insane, that you had to admire the man. He was the sanest of the lot, this sonneteer of the lost. If you did your job, however, he left you alone.

The men under him were not so agreeable. Most were lazy drunks who would idly push a broom around in the morning, listless and bleary eyed, sometimes ordering the boys around because the boss had "delegated" them to keep an eye on us when he had to go off somewhere in the town pickup. All the men drove off at lunch break, drifting down to Woody's, and sometimes they took two or three hours to replenish the fluid levels in their sagging bodies. When they returned, the old battered cars sputtering and zigzaging down the town roads like inexpert skiers maneuvering treacherous moguls, they'd park in the shade, eyes drawn into ominous slits, and watch us. When the boss returned, he either ignored them or listened to their tales of how they needed to take a "breather" because of health palpitations or "digestive attacks." They'd struggle out of cars, gain some semblance of balance, and pick up shovel or broom, and usually cover the same ground we boys had already cleared. We hated them and made fun of them. They didn't much care for us either.

I remember a couple in particular. Lennie, for one. A guy probably in his forties, he was always the jokester, genial, likeable, our fast buddy who liked to hang with the boys rather than the other "old farts." He had something to say about everything. Sometime in July his son was going through a messy divorce, and the son's wife sued Lennie for "alienation of affections," whatever that means, because he'd "interfered." For a reason I can't remember the story had lots of juicy gossip surrounding it, probably because the son or daughter-in-law had some public identity, and some sleazy Bridgeport tabloid made the story front-page news, with a garish headlines. So Lennie talked of nothing else and carried that paper around until it was frayed, soiled, and oil-smudged. "Who'd ever think I'd be famous?" he kept saying until we thought we'd have to kill him. His fifteen minutes had become the summer of our discontent. "Look at this. I'm famous."

Being famous in Bridgeport, I thought, was a little like talking about what you had for breakfast: nobody cared.

When he got drunk, he got nasty—low-down foul and narrow-eyed brutal—picking out your worst fault (usually a body feature you had no control over, like the nose that led you everywhere) and running scrimmage with it. No mercy. I wore eyeglasses with Coke-glass lenses, so I was an easy target. And I spoke English, which was not the language of choice among them, preferring as they did some ungrammatical, slangy *patois* where *fuck* was noun, verb, adjective, adverb, and the end of every periodic sentence. I'd been trying to improve my English for years since junior high school. At home my factory-working parents spoke a serviceable working-class English, and only when a classmate made fun of me in front of everyone after I'd said, "What are *youse* doing this weekend?"—only then did I realize I'd have to get my act together if I wanted to be a schoolteacher, my current occupational goal. So I listened to myself, did self-correction and penance, and as I pushed brooms with the road crew I spoke as if I had just escaped from elocution lessons with Eliza Doolittle. Lennie, who perhaps had a vocabulary of ten words, two of them *gimme* and *forChristssake*, mocked me mercilessly when he was plastered. When he was sober, he liked me, told me I was a good kid, smart as a whip, one of the good ones. Actually, the phrase he used was *fuckin' brainy*. I took it as a compliment.

Then there was the weasel, a small, compact mole named Henry, with a pinched, ferret face, tiny darting eyes, dripping nostrils, a tongue that slipped out of the corner of his mouth with a regularity that suggested he'd been a frog in a previous incarnation. He had a nosy streak wider than an interstate. He wore loose jeans that didn't fit right, hanging off his hips and bunched like an accordion over his shoes. And always a white T-shirt, too tight, so you could see his emaciated, all-ribcage body. He was originally from New Hampshire or Vermont, I remember, and he never stopped talking—rather, asking questions. "Why'd you say that?" "Your father's Joe, right?" "You got your license yet?" "Why not?" "Why you wearing them shoes?" "Who she boinking?" One of his favorite topics was love and marriage—his. He was especially fond of the article *the* and used it, I guess, in some down-East lingo: "I was talking to *the* wife yesterday." "I had a fight with *the* mother-in-law, the bitch." He peered into personal lives and seemed obsessed with our sex lives. Unfortunately, other than obligatory bravado and fancied story telling, we didn't seem to have any. Those that did—the tough boys who talked of gang-bangs, pipe jobs in the back seats of Fords, and city whores who loved them to death—were probably lying, too. Once Henry, tipsy after lunch, started grilling me. "Been laid yet?" I didn't answer him. A little later: "Not getting any, is you?" Later: "No haystack puntang for you, lad?" What? Then, annoyed by my silence: "Eddie's not into the women." I stared at him. "Don't like *the* women, don't you?" I walked away. That was a mistake. His eyes followed me all afternoon, vacantly, until one of the boys made a random comment about a girl in a passing car and Henry asked the boy if he jerked off. The boy gave him the finger.

For two weeks one of Henry's buddies worked with us, a temporary hire for reasons I never could understand. Pete did almost nothing except stand in place, a statue, lean on a broom, tell us what we were doing wrong, and talk incessantly about the hordes of women who wanted him. He was a garrulous jerk, a creep, a roly-poly confection of soft buttery corners, failing hairline, just a chubby gnome among men. *The* men, as his buddy Henry might say. Nobody could stand Pete. "So I'm walking by, see, and she opens her door to pick up the morning paper, and sees me and opens her robe and she's stark naked. Starkers." "I'm in the fuckin' market and the cashier—I swear she looks like Marilyn Monroe, all platinum hair and big tits, and she whispers that she'll do me on her break." "This old broad, maybe sixty, whispers that she's gonna do me in the back seat of her Edsel." On and on, all stomach turning. Images to make a soul swear off sex forever. Pete told us he'd been in a car crash, laid up in bed and unable to take a piss. "The nurse knew an old Indian trick. When I was asleep, she put my hand in warm water, and I pissed like a race horse." When he woke up, they "did it." A week later Pete was gone and his buddy Henry walked around asking everyone: "Do you think he's nuts or what?" I figured that went without saying.

But the one who made me most jumpy—and the one I often ended up working alongside of, and was proof positive that there cannot be a God—was a hairy guy they called Junior. He was a mountain of a man, a huge belly that always escaped his pants because of missing or undone buttons on his work trousers and shirts, scraggly beard stubble, salt and pepper, the eternal denim cap, and a scowl that could clean pots. Blustery, backslapping, he defined himself as a happy-go-lucky bloke—he always used the Brit term—who was everyone's friend. He actually was kinder than his scary visage suggested, to be sure, but he drank just a little too much. The back-slapping bonhomie got worse then, with him leaning in so close you'd think you'd die of asphyxiation from the alcohol and body order—and he often scratched himself a little too obviously, fore and aft, as it were. Then he'd put his finger up to his nose and say "Hmmm," like he'd created a new scent for Max Factor. I'd gag. But his worst fault was his low tolerance of noises—any sudden noise that occurred too near his shell-shocked cranium. A truck door slammed too loudly as he stood nearby, a passing car leaning on the horn as he went to cross the road, a pay loader clanging metal against metal as it dropped crushed stone into a ravine—all would set him off. Suddenly, without warning, the placid exterior would disappear, and he'd erupt. Eyes flashing, hands flailing, body twisting, teeth chattering, as he looked for someone to kill. This outburst might last a minute, but once you saw it, you never forgot it—and you learned to avoid him or run for cover. Junior was a madman. And often I had to sweep alongside him. The Lone Ranger and Tonto.

He liked to gossip about his wifey. Like many of these men, he'd been in the Second World War, the Big One, and like most of them, something had snapped. At the end of the "battle," he'd been in London, he said, where he'd married his "bloomin' wifey," a publican's daughter he'd met in a local tavern. She was a painted tramp, he said, but, squired back to America, they raised a passel of kids in a squalid mobile home park at the edge of town, a no-man's land of what the town considered unredeemable white trash. Junior actually made me laugh with his fantastic stories of sex and mishap with the missus. "'No, no, no, oh Lordy no, I don't want you at me again, like a randy rooster, no, no, no, I'm a tired woman,'" he mimicked, in a high-pitched Cockney accent, "as she's pulling down her stinkin' bloomers, thrusting out them sagging jugs, and rolling her bloodshot eyes at me." It was his favorite routine, and I never tired of it.

Once when Junior called out sick—"on a drunk," Lennie confided—Lennie told us a story that made us squirm. A week earlier he'd gone to the trailer to pick up Junior to go play cards at the VFW Hall, and he knocked on the door and was told to come in. Inside, paces away on a trundle bed, was Junior, a naked and sweaty heap, atop the British wifey, pounding away like a mongrel dog rutting in a field. "Wait a sec, Lennie boy," he'd said, pausing between thrusts. "Pull up a chair. Don't like to stop a job I start." From beneath him, the wifely stared, vacant eyed, and said: "Welcome to our home."

My days working on the hot town roads were often exhausting. Not only the back-breaking work—hauling stones onto trucks, spreading sand on tarred roads, sweeping sand on windy days until your eyes felt heavy with sediment—but the abuse from the old-timers. What I most feared was the suddenness—the arbitrariness—of an unprovoked attack. I could be having an easy day, working with a couple of the boys as well as Henry or Lennie, and then, in a flash, because of a random comment from a passing car, Henry or Lennie or the boss would terrorize us, swear like fishwives, insult our mamas and our sexual futures. "Can you move any slower, you fucking asshole?" "You really are a stupid sonovabitch, you know." "You're just a pile of shit, boy."

But the job was also a curious salvation, unexpected. Long the outsider at school, I suddenly became part of a *group*. I belonged. As I said, since I didn't shirk the grimy work, I'd paid my dues with the other boys. Now they included me in their

Trespassing in the Garden of Eden

conversations. Given the verbal abuse of the old-timers, it was *us* against *them*. And I held my own. I also had a mouth when need be, hurling sarcastic barbs against the bosses (although always behind their backs)—something that made the others laugh. A few years back the town instituted a Little League, and there was a *mandatory* meeting of all the boys on the town green. I went, vaguely recalled hitting a ball ineptly, and then sneaking away, headed home. Later that fall, back in school, I learned I'd been put on a "farm" team, the final repository of loser boys, which included Donnie Perillo. All that year the bragging, hotshot boys made fun of me—"farm team boy." Well, now I even made friends, especially with a James Dean wannabe, all ducks-ass haircut and cigarette rolled up into a T-shirt sleeve. We ended up talking about buying a home, of all things—I don't know why— and he said he was getting married and wanted a home for his wife and (unmentioned) expected baby. I'd seen a For Sale sign on my road, by the lake, and he got interested. He never bought it, I know, and he and his pregnant girlfriend disappeared from town within months, but that brief conversation made him, well, *nod* to me appropriately when we crossed paths in town. When all of us had lunch together, he talked to *me*.

Some afternoons were blissful. Trailing after trucks filled with hot asphalt mix, we'd learned to steal ears of succulent corn from farmers' fields, bury them in the boiling asphalt patch, and by lunch time the corn was cooked to perfection. We'd peel back the husks and munch on sweet, fresh corn, never realizing, of course, that we were probably ingesting toxins that would eventually kill us. No matter: this was ritual, this was bonding. We had a good time.

So I discovered roadside camaraderie, and it felt good to be a part of something for once in my life. It simply meant I had to lie and conceal and hold my tongue most of the time. I had to go along with the crowd, no matter how unkind. One unhappy example stands out. There was a nerdy older boy in town, at that time probably a junior or senior at Yale. Years back when he was in junior high, he'd been the schoolyard sissy and was shown no mercy by the kids. Once, playing at the grammar school lot, I'd seen him racing by, chased by a mob of insane boys his own age. As Rodney ran by me, at breakneck speed, I saw his face: set, determined, oddly triumphant. He outran them, but eventually they caught him and beat him up. They were always beating him up. This was when he was thirteen or fourteen. He was a "girl," "girlie boy," with his exquisite gestures, his effeminate turns and twists, his wispy voice. He was, unfortunately, the stereotype most Americans knew. Now I don't think that the pack of horrible boys who hounded him understood homosexuality, but they sensed *difference*, and it threatened because it somehow touched their boy-to-real-man sense of self. Perhaps. I don't know. But I always remembered that face: *You cannot defeat me. It just can't be done.* That was the message. I never forgot it.

So one afternoon, we're lazing on our shovels, working in the Northford part of town, near the one-room nineteenth-century little red schoolhouse, now a national landmark. Those days it served as a local library. And who should walk by but Rodney, home from college for the summer, cradling a stack of books against his bony chest, perhaps swaying to some tune in his head. Approaching the group of road-crew boys with their deep tans and naked brawn and suppressed fears, he paused a half-second, as though he would turn around, but I knew he wouldn't. I remembered his face from years ago. This kid had a kind of self-possession I could never imagine. He strode by us. He didn't even look at us. And, I swear, he exaggerated his sashaying, pursing his lips together, narrowing his eyes, and raising his skinny shoulders, left then right, like he was Lana Turner on a boardwalk. He was Gay Lib before it was an idea in the mind of God. As he strolled by, the boys whistled, made their wrists limp, blew sloppy kisses, and asked for a date. I'm sorry to confess that I was the one who asked for a date, a bit of sarcasm that struck the other boys as inspired. As Rodney lingered in the library, the boys circled around me, punched me, intoxicated. I'd obviously gotten off the most thrilling barb. Easy heroism, easy mark. Inside I wasn't that happy. Because I knew in my heart of hearts that I was still a member of the outcasts, the outsiders, the world removed from the hale-fellow-well-met cocky boys I worked with, simple though they might be. I was play-acting. I knew that Rodney and I inhabited the camp of the social leper—the brainy (my group), the runt (my group), the unorthodox, the nerd, the neurotic, the bumbler, the loser (ditto, ditto, ditto, etcetera)—and I'd probably be there for life. I wasn't happy—but my God in heaven, was I popular that day.

Near the end of the summer the tarring of the hard-swept roads began. Trucks spread a thin layer of oil, followed by sand trucks that covered the slick, glistening surface. Junior was assigned the job of spotting the isolated spots missed by the sand spreader. "I drove trucks in Europe," he said proudly. "At night with no lights on. Drunk." He drove a dump truck now, filled with sand, and I was chosen to be the creature who stood atop the shifting sand pile, staring ahead to spot bare patches of tar and then, somehow maintaining my balance, hurling shovelfuls of sand onto the naked spots as we passed by. That took some doing, but I mastered it. Junior drove the truck slowly, and I did my job. Teamwork. Now and then he'd flip out when some passing car blew the horn. He'd stop the truck, jump out, swirl around looking for a long-gone culprit, yell Fuck You, and go into his rage. I got used to falling back onto the pile of sand when he stopped short, and just waiting.

And then one afternoon . . . We were moving down a tree-lined road, a quaint lane of old sugar maples, and we came to an intersection where four or five boys were loading sand onto a truck. I waved and bowed as we stopped at the sign. All of a sudden one of the boys—a kid named Roger who was a troublemaker and all-round fool—jumped onto the truck, pulled my idle shovel from the sand, and used it to pound three or four heavy blows to the roof of the cab. In a flash the boy jumped off the truck, a smirk on his face. Stupidly, I stood there. This was, of course, the most awful taboo. We'd heard all the stories of trunk pounding from a previous summer, and such behavior had sent Junior into a tailspin that left him crazed for a week. Now—again. Junior jammed on the brakes, and I lost my footing and fell over. In a rage he flew out of the cab and, as I righted myself, he tried to grab at me. "It wasn't me," I sputtered, but we were beyond language now. His hands found the long-handled shovel at the very moment I hurled myself off the other side of the truck, and I toppled onto the ground. Junior, a maniac now, was making these grunting animal noises, a wild beast caught in a final trap.

I stood up, dizzy, watching him. Holding the shovel by the long handle, Junior approached me and swung at my head, insanely, one long menacing sweep of metal blade. The sharp edge nicked my skin on the side of my neck. I felt wind and death. I felt the burning sensation of broken flesh. A few inches more and he would have smashed open my skull. The foremen and the other boys were yelling at him to stop—I later learned—but Junior wanted blood, my blood. Stunned, I couldn't move. No one dared approach him. And then he swung again, this time grazing my shoulder. I staggered. He positioned himself to swing again, and instinctively I knew I could be decapitated by the sharp edge. Blindly, dully, on automatic pilot, I managed to duck and run, crouched over. One of the boys grabbed me and pushed me behind a tree. "Don't move," he yelled. I was shaking. When I looked back, Junior was swinging wildly at the air, the shovel flying back and forth like a machete slicing through sugar cane. He was making a whinnying sound, mosquito-thin, like a balloon losing all its air.

The foreman yelled for me to go home, and one of the boys drove me. In the rearview mirror I saw a trace of blood on my neck. "He's fucked up," the boy said. I looked at him. "Really fucked up."

When I walked into the kitchen that afternoon, I stood there, still shaking. "I was almost killed today," I announced.

My brother looked up. "What happened? Did you trip on a pebble?"

I told my story.

No one ever believed that Junior tried to kill me.

But decades later, waking from a fitful sleep, I sometimes feel a twinge of pain in my neck. At that moment I remember Junior.

"Yes, But—"

Three weeks into my sophomore year of high school, Rose Klein whispered that she planned on raping me. I'd already been nervous as I strolled the halls of Wilbur Cross High School in New Haven, getting used to the crowds of kids and the feel of a big-city school. North Branford had no high school, small town that it was, so the town paid tuition at the city school. To me, it was total culture shock: these kids—often Italian, Irish or Jewish kids—seemed more worldly, more sophisticated, more hip. They dressed differently, they spoke differently, and they employed more elaborate forms of abuse on lesser mortals. I felt like a bumpkin, in part because we country kids were called *hayseeds, turnip pickers,* and *yokels.* What I'd soon learn was that we burlap-sack babies were the ones who ended up regularly on the honor rolls, but that knowledge would come later. Instead I had to deal with Rose Klein, who made my first days hell.

Rose Klein was a big girl who began most conversations by saying she was not only Jewish but also crazy. "Even the rabbi thinks I should have electric shock treatment," she said, dissolving into giggles. Sometimes she'd sit on the floor, tucked into a corner of the room, a desk pulled near her as a barrier, and laugh hysterically. "I'm crazy," she said. Of course, we all believed her. She dressed in featureless smocks and wore what I assumed were her bedroom slippers. She let her long hair fall straight down, cut unevenly, and she wore eyeglasses with oversized shocking pink-flamingo frames. She was woefully nearsighted, and if you got close to her—which I tried to avoid doing—her eyes stared out at you like the moon on nights of utter madness. Now I'd always made it a point to steer clear of lunatics, as a general rule, but avoiding Rose Klein was not easy. Staring out from her maddened view of the world, she spotted me walking through the hallways. I bear some responsibility for being noticed, I have to admit. My grandmother had given me a shirt obviously bought from a departing band of unfashionable gypsies: bright scarlet, with gold metallic buttons, a lightning zig-zag on the breast pocket, with some dull gold stitching around the shoulders. It might have been appropriate at the Grand Ole Opry, if I'd had a guitar in hand, a cowboy hat on my head, and an unpleasant twang to my diction. I have no idea why I actually wore it, but I did—that one time. Keep in mind in the late 1950s boys (and men) dressed as blandly as possible, white shirts, white socks, black shoes, black pants. Eisenhower crew cuts, "flat tops" or even "baldies" were the haircuts of choice. So I stood out. Walking through the hallway I passed two girls who burst out laughing. "Now I didn't think God made such funny-looking creatures any more," one said. I glared back. And it was in such dreadful attire—*because* of that costume— that Rose Klein spotted me.

She was in one of my classes, an art class taught by a man who would fly into hysterics over anything, smash some innocent student's clay sculpture to the ground, and then sit at his desk, trembling over an old copy of *Time* magazine. When I walked into class in that shirt, Rose giggled, then bellowed, "Hey, Christmas tree." From that moment Rose watched me out of the corners of her eyes and then directly, and then—well, she was always at my side.

I was terrified of her, and that, I now realize, contributed to my charming allure, besides my tantalizing natural body musk. Whenever I stammered in response to a curt remark from her, she looked at me as though she could see into my soul. Of course,

I never wore that awful shirt again, so much for my audition for the Commedia d'Arte, but the damage was done. Rose Klein, that battalion of a girl, was smitten. And then, a few weeks into her giddy infatuation, she leaned into me and whispered, "I'm going to rape you."

Now I didn't know girls could rape boys—they'd left that out of my grammar school education—but her intent to rape me filled me with terror. I had no idea what look must have come over my sweet little face at that moment, but whatever it was caused her to burst out laughing. And, sadly, to hit the floor, retreat to a corner, pull up a desk, and declare her madness to the class. Now and then she'd point at me, shaking her head. She couldn't stop laughing. I'd obviously failed some test.

She never spoke to me again. Never followed me around, nor plagued me. It was as though I didn't exist. But I still feared her.

By the spring I was a traveler in the city, loving New Haven, staying late and catching the town bus back home. I felt the cool customer, wandering in the stores along Chapel Street, buying a quarter-pound bag of nonpareil chocolates at Kresge's Department Store, buying a paperback copy of W. Somerset Maugham's *The Moon and Sixpence* at Shartenburg's. Then I discovered a used bookstore called "29 Cents," which, not surprisingly, sold most books and magazines for twenty-nine cents. I lived there after school, watching other high school students shoplift magazines while I spent a dollar on books by Eric Ambler, James A. Michener, and A. J. Cronin, all the paperbacks missing the front covers. When they went out of business a year later, I bought a box load of books and, almost missing the town bus, ran against the light to catch the bus. Cars squealed to a halt, and the cop—why are there always cops around when you don't need them? —gave me a long and embarrassing lecture about "later life" and did I want to get there in one piece.

High school, I learned, was long hours of studying because I was in the academic accelerated program, but what made it really interesting was the aberrant personalities that inhabited those hallways. Watching these characters swirl around me, I came to understand that everything resonates from that mass of eclectic charges that constitute a person's nature—and the more idiosyncratic the better. It was, in other words, what made me a lifelong people watcher.

There was Mr. Neely, who taught Earth Science, a man who couldn't disguise his misery being in a classroom. A man determined to teach, he'd fill the blackboard with terms and diagrams, nonstop, but he hated facing the unruly class. An old man, forever wearing rumpled summer suits no matter what the season, he had a face so wrinkled, so deep-creased, he was hard to look at. Once he removed his thick eyeglasses and his red eyes seemed shrunken and hollow. The whole class audibly groaned, then burst out laughing. He had no control over the bad apples in the room, especially a boy I knew from North Branford, a handsome, dark-haired stud who effected the current James Dean outfit and attitude. Sullen, bitter, brutal, he hated Mr. Neely and sassed him back. Mr. Neely would tell him to leave the room, but the boy never did. And Mr. Neely never followed up on his commands. This smart-mouth kid sat at a lab table with a small blond boy, a German immigrant, who never opened his mouth and always looked lost and miserable. One day, when Mr. Neely was writing on the board, James Dean threw a banana and it hit Mr. Neely squarely in the back of the head. Enraged, he rushed to the back of the room, stood trembling over James Dean, who was smiling, arms crossed, taunting him. Mr. Neely lost it. He raised his old hand, held it out, as he stared into the impudent face. And then—to this day the act stuns me—he struck out, in a fury, but he had turned his body and slapped the little blond German boy across the face. It was one of the most awful moments I'd ever seen. The German boy, who'd been quietly watching the tense standoff between Mr. Neely and James Dean, erupted from his slumped position, flying out of his seat, beet red in the face, sputtering incoherent words, and then flew into Mr. Neely's bony chest. The old man fell against a wall, slipped to the floor and lay there, body twisted, as the bell rang, and we participants in a moment we could not understand fled the room. When we returned to class the next day, the German boy was gone, and Mr. Neely gave us a pop quiz that no one turned in.

Many of my teachers were old maids, to use that now-suspect term. Irish spinsters talking care of even older mothers at home—or so one told me one afternoon. They were a hard-driven sort, the last of a breed of truly dedicated women, often passionate about their students and intolerant of any deviation from some purposeful Roman Catholic norm they carried into public education. There was Miss O'Mara, a semi-hunched-over woman, who never smiled or joked, who stared at you with withering eyes, a woman I so feared that, years later, meeting her on Chapel Street and being greeted with a broad, friendly smile, I just didn't know how to handle her genuine goodwill. She liked me because I was one of the good students. In class, if a student did something amiss—a slight attempt at humor, for example, or the failure to follow an expected order—she would stop, freeze in place, and then walk out of the classroom. I figured she was going to the teacher's room for a cigarette. (After school I'd see her light up in her car in the parking lot.) Now you'd think we'd act up, given her frequent flights from the classroom, becoming boisterous after she departed. But no deal: we were so scared we always sat in silence, quiet, quiet. At one point she'd return, walking back into the classroom and resuming the lecture exactly where she'd left off. There were all kinds of urban legends about her. The most common was that, as a beautiful young woman, she'd been engaged to be married but was in a car crash that killed her intended, and she was left with those stooped shoulders and a life of solitude. It was a favorite story, and everyone really believed it.

Mr. Gotta taught us Latin, but he insisted that our previous Latin instructors had done so poor a job that in Latin II he had to reteach Latin I. In Latin III he also retaught Latin I. The only course he seemed to teach was Latin I. The fact that he was the one who had originally taught us Latin I, well, that did not seem to bother him. So I spent my last two years of Latin declining the simple *amo, amas, amat* world of September of my first year. Now and then he'd look up from his newspaper to tell us to be quiet. How did we expect to learn the greatest language of Western civilization if we couldn't shut up? Sometimes he'd make us go to the board to write out our declensions, but he never said anything about them. I could have written a dirty limerick and he would have nodded his head. Likewise Mr. Smith, who taught World Civilization and simply read from the text, which we then had to outline in class. He demanded the classical form. "If you have an A, you need to have a B. If you have a one, you need to have a two." Periodically he'd stop the class, ask someone (using our surnames) a question, and then, after a pause, smile and announce: "Not so, Miss Castillano, no so," and move on. *Not so!* I heard it in my sleep. I knew most of the answers, and so I rarely got a *not so*. He turned to me to get the right answer. But when I got the courage to say, "I don't know" once or twice, he'd shake his head as though I'd just uttered an obscenity in his presence.

I have images of them all, pieces of memory: Mr. Cerulli whose desk was always surrounded by the dumb athletes, picking up the essays he wrote for them. I'd seen him driving through New Haven, always with a football player in the passenger seat. Mrs. Gustafson, a retired substitute who seemed everywhere, an immigrant from some Scandinavian country, who had no control over any class. At one point, delirious, she'd scream at the class: "I hope you all *flank*," which, to be sure, sent most of us onto the floor in stitches. Sometimes boys in the hallways would yell, "Flank you," to confused other students. Miss Josephs, our geography teacher, glamorous and haughty, cold and annoying, had once been Miss Kentucky five or six years before, we were told by our homeroom teacher who was obviously lying to us. That kept us interested for five minutes. Miss Jones, the daughter of a famous Yale football player—whom I'd never heard of but everybody else did, weeping their adulation—who announced that she would never wear the same dress twice in one year—and didn't—and made no bones about having favorites in the class, usually the rich kids. She didn't care for me and gave me D's on my essays. At the end of the year she got married in a spectacular wedding at a chapel at Yale, and she invited a few of my classmates. I wasn't one. One of them collected for an expensive gift for her. I didn't give at the office.

Mr. O'Brien taught chemistry. *Doctor* O'Brien, I mean. There were rumors he'd been a Yale professor who'd lost his job because of drunkenness. I assumed the rumor had legs because Dr. O'Brien (a) talked of Yale all the time and (b) seemed a little tipsy the rest of the time. Once I actually saw him taking a swig from a flask when I walked into the back storage room looking for chemicals. An odd, squirrelly man with a pinched face with red blotches and ill-trimmed beard stubble, I always thought of him as Roger Chillingworth—that sterile little man of Hawthorne's creation. He had a peculiar way of talking. Each week we'd be tested on vocabulary, which he pronounced *vocaBULLary*. It really tickled me. He looked out at the world from boozy, jaundiced eyes, a remarkably unhappy man, who made no bones about his purgatory spent at the high school. We were beneath him, and don't forget it. On weekends, he told us, he did *real* chemistry at home in his lab. I imagined some assistant to Frankenstein, some Irish-American Igor mixing brilliant chemicals in vials and beakers, all calculated to end a world he never made.

He loved only one student, a freckled girl named Belinda Wyman, bright and dreadfully chipper, a girl who'd never lost her body fat and seemed proud of it. Dr. O'Brien tolerated the rest of us, and disliked a few. I was one of the few. Oddly, now that I think of it, there were just two lepers in the class: Melissa Lewis and me. I don't know why I was on his toxic-waste list—maybe because the first week I dropped a beaker of nameless chemicals on his shoe— but Melissa was the only black student in the class, one of the few in the academic program, and he made it obvious that her presence was a gross error on someone's part. So Melissa and I were relegated to the lab desk at the back of the room, a no man's land where we were dutifully ignored, except when he wanted to point out the ignorance of the new world, at which time he'd ask Melissa or me an impossible question. So Melissa and I became good friends, although she was leery of white boys

("My grandmother isn't too happy about this"), and I had never known any African-Americans as friends. She was intelligent girl with sharp, dark eyes, with straight processed hair that went to the small of her back, and with a flip, irreverent manner I thoroughly enjoyed. Dr. O'Brien disliked me, but his contempt for her was palpable—and a little ugly. She never let it get to her. Smiling, she confessed she called his home on weekends, and when he answered the phone she hung up. She couldn't help herself, she said.

Since we two were ignored, we played with chemicals, having a grand old time. Once, she mixed some forbidden chemicals in a beaker, asked me to look at the surreal, wispy colors, and when she drew it near my face, I inhaled, got totally light-headed, and knocked it out of her hands. It broke on the floor, and the entire room had to be evacuated. Had Melissa done that in today's world, HazMat officials and bomb squads would close off the neighborhood, and CNN would send in a satellite truck, but back then, we lingered in the parking lot for the rest of the period, and then went onto Algebra. It was a different time. Another time, right after Christmas, I was wearing a new button-down sweater, some hybrid synthetic creation. Melissa had concocted a new amalgam in her test tube, little clots of moving, swelling toxic fury that eventually shot out like balls from a Roman candle, striking me dead center in the chest. The sweater started to disintegrate, and I pulled it over my head. Within seconds a bunch of lovely buttons rested in a heap in the floor. In the front of the classroom Dr. O'Brien prattled on, obvious to our errant behavior.

At the end of the year, I heard him talking to teacher's pet Belinda Wyman in the hallway, his gritty alcohol voice trying to be sweet and lively. "You going to the prom?" he asked her. Was he going to ask her out, the lech? Was he jealous that his darling had a life without him? She said yes. "Who with?" said the dirty old man. "Eddie Ifkovic," she said, hesitating, knowing his dislike for lesser forms of biological life. He recoiled like, well, Roger Chillingworth, face to face with Satan himself. "Can't you

Trespassing in the Garden of Eden

do any better than that?" he said. I swear those were the words that tumbled out of his mouth. I strolled by, tucked myself into Belinda's side. He turned away.

At the end of the year, we had to ask out senior instructors for recommendations to college. All my teachers said nice things, but Dr. O'Brien wrote that college would be a waste of time for Eddie Ifkovic, a boy with no ambition, little smarts, and a bad attitude besides. My guidance counselor showed to me. Even she was horrified. Melissa went onto the University of Connecticut and became a nurse practitioner. Belinda Wyman left the state after graduation and became a Mormon missionary. Dr. O'Brien slipped on a broken egg someone had tossed into his back lab, and his flask slid across the room. Some student pocketed it, and Dr. O'Brien never got it back.

But I really want to talk about Miss Reilly, one of my English teachers. The first day of class she walked in promptly and yelled: "Everything you've heard about me is true." Most of us had never heard a thing about her, so the news was shocking. Hadn't we done our homework? A tiny, birdlike woman, all jittery and wide-eyed, she was a wonderful teacher of Shakespeare, I must admit. I still recall her fiery rendering of Hamlet. She told us marriage was never in her "cards," but teaching was, and that took all her time. She said that the English Department would falter, stumble, dissolve, if she missed one day of school, so she came to class with migraines, running nose, boils, jaundice, and gout. In the early 1960s she drove a classic Model T Ford, possibly the original owner. "Some people are just important," she said, and she was obviously at the top of that list. She was driven to distraction by students who did not follow rules, for rules were the name of the game. "Rules are civilization," she said. "Without law there is only the abyss." One of my buddies, a smart-as-can-be Jewish kid, was also the captain of the swim team and always had to leave early for swim meets. It drove her mad because she had no control over it, but she clicked her tongue as he gathered his books, as though he were really sneaking off to a girlie show downtown. (In homeroom Jake was the only Jewish kid and he sat next to me. When we stood for the Lord's Prayer and Pledge of Allegiance—which struck me as mindless rote—I suddenly noticed his shuffling, his discomfort. While the rest of us intoned *Our Father who art in heaven,* Jake stood there a little sheepish, alone in Christendom.) A black kid named Arturo also drove her nuts because he carried piles of daily newspapers to class. He was a news hawker on a street corner downtown, and *loved* newsprint. He'd pile his desk high with the New York editions of *The Daily News* (extra thick with ads), *The New York Times, The Post, The Bridgeport Herald, The New Haven Register, The New Haven Journal Courier*—you get the picture. He did almost no schoolwork, but circulars and real estate sections broke loose and slid across the shiny floor. Miss Reilly screamed as though Huns were invading us.

We had a love-hate relationship, the two of us. I was bright, articulate, well read, and reverentially obedient, this last characteristic being the most important in that *Leave it to Beaver* decade. I knew *answers* to all the right questions. One day the principal stepped into the classroom, and we all dutifully got quiet. Like he's Alex Trebeck, he yelled out an obscure, archaic vocabulary word—something like *anon*—and, at random, pointed to me in the front row. Without missing a beat, I answered: "Shortly, soon." I was a crossword puzzle aficionado, so that wasn't a stretch. He nodded his approval to Miss Reilly, and disappeared. She beamed on me like she'd stumbled onto Atlantis.

But such facile approbation only went so far. You see, Miss Reilly had another pronouncement: all literature ended with James Barrie, author of *Peter Pan.* I'm not making this up. As if that was not startling enough, she'd go into a rage mentioning George Bernard Shaw who, she said, had announced somewhere that he was a greater writer than Shakespeare. "Who will read Shaw in one hundred years?" she screamed. "I ask you. No one. Repeat after me. No one!" Of course, most of us hadn't even heard of him to begin with. So we read Shakespeare, Sydney, Marlowe, Pope, Browning, and the rest of the expected canon, but veered totally away from the decadent twentieth century.

Thus the lines were drawn. I loved modern literature, good and bad, and had read a ton of it in my junior year honors class (Virginia Woolf's *To the Lighthouse,* James Joyce, E. M. Forster, Arthur Miller, Sinclair Lewis' *Dodsworth,* on and on), and, prowling through my favorite used bookstore (29 Cents) I had found a guide to world literature, which listed every book I was supposed to know as a literate gentleman of the Republic. I read and read, and checked off the likes of More's *Utopia, Gargantua,* Moliere, St. Augustine's *Confessions,* and modern out-of-the-way novels like *Zenoiba Dobson, Antic Hay, My Name is Aram,* and a host of other moderns. Much of it was, well, Greek to me. I devoured F. Scott Fitzgerald, Hemingway, O'Neill, Thomas Wolfe, Lillian Hellman, all of whom I read on my own, my paperbacks lined up like milestones on my shelf. Throwaway bestsellers from Frank Yerby to *Forever Amber.* I was looking for answers: I wanted to become a writer. I never did get to read the best-selling *Not as a Stranger* until I was in my thirties. I brought home the paperback, and my mother took it away. Not appropriate, she said. So I bought a second copy, hid it, and my mother found it and took it away. When I bought a copy as a grown man, I found I couldn't get past chapter three.

Inevitably, there would be battle in Miss Reilly's fiefdom.

One day she was decrying the state of the world and bad-mouthing, of all works, Mailer's *The Naked and the Dead,* which she had not read—and never would—but which I'd just finished late into the night. I loved every word of it, intent on imitating his quirky, newsreel style when I became a great writer, intoxicated as I was with his characters and plot and—well, ballsy verve. I'd bought a library discard at the used bookstore.

I raised my hand. "Yes, but Miss Reilly, I said, "what if you happen to think it's a great book?"

"It isn't." Flat out.

"He does this thing with characters, like they were talking and—"

"No."

"Yes, but, Miss Reilly," I said, brazenly, "I've read Hemingway, and, and Fitzgerald and they tell a story that's—"

"Stop," she screamed. She stood up from the stool she always perched on. "You will not—hear me—not discuss pornography in my classroom. That is porn-og-ra-phy. You hear me?"

I started to sputter.

"Stop," she screamed. "Not one word more."

The subject ever came up again.

But I argued with her all year, and, interestingly, she let me, so long as we avoided modern literature, the world at large, public morality, the Second World War, infidelity, the kidnapping of the Lindbergh baby (I have no idea why), and other topics on her black list of the forbidden. I was an argumentative sort, I admit, and she infuriated me. In retrospect, I think she allowed much of it because it did engage her on some teacherly level, kept the class lively, and she could segue into a new assault on the disintegrating culture via my almost "mesmerizing naiveté"—her phrase for me.

She stopped calling me by my name. I'd raise my hand, and she'd say, "What is it, Yes But?" Because I began most of my rebuttals to her comments with a raised hand and a pleading: "Yes, but Miss Reilly."

Soon the whole class was calling me Yes But. I could see it amused her.

If any of my modern views infiltrated my essays, she'd red ink them out, grade the paper down.

"Yes, but Miss Reilly, I have a right to express my ideas."

"Who says?"

"You're not being fair."

"The world is not fair. I'm preparing you for that world. You should thank me."

Despite her proclamation that the school could not go on without her, she suffered a slight cerebral hemorrhage in March, and disappeared from the class for two months, replaced with bumbling substitutes. Miss "I Hope You All Flank" Scandinavia taught us how to diagram sentences and informed us that adverbs are not really necessary. That Shakespeare should be spelled Shakespear (or something like that). That the word *wind* (as in air current) in poetry must be pronounced *wind* (as in "wind the clock"). That J. B. Priestley was a twentieth century master. That there was something really wrong with Eleanor Roosevelt that people hadn't noticed yet. That *Gone with the Wind* (pronounced *wind*, you choose, I guess) was a book we should all have a personal copy of. That students should never use prepositions to end sentences with. That Edna Ferber was a royal bitch (she'd refused the substitute an autograph when she was in town for an opening of one of her plays at the Schubert).

Near the end of the year Miss Reilly returned, a pale, wavering shadow of her former feisty self. Her hair pulled back into a tight bun, her skin the color of old bread, she looked like death. That afternoon our honors class trooped in, and there she sat, perched on a stool, talking, book in her hand. We were quiet, respectful. The doctors, she said, told her to stay home during her successful recovery, but she had a solemn duty to her students. That was why she was there. She was a Teacher. We remained quiet.

"Forget what the substitutes taught you," she said, icily. "Open to page 257." It was a poem by Robert Louis Stevenson, I remember—*Home is the sailer, home from the sea.* She read it—she always read beautifully—then talked of its meaning. From there, oddly, she segued into some travail in the modern world. Something about how no modern writer came close to Stevenson.

I raised my hand. "Yes, but Miss Reilly, what if—" The look on her face stopped me.

Quietly, she whispered, "You know, all day long I taught the students in the general program. Other classes. The slow kids. They all know what I've been through, and they treat me with respect. But I come into this honors class and right away I am attacked." She stared at me. "Just how were you raised? In a barn? You just have to badger me, don't you? I was at death's door, and you have to—to—abuse me." She glared at me. "A barn," she said. "A barn."

My blood boiled. In a totally tasteless moment, I blurted out: "If you're so sick, why don't you stay home?"

Her face colored, her shoulders bunched up. Her hands trembled. I'd never seen such anger rise so quickly in a person, and as she slammed her book closed, it fell off her lap onto the floor. She reeled. I have no memory of how we all got through the rest of that period, but I know she and I were doomed warriors.

The next day she was absent, and during the summer that immediately followed I learned that she had died.

One friend phoned to tell me that I'd killed her. He seemed happy to give me the news. I kept my feelings to myself, but I did grieve for her. After all, I wasn't raised in a barn. I wasn't. I swear.

Years later, a friend remarked that Miss Reilly, when she answered my raised hand, was not saying, "Yes, but?" She was saying, in fact, "Yes, butt?" I like that, and I smile to think of it. Of course, she'd be horrified with this bit of posterior slang, but so be it. It made me think of Miss Reilly in a whole new light. Norman Mailer, I guessed, would have enjoyed it, too. Maybe even Bernard Shaw. But frankly, who the hell remembers him anymore?

Piece Work

The first time I heard the lascivious wolf whistle I smiled. After all, I was walking across the floor of the factory where banks of burly men were aggressively producing the sand cores that were part of the production of iron and steel fittings. A tough job, sweaty and miserable.

But then I realized that the whistle was directed at me. At me.

I got red in the face and nearly dropped the wooden container I toted, with the eight round slots holding eight round jars, sort of like one of those old milk-bottle carry-alls. I looked straight ahead and made my way to the middle of the shop, where I stopped. My job was to pick up representative samples of the sand being used to produce the "cores" that helped shape the iron and steel fittings produced elsewhere in the foundry. It was my first time on the floor.

I approached one station. "Excuse me."

"Not me, kid."

This was not going to be easy. In fact my foreman had warned me. "They might give you a little trouble."

"Why?"

"It's piece work," he said. "They make their money by the piece. You stop them for one minute and they lose money."

Great! Well, I thought, it's only one minute. Maybe even less.

I stood by the man. I'd been told they *had* to let me take a sample. And I should choose different stations on different days. "Go somewhere else," the man grumbled. I stood there, ill at ease. He was a wiry man, lanky, with a gaunt face, spotty scalp and a huge belly. I suppose I chose him because he looked weaker than the other beefy men.

"I have to," I pleaded.

He stopped his machine, bit his lip, stepped back. I rushed, filling one of the eight jars with the sand he was using, spilling most of it, apologizing as I stumbled. He looked like he was going to kill me. Quickly I got out of his way. Only seven more men to offend. Three days a week—the ironclad routine. I came to dread it.

I had been very impressed with myself, bagging a summer job in the chemical lab at an iron foundry in Branford, the summer between my freshman and sophomore years of college. The Malleable Iron Fittings Company—called affectionately (or derogatorily) the MIF—was a vintage Civil War brick structure then entering its last, faltering decade, although no one knew it at the time. My being an inept summer worker in the chemical lab had nothing to do with this impending bankruptcy. Well, maybe just a little bit—if you believed the yard foreman whose life I made miserable.

It had seemed like the perfect job—it really did—working in a chem lab where I'd mix impossible chemicals with packets of sand and then write reports and feel very important. An American Literature major dealing with test tubes of hydrogen and sodium and sulfur. The lab was tucked into a corner of one of the factory floors, a shielded oasis of quiet and cleanliness, with only a patina of gray dust on the windowsills. Outside the lab, the presses and conveyer belts clanged and thumped, but inside the enclave the foreman played Mozart and Bach. Of course, my workstation was just *outside* the lab, a bench adjacent to the lab windows where I processed the sand I gathered at great risk to my well-being. So I was in some borderline purgatory, some suspect territory between the rowdy, cacophonous workers (who, thank God, drifted over to joke with me) and the refined regions of chemical Camelot (who were polite and decent to me). Each day when I clocked in, I tucked my time card at the upper left of the board, separate from the hundreds of factory workers, but at the bottom of the collection of chem lab workers. After all, I was summer help.

I liked the people in the lab, as little as I got to know them. Sometimes I was invited inside, as for a special occasion—cake served for someone's birthday or promotion. My June 16 birthday, however, was unheralded. I longed to know them better. When I deposited my quality-control sheets on the desk inside, neatly stacking them so they'd know I was scientifically-minded, I noted that one of the women was reading Lawrence Durrell's *Bitter Lemons*, a tiny paperback with an unflashy cover placed among her other belongings. For some reason that book spoke volumes to me. She was a tall, willowy woman with a British accent who said maybe ten words to me that whole summer, a woman who nodded her conversations. I was singularly impressed that anyone could be that distant. I longed for a talk with her about Durrell, some of whose work I'd read. But the book never moved from its spot on the table, eventually acquiring a faint hint of factory dust. When I left at the end of August, it was still there, untouched. It's probably there to this day, hidden behind the boarded-up windows of the abandoned building.

The only lab staff I wished to avoid was Mr. Jacobs, a man who announced in virtually every conversation that he had turned seventy-three and still was able to work better than men half his age. Doubtless this was true, but he also worked my nerves. Obviously everyone else had successfully tuned him out sometime back during the Great Depression, but I was fresh fodder for his rolling tongue. He'd stroll out of the lab and linger at my station, where I was filtering sand into test tubes and applying chemicals and awaiting wonderful reactions. I'd copy down the fluctuating numbers onto pads. Mr. Jacobs always waited until I paused and looked up, and then there was no pause. A short man, with leathery skin, gnarled, much like bitter lemons, and as yellow, he combed his hair in one of those brave comb-overs, two strands of wispy white hair making the transcendental journey to the other side of the mountain. And the man actually carried a comb in his shirt pocket. I think he must have placed it there sometime at the end of the First World War and forgot it.

"Working hard?" he always began. "Or hardly working?"

"Yes." I squinted through the eyeglasses at my numbers, as though depressed at the gross national debt.

And then began The Talk, capitalized. "This"—he pointed to the test tubes— "will all pay off down the road in later life." Later life: his favorite phrase. Which I'd heard from Mom, from teachers, and from John Q. Public. I'd nod. His most cherished metaphor was the convertible. "Other college kids spend their summers in convertibles, going to parties, drinking. But not you." I'd nod foolishly, starting to get depressed. Thanks for the info. Yes, it's true: my life is drab and unexciting. "They live for the moment," he said, "racing their convertibles up and down the streets, squandering time, breaking eardrums, annoying people on sidewalks." I'd nod. That sounded good to me. "But college kids like you, in later life you'll be successful, have a home, car, money, respect, dogs." I'd nod. Dogs? Did he say dogs? "And where will they be? In the garage trying to get the twenty-year old convertible going. *Working* in the garage, grimy and dirty."

The problem was—he'd go on and on and on, a deadpan monologue, repeating himself. I heard the same line day after day. He was one of those people whose droning speech sucks the very life out of you, exhausts you. After twenty minutes I wanted to take a nap, just lie on the grimy oily floor and doze for an hour, my snoring wafting up to the beams overhead. Eventually—I got to recognize the sign—he's crack a thin smile, and I knew his break was over. He'd disappear into the lab where he'd hover over his table, mumbling to himself. Everyone ignored him. I couldn't.

He was preferable, to be sure, to the men working piece work, where I had to collect my samples. The dreaded piece workers. I suppose I must have looked a sight. Here I was, a skinny,

Trespassing in the Garden of Eden

four-eyed college kid, geekdom to the nth degree, but I made it worse without realizing it. For some reason, I wore a white dress shirt—old and faded though it was—inside black dress slacks—also old and faded. Not jeans or work shoes, not a T-shirt, not the normal attire of any college kid. I never really thought about it. The workers in the chem lab dressed similarly, and I suppose I thought I was one of them. These were clothes I no longer wore anywhere else, ragged that they were, so I suppose I thought it appropriate for my days in the factory. But it must have seemed odd to the sweating, undershirt-clad piece workers, this rail-thin black-and-white vision sauntering through with what looked like a milk carrier, swinging it to the beat of some Everly Brothers tune only I could hear. *Wake up Little Susie wake up.* Dust flying, noise deafening, grease coating everything, and in walks this college twerp, all drive and demand. I suppose they assumed all college summer workers were just plain obnoxious. I certainly was.

When I strode onto the floor, I'd hear the groans because I was taking money out of their pockets and making them break stride. It didn't take long to learn which men were most likely to abuse me. One guy would actually spit to this side but near enough to my creased pants leg to make me nervous, and then, in a nasty whisper, say: "You don't have sex, do you, kid?" I avoided him after that. He knew too much about me. One time, stopping four or five stations away from him, he still got to me, yelling out the same embarrassing line in a booming voice. Everyone laughed and I did the fake I'm-one-of-the-boys-and-I-get-the-joke phony smile.

My favorite stop was the station of a huge black guy, with bald shaved head and the roundest face I'd ever seen. He looked mean and deadly, but I was drawn to him because he'd scribbled in chalk on the side of his station some magical words:

The Duke of Earl
Has lost his girl.

I loved it! I'd always been fond of doo-wop music from The Five Satins to The Marcels—*there's a moon out tonight!*—and Gene Chandler's *Duke of Earl* was a song I often sang in the shower. *Duke*

duke duke duke of Earl duke duke, duke of Earl duke duke, duke of Earl duke duke. For me it wasn't hard to learn the lyrics. So I gravitated initially to the man, who would fret and scowl and sputter, but, I learned, was actually very nice to me. When I walked away with my packed sand specimens, he always *said* something. Take it Easy. See you later. Okay. Some words that made me relax before tackling the more violent and inaccessible workers down the line.

Back at the lab I'd play in the sand. I was horrible at the job, I confess. I was given control numbers against which I had to compare my figures. Sometimes nothing matched. I'd total all the figures and nothing reached the acceptable standards. I'd redo the tests. The numbers were totally different. After a while I simply doctored the numbers, making everything come out hunky dory, and making the foreman happy. Years later I'd have these flashes of memory and guilt, believing I'd help create faulty iron fittings which resulted in the collapse of a bridge in New York City, over which an impoverished family of ten was driving to their unsuspected demise. When I read Arthur Miller's *All My Sons*, about a man who knowingly sold faulty parts to the war effort, which ironically led to the death of innocent lives, I knew the playwright had me in mind.

Once every two weeks, I had another unpleasant job. Freight trains carrying loads of sand frequently chugged into the yard, were off-loaded onto trucks, and moved on. But that sand also needed analysis. I was given the number of a particular railroad car and told to watch for it. "This week it's 947," I was told. Each time I heard a train approaching the yard, I'd run to the window, stare out, repeating, ""947, 947, 947," like a mantra, afraid I'd miss my train. You see, I had to get there before it was unloaded so that I could test the sand in various places—top, middle, sides, bottom—for the sand would shift inside, the heavier in one pile nearer the bottom, the wispy in another near the top. I would take eight different samples from 947. For some reason, I always panicked, rushing out with my pail as though I might miss it. I always made it there before the yard foreman. Yet sometimes the car just sat there all day.

Trespassing in the Garden of Eden

The yard foreman was Johnny Ginko—"Gin" to his friends and enemies. I once called him "Gin" and he said only his friends called him that. "What shall I call you?" I asked. "I'd like it if you don't ever talk to me." He hated me because, once again, I was this twerpy, no-sex-getting college nerd who made him interrupt his schedule of unloading, forcing him to wait on me. He was a rugged, hairy mountain of man who always had a cigarette in the corner of his mouth. He couldn't unload sand until I took my sample. It pissed him off royally. When he'd see me scurrying across the tracks, tripping in my black shoes, swinging my milk pails, he'd turn his back on me. He claimed people like me would make the good old MIF go under. "They hire you and the end is near," he said once, putting his face close to mine. Of course, that made no sense, and I'd smile. His eyes were small and close together and that scared me: I'd seen faces like that in my nightmares. "The end is near." I didn't understand the logic of that thinking, but I often thought about it, a decade later, when, indeed, the MIF disappeared. I wonder if "Gin-and-Tonic," as I nicknamed him in my head, then nestled in a retirement home where he was spoon-fed strained peas, thought kindly of me, his nemesis.

Within weeks, I started dreading the factory, unhappy to be there. Always a loner, I felt like a true outcast there. This strange boy wandering with milk pails into the nether regions of hell. Working alone at my station, I longed for someone to talk to, some lunch companion, someone to clock in and out with, and someone to whine about working conditions with.

"You got a little dirt on your pretty pants," one of the piece workers yelled, and I was depressed all afternoon.

I'd cross paths with Gin-and-Tonic in the parking lot, and he gave me the finger. But at least someone took notice of my being there.

But it got worse. At midsummer, when parts of the factory closed or were on modified schedule, the chem lab shut down but I was assigned to assist with "inventory." What that meant was that I had to help count the various-sized fittings stored in vast horizontal bins that lined the walls of a long, dim room. Two weeks of that relentless, monotonous, dirty work. I was teamed with two other college students, the three of us working as a team. One was a junior at Yale, one a junior at Oberlin. Why they were working at a menial factory job during summer break I had no clue—perhaps their convertibles were in the garage—but I learned so little about them, largely because they ignored me.

The first day we were assigned together, we introduced ourselves. Jeff (our envoy from Yale) and Henry (our esteemed ambassador from Oberlin) began by mentioning their schools first, and then their names second, as in, "Hi, I'm home from Oberlin. My name is Henry." I thought that a curious construction but so be it. When I mentioned that I was Eddie from Southern Connecticut State College, they stared at me as if I'd been released on parole from a boys' detention center. Now Southern Connecticut had only recently been New Haven State Teachers College, a few hours removed from its Normal School lineage, and many obviously held the college in lowest of regard. After all, most local colleges withered under the glare of prestigious Yale domination. Guidance counselors warned students that you shouldn't go *there*—and there was any school other than Yale. So obviously did Oberlin and Yale buy into that idea—I mean Jeff and Henry. I swear it took a nanosecond for those two to bond, and summarily dismiss me as unworthy. Within seconds they were sharing school stories, very happy with the academic lives they led. Let me give one typical example. Yale said to Oberlin, "You had Anthropology last spring? Did you use *Societies Around the World* as a text? By Irwin Sanders." "Of course." Overhearing this exchange I said, "I used that same text in my class," but we were a half hour into our two-week arrangement, and by that time I'd been totally forgotten. Totally. Neither answered me, digesting, I suppose, the news that I had actually been taught how to read. While we went about our preliminary duties, they chatted and laughed and seemed destined for marriage, savoring the blissful honeymoon before my very eyes. Already pummeled by Gin-and-Tonic and the Piece Workers Union, I had no resources to fight them. What was worse, I started to stumble, do inept calculations, make the wrong notations. I'd catch them eyeing each other with expressions that indicated they were not surprised: after all, he was at a teachers college. That was like, well, day care for the dull and intellectually disabled. I burned in silence.

Then I really fumbled. All three of us were kneeling before a huge gray bin, filled with oily fittings. We had to produce a rough count. I was on the end and started emptying the contents into a pile behind me. Yale and Oberlin did likewise, though they paused to make offhand remarks to each other; and when we were finished, Oberlin and Yale each announced the number of fittings they'd extracted. I'd simply emptied the bin, planning to count carefully when I replaced them. "You weren't counting?" Oberlin screamed. "Now what do we do?" Yale echoed, like he'd been denied membership to a table down at Mory's. I'd had it. Yale had around 473 and Oberlin had 495 or something like that. I turned to both of them, kneeling there, arms folded over their smug chests like Cotton Mather and Increase Mather sharing a sermon, and said quietly, "Well, we have an easy solution. Since I was working twice as hard as the two of you, with all your gabbing about nothing, let's estimate my count as 1,000."

Not a word was spoken to me that afternoon.

I didn't know why I let them get to me, but I did. I started dreading dealing with them, lest my speech betray my working-class origins. My father worked at the same factory—that was how I got the job, of course—but as a pattern maker at the other end of the building, so I rarely saw him. He'd been there since he was fourteen, a boy who dropped out of school to help support his immigrant family from Croatia, a boy who began sweeping floors and worked himself up to the skilled craft of fashioning patterns for fittings. For a few years my mother worked in the core shop, inspecting and trimming the sand cores made for the piece workers. (Years later, during the Anita Hill revelations about Clarence Thomas, she confessed to me that the shop foreman, a slimy old guy named Dominic Tomassi, would sidle up to her when she clocked out and touch her breasts. She never told anyone about it, horrified as she was, until the Anita Hill debates helped her find her voice.) So we were a typical hard-working MIF family, and though I was an English major who spoke the President's English, I still would slip occasionally into ungrammatical territory. Sometimes I'd use words like *youse* and *ain't* and I'd even split my infinitive, heaven forfend. Living in the Italian-Polish neighborhood I sometimes didn't know what was English and what was not. I referred to *basil* with a New Haven/Neapolitan dialectical rendering: *basilagoia*. My mother called me a big *kootch*—or something like that, which, I learned, was Italian for horse. When, in the third grade, the teacher held up a spatula and asked what it was, I kept my hand down, thinking the word *spatula* was Italian for the kitchen implement before me. So I always felt I was one step away from slipping back into childhood speech patterns, that deep well of colorful if ungrammatical expression. In moments of tension I reverted so easily, just as I would sometimes stammer and choke up. Oberlin and Yale spoke like they'd been weaned on the Oxford English Dictionary.

One Friday as I prepared to clock out, I was talking to someone who knew my father. I hadn't driven my own car that day, and I was going home with Dad. The guy said he'd walk with me to meet my father at the gate, so he could say hello.

"Your father works here?" Oberlin said, out of the blue.

I nodded.

"Mine, too." But his father, I soon learned, was one of the vice presidents. That information explained in some small measure why he was slumming at this iron mill, although I wondered why Daddy let him crawl into dusty bins.

I didn't know why I saw this brief exchange as some avowal of friendship because I suddenly blurted out, "We're going for abeetz."

Yale, nearby: "What?'

I didn't know what was wrong with me—why I even spoke. Now *abeetz* is the Neapolitan dialect for pizza—apizza, actually. Everyone where I lived called it *abeetz* (my spelling here, of course), "Let's get abeetz at Pepe's." Pepe's in Wooster Square had the best abeetz in the world. Still does. And some nights my father would pick up a cheese pizza on the way home from work, with a bag of peppermint patties (which we refrigerated), and that was a meal fit for the gods. Moreover, we'd troop to Pepe's on a Sunday afternoon, a beloved family excursion. "Abeetz," Yale screamed, out of control. Oberlin shook his head.

I nodded away, flummoxed. I could hear Yale chortling. "Abeetz. Did you hear him?"

That night my slice of abeetz tasted like, well—bitter lemons.

I later learned that Yale was himself a poor boy, a scholarship student from a factory family in the Midwest, a fact I learned from the payroll manager when I went to whine about not receiving in my last paycheck the two-cents raise I'd been promised after working four weeks at the factory. Yale and Oberlin had gotten it, as I overheard, both making fun of the miniscule increase. So Yale had hidden his origins, at least from me, and I wonder if Oberlin knew Yale had once possibly spoken the same questionable Americanese I did.

When the two weeks were over, I happily ran back to the sanctity of the chem lab, my refuge from the storm, and immediately I found a note telling me to watch for train car number 741. The usual panic set in. Within the hour, hearing the clang-clang of a lumbering train, I spotted 741 pull in. In a frenzy I grabbed my pails and rushed out.

"Not today," Gin-and-Tonic said, holding up his hand. "We ain't opening it until tomorrow. Come back. We got them three over there to unload first." He pointed at cars that were opened, with payloaders getting in position, "I gotta do it today," I announced, imperious.

"Do you now." Sarcastic.

"I gotta run tests." Then, smugly: "You *have* to." It was an awful line, but I knew he had to. I could report him, snot that I was.

Cursing, spitting, shuffling, he undid the car's seal and pushed back the door. I faced a mound of brilliant white sand. "Hurry it up," he said.

"I gotta take it from different places."

"Hurry it up, will you." He backed up.

Usually I had a routine, maneuvering around the unstable pile, extracting my sample. But when I looked back at Gin-and-Tonic, he was shaking his head as though I were a worm-white creature he'd unearthed from under a rock. Stupidly, I strode up the hill of sand and filled a jar with the sand at the top. I lost my footing and slid, toppling onto my side. Suddenly, with the growing momentum of an avalanche, the sand started to shift, break up, move towards the open doors. As I jumped out of the car, my feet dug in and served as impetus to the monumental flood. The sand started pouring onto the siding. Gin-and-Tonic lost his mind. "Get the fuck outa here, you fucking loser. You asshole." I ran away.

I learned later that Gin-and-Tonic had to redirect the payloaders from other cars, hurriedly move them into position, and attempt to salvage the avalanche of sand. He ranted and raved all afternoon, filed a scathing report against me, and I was told by my lab foreman—with an odd smile on his face—I'd "misstepped." Well, I couldn't argue with that. But it made me fearful of reentering the rail yards after that, but I was told someone else would take over that assignment. Gin-and-Tonic had said he would kill me on sight. I was happy.

One Monday morning, a hot August day with the heat already rising on the land, I woke up depressed, showered, but I dragged myself to work. I was ready for summer to be over: I wanted autumn, textbooks, cafeteria life. It was going to be a surrealistic day, I knew, because I had to do a task I dreaded. I had to climb a narrow ladder, walking up to the very rafters of the vast factory, up along the criss-crossed interplay of steel beams, and tread carefully along a narrow catwalk that was suspended in that upper atmosphere of thin air and peril. I was told never to look down. A dangerous thing to tell anyone, of course. My job was the collect samples of dust and sediment that had accumulated there.

I was terrified, to say the least. It was an awful job. I never liked heights, and trapeze artists always struck me as natural-born fools. Holding onto my pails with one hand and grasping the thin cable railing with the other, so tight that my skin bruised, I moved like a slug, one tentative step following another. Halfway across, remembering that I was not supposed to look down, I inadvertently did so. And was stunned, locked in place by the world below me.

I haven't mentioned the big news that morning, the news that had electrified the hallways of the factory—and, I suppose, America itself.

For on every station below me—and I mean on *every* station of the piece workers, redundant lines of sweaty workers— there rested a copy of the morning issue of *The New York Daily News* with this sensational headline: MARILYN MONROE KILLS SELF.

It was August 6, 1962.

The film star had died Saturday night or Sunday morning, and the glamorous image of that lost beauty was headline news. Here it was below me, one newspaper after another, a checkerboard replay of the bold type and the black-and-white face.

As I walked the catwalk I could not take my eyes from that headline. One after the other, lying there, face up, a hundred newspapers, a lot of them already coated with the blue-black dust of the factory, that same headline over and over and over, and that stunning photograph of the dead blonde beautiful goddess. It was mesmerizing, alarming, even intoxicating, that snapshot that tugged at the heart. It hurt. I had always loved Marilyn Monroe. Now she was dead, and the floor of the piecework foundry was a tapestry of headline and graphic photograph.

I stood there, my grip tight on the pails, but unable to move. The brutal August heat, coupled with the furnace blasts from the ovens below, rose like vapor around my head. I had to get on with my business, but I just stared from one front-page to the next. Looking for what? A different headline? A happier fate? A different ending?

Finally I glanced up from the floor. At the end of the vast hall, I spotted two floors of small offices sheltered from the piece workers by stairwells and huge plate-glass barriers. Looking through the window of the second floor, I saw my boy Oberlin sitting at a desk, shirt-and-tie and neatly combed hair, as he leafed through a pile of papers. He looked important. I just stared.

For some reason at that moment he swiveled his chair, placed his hands behind his head and stretched, staring down into the foundry. Then, perhaps because my eyes were burning a hole into his head, he looked up over his head and seemed startled to see me standing above him, looking down. For a second we stared at each other, neither moving. Dumbly, grinning nervously, I waved. But in an abrupt dismissal, he swiveled his chair around and started filing papers into a cabinet, his back to me.

I found myself looking at his stiff back, and I didn't know why but I felt an awful chill sweep through my body.

Dante's Hell

November 1963: I am sitting in my World Literature class at Southern Connecticut State College, surrounded by other English majors training to become high-school English teachers. We're a dreary crowd, purposeful but oddly indifferent to the literature. My one friend in the class, a man who would someday murder his wife and be sentenced to life in prison, always said the same thing: "These are not the lovers of literature—these are minor league players who prefer being credentialed than educated." I don't care. Dr. Davis is teaching the class, and she's earnest, unflagging, an old trooper who takes literature very seriously. With her iron-gray hair pulled back into a tight, puritanical bun, with dumpy sweaters and the kindest eyes you can imagine, she is witty and clever. She'd met Yeats early on when she did a dissertation on him, and her voice got sad and distant when she mentioned how her house burned and her inscribed copy of his poetry burned in the inferno. She would toss little asides into the often-ponderous lectures, and her remarks, filled with the stuff of human experience, endeared her to me. Most students found her boring: to me, she was Literature, writ large. As I looked around the classroom, I saw barely stifled yawns, raised eyebrows, and some students doing their Spanish homework.

We'd already trudged our way through Homer's Iliad, almost line by line, too long a beginning for the semester, but she'd gotten excited with the epic drama, as though she were reading it for the first time, and she wanted to share her undisguised rapture, though low key in presentation as befit a woman with her hair in a tight gray bun. Whenever she looked up from her notes or text, she sought me. Perhaps she knew I was the only one who read every word. Now, late in November, the days cold and windy, the promise of Thanksgiving around the corner, we were deeply mired in the grotesque levels of Dante's Inferno, seemingly moments away from approaching paradise. As we moved through the increasingly ominous rungs of Dante's stratified hell, she would nod knowingly: each rung seemed to elicit from her an amusing commentary on the degeneration of the contemporary world. To her, life in some distant era doubtless seemed more salutary, but her wry, often slight dismissal of current mores always tickled me. Yes, I believed, if you have to live in degenerative times you might as well have a sense of humor about it.

The door to the classroom opened, something in itself unusual. We all stopped and stared as a young coed, not a class member, screamed: "President Kennedy has just been shot!" Then the door slammed closed. I don't know whether or not she was running the length and breath of the hallway, some collegiate town crier with disaster on her lips. But we sat there, stunned. We had no information. Dr. Davis fingered the pages of Dante's Inferno. She looked at the text, then at us. I could see she was debating whether or not to dismiss the class, something she obviously was not inclined to do. Then, in a strong, horrible voice, she said:

"Well, we certainly are in the right place." She tapped the text.

She continued reading and commenting, even asking questions. But the class was antsy, fidgety, whispering. She tried to keep control. Outside, in the hallway, swarms of dismissed students rushed by, voices louder than usual. I wanted to be out there, among them, part of that swirling eddy of emotion. I felt as though I was missing something. In the classroom we hovered on a rung of Dante's hell.

No one paid any attention, but Dr. Davis plodded on, at one point, I noted, touching the bun at the back of her head, as though she believed it was coming undone.

A short time later a boy at a desk behind me broke into her reading. "Kennedy's dead," he shouted, and his voice cracked. He held up a tiny transistor radio he'd been secretly listening to. Dr. Davis looked up, focused on him, and then said: "Then we have no choice but to leave." We streamed out the room, and, looking over my shoulder, I noticed Dr. Davis sitting there, in place, and she was reading Dante's words to herself.

I got into my car and started to drive out of New Haven to North Branford. I was a commuting student, living with my parents. I desperately wanted to be home with my family, in front of the TV or near the radio. But the streets of New Haven were mad with unexpected traffic jams, as though everyone had jumped into a car and had to drive somewhere. Gradually, eventually, I inched my way through lights that went red then green and then red again—though I scarcely moved. I noticed that no horns blared, no one raised a middle finger, and there were no fits of blind road rage. We waited as though in a funeral cortege, peering through windshields at one another. It was eerie, and horrible. The radio spoke of his dying, his death, his passing, his leaving us. The void, the abyss, the pit. I was stuck in a rung of Dante's hell.

It lasted for weeks.

I'd been a big fan of John F. Kennedy. During the campaign in the fall of 1960 I had become energized by his campaign, thrilled with his metaphor of Camelot, happy to be young, American, and I wished I could vote. My family, inveterate Democrats to the death, were enthusiastic followers, but, for me, the campaign was rich with the promise of an America with a glorious future. I was editor of the high school paper then, and the old unmarried Irish teacher who ran the paper with a gentle fist would swoon at the mention of JFK—"Have you looked at those beautiful eyes?" In school I was surrounded by Republicans who thought Nixon was The One. Well, he certainly was the one, although we didn't know it at the time. My mother, in particular, found him reprehensible, a slimy creation of the post-McCarthy, post-Eisenhower pan-dripping era. With the first televised political debates—I can recall the sheer thrill of that new spectacle, equal to the later killing of Oswald by Jack Ruby (which I also saw on TV) or the first moon landing—all of us sat glued before the small twelve-inch black-and-white TV. And we all agreed JFK blew the sallow-faced, shifty-eyed Tricky Dick out of the waters of paradise. As editor of the school newspaper, I (with a co-editor and another student) got an invitation to sit in the press box for Nixon's visit to New Haven. He walked within four or five feet of me, and I swear I felt nothing but repugnance that America could nominate such a man to a high office. On the front page of the next day's *New Haven Register*, there was a grainy, long shot of the rally. If you looked really closely—if you squinted through the faded gray spots—you'd see a table with three mute figures sitting dutifully. I was the one in the middle. When Kennedy came to town, the Democrats refused us "press passes," which stunned me. I felt momentarily betrayed by my own people. No matter: at the rally, I stood atop a car and screamed my lungs out. I don't think he heard me.

So now he was dead, and something did, indeed, die in my young generation, that storied end to Camelot, although it quickly became a cliché to state such a sentiment. That weekend we watched the TV, wept, and waited for the light. On Sunday afternoon I was in the front yard with my father and brother Bob, standing by a local man who'd come to cut down an ungainly white pine. A man in his thirties from Vermont or New Hampshire, a hard-bitten Yankee, wiry and jumpy, he rocked back and forth with a tobacco wad in his cheek and the red bulbous nose of a heavy drinker. After he cut down the tree, we stood there, eyeing the fallen boughs and pine-needle debris, and I didn't like the bare openness of the space where once a tree stood. This had been a childhood shelter, a haven of leafy branches you could get lost in, a place where I could hide. It was a cold and clammy day, and I shivered. My father, lighting a Camel from his pack, said: "Too bad about Kennedy." The man narrowed his eyes, spat tobacco out of the side of his mouth, rolled his tongue over stained teeth, and said: "They shoulda shot the bastard years ago."

We just stood there, the JFK fan club, and not a word was spoken. Dad just walked away.

Returning back to class was a disappointment. I don't know what I expected, but more, certainly, than the silences and perfunctory nods and *tsk-tsks* I heard. But then I realized that most of my teachers were foreign-born, often doctoral candidates at Yale or wives of visiting professors at Yale. Could they understand what JFK meant to us? I was a Spanish minor, and I had two classes—one on Spanish grammar and one on the Generation of '98. Senorita Lorca taught the grammar. A distant, imperious woman with hazel eyes in a dark face, she only came alive when she discussed her own paintings—her major passion. I'd gone to one of the group shows Yale mounted and her oils and acrylics hung like vast splashes of bacon fat on enormous canvases—everything in gray or black hues, dripping over the edges, the paints coagulated like lard that lingered too long in a pan. In class I waited for her to say something about Kennedy but she didn't— she shrugged her shoulders in some European fatalistic gesture, as though she were sitting in a Barcelona coffee house and someone mentioned that spring would be late this year. She immediately launched into her Socratic Inquisition, a question-and-answer routine in which she'd zero in on one or two students and fire conversational lines at them, hoping they'd commit some egregious grammatical *faux pas*, at which time she'd close her eyes, as if to ward off a personal effrontery so horrible it could not be borne, and shake her head back and forth. I could read her mind: we were American nincompoops, all glitter and shine, no depth, no intellectual rigor. Often she began her sentences with: "When I learned English grammar as a child—" And we knew she was ready to launch into the superiority of European schools over the American.

She had a special fascination with Cindy DeCarlo, a petite little cheerleader type, all fluffy hair, red-lacquered nails, and dreamy

I'm-yours eyes. Her mother was Puerto Rican, we were given to understand, so (she said) she had no need to do homework in Spanish. But at first Senorita Lorca would sail off into cataclysmic disgust when Cindy muttered her street Spanish, the Spanglesh born of New Haven poverty. But then Cindy could do no wrong. Something else was going on, I sensed—worldly cosmopolite that I was. For Srta. Lorca often chose Cindy for her fifteen-minute question-and-answer assaults, and though Cindy butchered the lovely language of Cervantes and Unamuno, Srta. Lorca just smiled through it all. Had I done so, I'd been on the rack. But Srta. Lorca was smitten with the vacuous Cindy, and the questions often got very personal. The worst time, I remember, was an afternoon, when, after asking some questions about hobbies and movies—and not the death of Kennedy—many phrased in such a way to force Cindy to use the resistant subjective case, Srta. Lorca paused and said, in elegant Castilian: "Are you wearing underwear?"

You heard me: *Are you wearing underwear?*

Of course, few of us knew the word for underwear so we didn't understand the question, and we all reached for our Spanish-English dictionaries. All across the room light bulbs switched on over our cartoon heads as the full (and itchy) meaning of the question became apparent. Cindy, our resident *puertoriqueña*, did not need the dictionary. Her face got beet red and she stuttered, "Yes, I am." Srta. Lorca was grinning.

So much for the assassination of JFK as a review topic!

Then I went into Señora Maridu's Generation of '98 literature class, where I was the only Spanish minor in a class of ardent Spanish majors. My good friend—the one destined, as I've said, to murder his wife down the road in a struggle involving property and cocaine—and I were the only males. Señora Maridu waited until we were all seated and stood before the class. She shook her head: "A sad time for America," she said. "A sad time." And then we launched into the lesson, although periodically she seemed distracted.

Señora Maridu had a bizarre manner of grading. Since we were discussing literature and I was an English major, she insisted I had an advantage over the more parochial Spanish majors, whose focus was not so much literary but linguistic. Once she gave a ten-essay exam, and I wrote detailed comparisons between Spanish literary movements and similar movements afoot in Russia, in Europe proper, and in the United States—bringing in William Dean Howells, Henry James, Gorky, and even Oscar Wilde. When the blue books were returned, huge celebratory correction marks graced each answer, despite her red-penciled grammatical errors. But the grade was a "B." Next to me sat my friend John, and he had one whole essay x'd out—his response was totally wrong. But his grade was an "A minus." That rankled, to be sure. The same was true throughout the class. So after class I approached her and questioned my grade. Now keep in mind all conversations had to be *en Español*. She explained: "A brilliant exam, one of the best I ever read. Your comparison of Pio Baraja to the realism of Stephen Crane was inspired. I read it to my husband." Her husband was in the Spanish department at Yale. "He said it was better than what his doctoral students write."

I interrupted. "But Señora Maridu, you gave me a B." There was a pleading in my voice.

"Of course," she said.

"But why?"

"There no grade beyond A," she said.

"What?"

"All the Spanish majors wrote A or A minus essays—wonderful answers, but yours was much better. I could not give you an A."

"So you gave me a B?"

"I had to give you some grade."

We went aback and forth until, in despair, I petitioned her to speak in English because I thought I was missing something in the frantic translation. She agreed, and largely said the same thing. I got nowhere. My grade stayed a B. At the end of the semester she did give me an A for the class and an autographed copy of Borges' *El Aleph*. "I'm from Argentina," she said. "I am a friend of his." She'd read one of my short stories in a college literary review and said my erratic, surrealistic style reminded her of passages in Borges.

I still own the book.

A year later, a senior now, there was another Presidential election, but I had little heart for it. I didn't like Lyndon B. Johnson, didn't like the drift of the country, and so I campaigned for a third party candidate, an Independent Socialist, a sociology professor at Yale whose radical ideas appealed to me. His candidacy was a lightning rod for all those who sensed the tenor of the evolving 1960s—the nascent youth movement, the ugly war in Vietnam, the breaking away from staid 1950s blandness, perhaps the dawn of the Timothy Leary drug culture. To mention the candidate's name in certain quarters was to invite attack and censure—and the charge that you were a downright Commie pink faggot loser. With a small band of warriors, we invaded upscale suburban confines and posh expensive apartment complexes in downtown New Haven, where brand-new Lincolns occasionally (I noticed) sported George Wallace bumper stickers. Ours, we believed, was a cause for the common man, but we were bullied, shoved, ignored, despised. When I knocked on doors in North Branford, housewives actually told me they knew nothing of politics: "My husband tells me how to vote." Obviously feminism was slow to take root on the crabgrassed lawns of town. I was deliriously happy: I really believed this was a man with working-class vision, someone who could effect change in the world, albeit locally.

A few days before the election, my grandmother died. She'd been sick for a long while, bedridden after her two legs had been removed to the thigh, a long progression of painful amputation that began back with gangrened toes. I'd been outside all day long, disseminating our campaign literature, feeling very proud about my role as worker in local politics. With a friend I stopped at the family liquor store, the North Branford Package Store, and my uncle Branch told me: "Your grandmother died this morning." This statement came out of the blue, and for a minute I remembered the trouble I always had with her, especially years back when I trespassed in her garden and observed the internecine family warfare she created. "I'm sorry," I said. And I meant it, I suppose. But I felt nothing, and that made me ashamed. A year before I wept at the death of JFK, and the mere thought of his departure—a full year later—sometimes got me chocked up. But my own flesh and blood, well, nothing at the pit of my soul, nothing, a void. Except for a sorrow for my mother, who would be grieving. I was sorry for her pain.

The night of the wake was on Election Day. I'd spent the morning at the polling station in my small town, standing the requisite distance from the machines, idly spending my time with more substantial Democrats and Republicans, nattily dressed and confident. I was a college boy with a loud and insistent two-inch campaign button on my chest, advocating Mr. Independent. They glanced at me as though I were an annoying relative, overstaying my welcome. "Do you ski at Powder Hill?" Mr. Republican asked me. Confused, I said: "As a matter of fact, I do. Why?" "I hear the owners are Communists." He stared at Miss Democrat. They smiled conspiratorially at each other, for a moment bedfellows of the vast and good Republic. I started tell the current dirty joke about Nixon's wife but stopped. My Mom raised me differently. And that night when the polls closed, my candidate lost—I don't know why I was shocked! —and in North Branford I believe he garnered eleven votes, which included mine (and, I believe, my mother's).

Around eight o'clock I rushed into the wake at Clancy's Funeral Parlor in Branford, where my family had gathered. I caught my mother's eye—she'd been watching for me, fearful I'd skip the necessary evening, not because there was a victory celebration I had to attend but because lately I'd been drifting away from family ritual. I could see relief on her face, and a slight smile. I nodded to my aunts and uncles, to cousins, family friends. I suddenly realized I was still wearing my huge campaign button emblazoned on my skinny chest, but I left it on. But I noticed eyes drifted to it, some looks of annoyance, to be sure, but some just idly curious. I would hazard a guess that everyone in the dark and scented room had voted straight Democrat that morning, knee-jerk voting a family tradition. Here I was with: *Howard Simons for State Senate. Vote Independent.* And this, many insisted, was some blatant code for "Vote Communist and watch America sink further down the crapper."

I waited my turn to approach the flower-draped casket. An old farmer was kneeling at the coffin, dressed in his go-to-field clothes, manure crusted on the soles of his boots, and he looked unwashed. It was Arnie Buzelli, a neighbor who'd lost his mind years back. But a sweet guy. He was famous for driving his farm truck up and down the highway at two miles per hour and enjoying the traffic jams he created, such that they were in the small town. Now, for some reason, he was giggling loudly, privy to some inside joke only he and my grandmother obviously shared. Someone nudged him away. My turn. I stood before Grandma's casket, sort of nodded a silent prayer, and stared into the waxen, round face, the morticians' hand making serene that bitterness that had long settled into the creases and folds of her face.

Someone yelled from the back of the room, and everyone turned. Aunt Sonja, my mother's sister, had spotted my Vote Independent button on my chest and wasn't happy. "How dare you come in here at my mother's funeral with a Communist button on your chest?" she yelled over the heads of the mourners. She went on and on, in the same vein, as she moved through people toward me. "You're a Communist." Pause. "Pinko." Pause. "Anti-American." Pause. 'Commie, Commie, Commie." She was filled with rage. Her voice echoed of the velvet draperies and thick carpets, amplified in a room designed for people to speak in reverential whispers. Now Sonja was the family firebrand, the only really outspoken sister, opinionated and forceful, yet at times generous and kind. Except when politics entered the equation. She still worshipped the memory of FDR, the last American hero. She and I had had our skirmishes, and we never saw eye to eye. But we'd always sort of liked each other. Years back, when I was a boy, I heard

her sing the chorus of a ballad about a lonesome cowboy who'd died on the range:
And he'll not see his mother
When the work is done this fall.

I told her I loved that sentimental ballad, and the next day she placed the sheet music into my hands.

Now, however, her hands were clenched into fists and she was shaking them at me. "How dare you! Mama is in her coffin and you are here with that damn button. Traitor!" She launched into is-this-why-she-suffered-an-immigrant-coming-to-America-only-to-see-her-grandkids-want-Communism-to-take-over-America? routine.

Angry, defensive, I fought back, yelling that this was, indeed, a free country and I had a right to vote for anyone I chose—and my guy was not, repeat not, a Commie, and if he were, so be it. We stood, two stubborn fools with the same hot blood of my dead Grandma, a foot apart and a foot away from that very Grandma, fighting the political wars of the decade. Loud, loud, stupid and foolish.

Suddenly I felt a touch to the elbow. I looked over, and my mother stood by my side. There were tears in her eyes. She whispered: "This is my mother's wake."

"Get out," said Sonja. "Just get out."

My mother whispered: "She won't stop unless you leave. Please."

So I left, shamefaced and hound-dog looking, the family leper slinking through disapproving eyes of my own blood. I found myself on the sidewalk, shaking, angry, but a little bit sad.

Late that night I joined my college buddy John at his apartment in New Haven, hanging out with Budweiser and toasted tuna-and-cheese sandwiches, the only food he knew how to make. I was in a foul mood, recounting not only my sadness over the loss of my Socialist candidate—John refused to vote—but the debacle at Grandma's wake. John clicked his tongue: "This is the grandmother that always gave you trouble?" "Yeah." I'd told him about trespassing in the Garden of Eden.

He laughed. "You take this thing too seriously."

"What does that mean?"

"Fighting in front of your grandmother's coffin? You don't see anything odd about that?"

I smiled.

"Nothing is that important," he said. "Let it go."

"But it *is* important."

"Not really."

I looked at John. In the two years I'd been his friend, he'd been the leveler, the balancing act, the man who calmed things down. His slight, bemused philosophic nods ended petty college tiffs. We used to joke that nothing could touch him. Dark, short, and off-beat handsome, of Puerto Rican parents, he used to tell people that he was the son of the Spanish ambassador to the UN, that his parents were Spanish royalty, that he was destined for royalty himself. He made it all up, but he said the spiel so often you had to wonder. He started believing it himself. I never took it seriously, seeing it as a line to meet girls. "I'm going to be rich someday because I *choose* to be rich," he said. "And it has nothing to do with working for a living. Wait and see." After college we drifted apart, my going to graduate school in the South, he disappearing into a world of white stretch limos, upscale New York friends, East Side Manhattan bars and world-weary European émigrés—or so I was told. Years later I read in the newspaper that he'd married an older woman, enormously wealthy but sickly, and he lived off her vast fortune. He traveled in Eurotrash circles in Manhattan, posing as the son of the Spanish Ambassador to America. He wore the Spanish coat of arms emblazoned on his Barney's sports jacket. He owned a half dozen watering holes in Manhattan and Florida. In a fit of reality, perhaps, the dowager money machine turned him out, but he returned one night to their penthouse, charmed his way into letting him back in, and something happened. The police surmised that he sat on her bony chest and stuffed cocaine into her nostrils until she had a heart attack and died. He was in jail for life.

But on the night of Grandma's wake and the loss of Socialism in the Connecticut part of America, John turned to me and said: "After all, she *was* your grandmother. Say something good about her."

I was quiet.

"Come on," he said, smiling. "Because of her you are here."

I said nothing.

He raised the bottle of Budweiser. "To the life that she lived the only way she knew how." He nudged me. "To Grandma."

I raised my bottle. "To Grandma."

Zeke

I was terrified of Zeke the first time I met him. It wasn't that he was too loud, even though he did have that booming voice, or that he had that almost impenetrable Down East Maine accent, or that he was a nonstop talker. No: he was immediately in your face, up against you, buddy buddy, a backslapping kind of guy but too wide-eyed and nosy. He wanted to know all your business the minute he met you. The problem was—I had no business to share. I felt like a cipher next to him. Mildly illiterate, living in a trailer park somewhere in town, barely living above poverty, he swaggered, he strutted, he pontificated, he seemed to have lived a dozen lives. And, I suppose, I feared that he would see right through me. I was always afraid he'd call me on it publicly, announce that I was a fraud. But I didn't even know what that *meant*. More so, he spent most of his time talking about sex, which I thought a lot about but knew practically nothing on a practical level. I expected him to embarrass me somehow, to draw attention to—I guess what I'm trying to say—my wimpdom.

But that was not the case at all. In short order, we became friends, as close as two disparate souls caught in the brief interlude of a fleeting summer job can be friends. I was in college now, twenty years old. He told me he'd never gone to high school. "What's in it for me?" Growing up on a starved, pinched farm somewhere in the boondocks of Maine, Zeke had drifted around New England since the time he was thirteen or fourteen, in the army for a stint that didn't take, this factory job, that one, until he ended up in Connecticut, a man now in his late twenties, married to a woman he fought with constantly, living in a trailer park, where two colicky babes kept him awake all night long. He told me he didn't know how he ended up married, but that it was all right—his wife took care of him, fed him, and was available for sex on demand, because, he said, "She wants it more than I do. And I want it a lot." So he got a job as a handyman of sorts, Mr. Fix It, the guy that mowed the lawn.

We were both working for Mr. Leiderbacker, and that was the class field trip to lunacy. Harmond Leiderbacker was then a man in his late seventies, a lanky man with stooped shoulders, baggy dress trousers topped with a wrinkled white dress shirt. His uniform. A head of yellow-white hair puffed up like a soufflé. He also was never without a cigarette hanging from his lip, but the joke was that he'd never die of cancer because he hardly smoked the infernal butts. He'd light one, place it between his lips, twist it side to side for a few seconds, and then drop it to the ground, where he'd squish the tobacco into the asphalt. Almost immediately he was lighting another. Pack after pack, daily.

Mr. Leiderbacker had invented some miniature mechanical device that was used in the production of state-of-the-art hospital respirators, and this was his claim to fortune—or at least reasonable fortune. He'd bought this monstrosity of a house, hidden in the woods of rural Connecticut, a rambling house nestled under decaying pines, at the end of a long, long single-lane driveway that meandered off the main highway. It was very easy to not know it was there. During Prohibition, I was told, the house had been a speakeasy-cum-dancehall, with a cavernous front room where flappers with bobbed hair and zoot-suited flash-boys danced the night away. Or at least that was the story handed down to us laborers. Mr. Leiderbacker moved out of New York City with his wife Ludie and began the warfare that was their marriage. But he also carved little bungalows out of the hills, little white clapboard one-room buildings—at least six or seven of them—that became his "factory" where he manufactured his invention. Looking like some bucolic cottage industry, shielded by glorious maples and towering mountains, the business—Revolution Cycles, Inc.—flourished with local workers, mainly housewives who worked on and off for a few years, paid off the dishwasher and dryer, and then moved on. Most worked for a few months. Others stayed for years. Nevertheless, the business thrived, seemed to make a lot of money for the Leiderbacker clan, and Mr. Leiderbacker suddenly had the leisure to indulge his desire to prettify the landscape surrounding the old homestead at the far end of the long driveway, up against the hills, as well as decorate the grounds around the tiny bungalows.

That was where Zeke and I entered the picture. With such massive growth and meandering turns, a groundskeeper was needed. Zeke was hired to mow the lawns, create new lawns, build cement walls, plant fir trees on the hillside, prune the hedges, rake the leaves, and plow the snow. Even spending one day (successfully) looking for Mr. Leidebacker's false teeth, which one of the dogs had run off with. Boys like me were summer helpers, gofers seemingly without a care in the world. I was actually working there a few weeks before Zeke was hired, replacing a disgruntled old-timer who'd had enough. Every so often people who worked for Harmond Leiderbacker "had enough"—and disappeared. Sometimes Mr. Leiderbacker would give you two contradictory orders. It was easier just to quit. My initiation was to dig an asparagus bed in the vast vegetable garden near the house, removing a foot of dirt and replacing it with the finest loam, a backbreaking task—Mr. Leiderbacker stood over me and kept shaking his head slowly— that should have warned me to take immediately flight. I didn't.

My first job with Zeke was to build a stone wall, chiseled out of an expanded driveway through hilly terrain, mixing cement, setting it, imbedding granite rocks (dragged down from the hills) into the wet cement. Within two days I had no flesh on my fingertips. This was going to be a long summer. Zeke pulled me aside. This was when I still feared him, so I was immediately leery. "What?" I asked. In this thickly accented voice, he said, "You don't own the place, kid." "What?" "You're working for rich people," he said. "Just do a little and it goes a long way. They don't give a fuck for you." So I was working with a homespun socialist, some down-home cracker-barrel Marxist. But he often covered for my glaring ineptitude, shielding me from disaster, stopping me from being foolish, and suddenly we were enjoying each other's company. When the tractor wouldn't start, despite my coaxing it, I stood on the seat and screamed to the wind of poem of my own creation:

This
Is
A hunk
(long pause)
Of junk

Based on the rhythm of The Rolling Stones' musical line: *I want you back* (long pause) *again*. Zeke nearly wet his pants. Okay, you probably had to have been there. But from that point on, we found ourselves laughing over nothing, pushing and shoving each other like we were both ten instead of being in our twenties, and one of us in his late twenties, at that. No matter: I'd never felt such acute camaraderie before, and I found it intoxicating. It took me a while to master his difficult dialectical speech. I couldn't believe we both came from the same country—but I got most of it.

Of course, most of his vocabulary was the word *fuck*. He could be mouthing off on a number of topics—and he had quite a few ready-made boiler-plate sermons, from the superiority of Chevrolet over Ford or the reasons women needed to stay at home with the kiddies—and anyone passing by would simply hear a spurt of unintelligible down-East gabbing, except for the word *fuck*. It would ring out, loud and clear, with all the force of a ceremonial gong being struck. He would go on and on. One rainy afternoon when we were forced inside and were given jobs at the drill presses in one of the cottages, he talked a full three hours on how he would spend one million dollars—this was not some generalized catchall of yacht, mansions, trips to Paris, and fancy call girls. No: it was an itemized list. He'd done his homework. By late afternoon, when I was comatose and drilling small holes in my palm—on purpose? —he was down to "three cans of W40 at $.79 a can, $4.27 for some .22 ammo." I thought I'd go mad. When it was all over and he sat back, triumphant in his catalogue, announcing that it all added up to a cool million, I burst his bubble by saying, "I think you forgot the sales tax." He didn't talk to me for three days.

I made the mistake of inviting him to my home—that is, my parents' home. He'd been asking me to hang out some nights, despite the fact that he had a wife and two kids at home, but I was not the kind of kid who "hung out." I didn't even know where kids hung out. For God's sake, in the little town of North Branford, population maybe 1,000, you hung out in the backyard. But he persisted, and so one night we just drove around, and, bored, I invited him back to my house where we sat idly in the kitchen. I didn't know how to get rid of him. He was rattling on about something and segued into his opposition to the death penalty, then a hot topic. Now I personally opposed the death penalty, but, irritated by his strident, insistent tone, I played devil's advocate, purposely building a case for the categorical taking of human life, willy nilly, in fact. No matter what he said, I countered with spurious argument. At last I silenced him and felt a little foolish. I liked him. I didn't want to hurt him. Then he launched into some diatribe against women, peppering his remarks with the obligatory fourth word in every sentence—*fuck*. Late at night, in the bright kitchen, I panicked: one room away, separated by a small hallway, my parents lay in bed. I suddenly realized they were most likely wide awake, uncomprehending most of Zeke's rambling, but certainly cringing at the machine-gun fire of *fucks* exploding in the night air.

And then there was the missing piece to the story: Ludie Leiderbacker, the alliterative wife of the owner, a woman who hid in the massive home throughout the day, emerging only to speed—and I do mean speed—down the winding driveway, through the bungalows, in her sleek black Cadillac convertible. Invariably she was a presence in that campus of buildings only because she thought she was, to use one of my mother's phrases, "high and mighty." The Leiderbackers had one son—we all wondered how that ever happened—and there was a granddaughter named Susie, who visited from out of state with both her parents, and one of the workers overheard the child call Mrs. Leiderbacker by a nickname—LaLa. Baby talk, I guess, for Ludie. So, of course, she became LaLa to us all—sometimes Lulu or, I don't know why, Wing Nut. LaLa Leiderbacker. Every so often she'd stroll majestically—there's no other word for it—from the huge house, sashaying down through the flower beds, and wandering into one of the bungalow-factories, nodding her *noblesse oblige* head, rarely speaking, sometimes giggling as though she'd been told an amusing bit of repartee. We hated her more than dust. When she spoke at you, she looked over your shoulders at some distant mark, as though she'd spotted a totally absorbing scene that had nothing to do with you. We all felt tremendously small in her presence. At one point she took over one of the small bungalows and turned it into an artist studio, where, idly, she'd paint canvases that looked annoyingly like a baby's digestive surprise. But her visits to the kingdom of art were rare, perhaps once a week, and we knew such dilettantism would pass, like a gallstone.

Her aged husband indulged her because he, well, had a girlfriend who lived just down the hill. If any worker said anything about Mrs. Leiderbacker, he'd defend her, rise to anger, and that was that for the worker. "She's my wife," I heard him say once, "no matter what she is." I thought that a wonderful testament of marriage vows. They battled all the time like alley cats—or endured weeks of numbing silence. They co-inhabited the large house, but did not sit together at the dinner table. At noon I'd see Mr. Leiderbacker get into his black Cadillac (not a convertible) and leave the grounds, turn onto a road down the hill from his property, and pull into the driveway of a small ugly ranch house, where a fifty-something matron lived alone. Then he'd have lunch—two or three hours—and then drive around the corner and back to the office. From the big house windows LaLa could certainly spot the Caddie making its daily rendezvous, but nothing was ever said. No one wanted to upset the stasis of serenity and money. There were rumors that Mr. Leiderbacker was paying the woman in the ranch house a goody sum of money, but who knows?

This is not to say that LaLa lacked dinner companions. Every so often I had to go to the big house for something, and, working late on occasion, I'd knock on the kitchen door and LaLa would merrily intone, "Enter." Not "Come in, who the hell is it? We don't need any Fuller Brush products," but "Enter," stretched out to five or six syllables. She'd be at the large table, picking at some food, and three other chairs were occupied by French poodles, dutifully poised, munching their food, glancing at their Mommy. There was a full-size pooch named Duchess, whom I really liked—regal, sweet, friendly. There were two miniature pooches who had snooty attitudes: Tessa (Countess) and Princess. Are you starting to detect a theme here? The miniatures would yelp and go for the ankles—what kind of dinner guests were they, after all? —but Duchess would just keep eating. She knew where her Alpo was buttered. Now Mrs. Leiderbacker was also a poodle, in that she'd had her hair permed into a close-cut, kinky-hard style that did not distinguish her at all from her menagerie. She and Duchess both had creamy white hair. She doted on them, "my children." One time, as I watched her having a conversation with them—even asking questions and somehow getting answers I somehow missed—she turned to me and said, "They're people, you know." "What?" "They really are," she said. "People." I took her word for it.

Now Zeke and I—and a couple other high school boys that summer—tended to avoid her, but it was nearly impossible. She'd stroll down to the fields where we were working and say: "I'm expecting a famous artist here this afternoon to visit my studio." We'd wait: so? "If I have to leave for a while, could you direct him to the studio?" Sure thing. She told everybody the same thing, just so we'd know and ooh and aah. The famous artist—he may have been, how did I know? —appeared at three with LaLa sitting in the open doorway, waiting, hands flying as though she were landing a plane. He looked like a Mafia hit man, with dark sunglasses, a black shirt with a white tie, and black pointed shoes. We heard laughter coming from the studio, and Zeke insisted the man was out of control, hitting his sides at the sight of LaLa's mud-pie abstractions. "He ain't gonna pick up a paintbrush again in this life," Zeke said. Another time she summoned me from the asparagus bed. In my grungy work clothes, scrapping mud from my work boots, I walked through her cavernous living room where she pointed to a small oil painting—"I just acquired it"—perhaps a one-by-two-foot painting, a ghastly confection of cider mill-cum-New England ice storm, done with large dots a la Serraut on steroids. Only an all-night drunk could create such a painting, I thought. "I can't reach the spot," she said. Of course, the spot where she intended to hang it was only shoulder high, and I lifted it, hung it on a nail, and she said, "Perfect. It just didn't hang right for me." Well, hanging is one of my talents. She waited. "Anything else?" I asked. She waited. I fidgeted. "Do you like it?" she asked, almost timidly, but with a trace of anger: I was not doing my job, which was to serve as art critic in the provinces. "It's very nice," I lied. She frowned: "Art isn't nice." She dismissed me. To my back she said: "Just like some people aren't nice."

Zeke loved to put her on, carrying on conversations in which he got the best of her, and, of course, she never knew it. Once we were working in a flowerbed just outside her kitchen (for some reason nothing grew there, despite fertilizer and water and TLC), and LaLa was sipping coffee in the kitchen, watching us work through the screen door. Zeke was singing, as he often did, dreadful country western ditties. *I'm breaking my back putting up a front for you.* I think that was one of the lines. LaLa asked him what it was. "Opera," he said. She chortled. "Oh, really." She started in on Wagner and his ilk, going off the deep end, all *Sturm und Drang*, and Zeke slowly interjected what sounded like stupid rejoinders, egging her on, cultivating his ah-shucks country bumpkin role for the lady of the manor. She ate it up, patronizing him. I listened in horror, knowing Zeke was up to no good. As the conversation moved on, Zeke started mocking her, playing off her words—Parsifal became "that opry Parsley-full"—and I could see she was getting uneasy. He ended by somehow making Wagner some lackey at the Grand Ole Opry—"You've heard of that opera house, no? —and having the last say. It was magnificent, in its own way, so singularly seamless in its cruelty, and I felt for her—but not that much. She seemed to suddenly realize a game had been played, and she was the loser. It was just a case of one cruelty topping another. She never saw it coming.

One day she tried to get me fired. She was having an afternoon tea for friends—we'd never seen anybody going into that house to see her—but we assumed she'd rounded up some locals, given her husband's standing in the town. That morning her maid quit. They always quit, the local Polish women who vacuumed and dusted and put up with her pretensions and accusations. Well, that morning, with her nerves on end, LaLa had pushed Stacia over the edge, and the buxomly immigrant woman with rolled-up stockings and obligatory kerchief—and more body hair than Paul Bunyan—got into her beat-up car and made a one-finger exit from LaLa land. Mrs. Leiderbacker dragged me from the fields and commandeered me to clean her vast living room. Now I had never touched a vacuum before, nor feather duster, nor sniffed a bottle of Pine Sol. I was filthy, bedraggled, mud-covered, and she dragged me into the oversized rooms.

Let me describe the living room. It was so long that it had seven distinct sofa-and-armchair-and-coffee-table arrangements. Seven. One for each sin. None of them had any style, at least to my untutored sensibility, but it was as though LaLa had inherited the once-glorious Prohibition dance hall and felt the need to fill it with bland, unobtrusive parlor sets. The only eye-catcher was the huge fieldstone fireplace, situated in the back wall, with, of course, one of the living room sets positioned dangerously close to it. I doubted whether a fire was ever lit on a blustery winter night. What made the hall bleaker was the sheer amount of clutter, porcelain and ceramic bric-a-brac, dewy-eyed shepherdesses with staffs, pink Elizabethan ladies in flowing skirts, Keene-eyed plaster-of-Paris doggies. The whole place looked like the storage room at the local Goodwill store.

At the entrance to the kitchen rested a vacuum cleaner. "I need you to vacuum the living room," LaLa said, pointing. "I'm expecting guests this afternoon."

"Mrs. Leiderbacker," I said, helpless, "I've never vacuumed."

"Of course you can," She doubtless assumed that the working class knew all manual operations by birthright.

I stared across an expanse of clutter and angle, and despaired. I was in my crusty work boots, I was wearing a soiled T-shirt and torn jeans. I was, well, built for the great outdoors. Nevertheless, sighing to let her know this was not acceptable, I found the "on" switch, contemplated the hose with the brush attached—like Aristotle Contemplating the Bust of Homer—and placed it on the first of the oriental carpets. I was surprised that it worked. Stuff was being sucked in. But there was only one problem: the cord. It kept getting tangled on the legs of the sofa, or it mysteriously unplugged itself and came whipping back at me like an insane rattlesnake. I had clumsily made it past one of the living room sets, jerkily maneuvering the Hoover, when, turning to avoid a frightening looking Oriental-style dog figure, the Hoover slammed into an end table, sending the lamp to the floor, smashing it into pieces. In trying to rectify the mishap, I banged a table, sending the cutesy figurines to the floor. Like a chain reaction, all the accoutrements that graced parlor set number one collided and caromed and crashed. Mrs. Leiderbacker, hearing the noise, came rushing in, screaming at the top of her lungs. The poodles howled in sympathetic chorus. She grabbed my shoulder and sputtered—I swear! —"Desist." She didn't add, "lout" but the inference was clearly there. "Get out, get out," she yelled, and I scurried through the kitchen and into the great outdoors of freedom. Later that day, Mr. Leiderbacker found me in the fields and said that LaLa insisted I be fired for—not the destruction of "priceless artifacts from New York's Chinatown," bought (and described as such) by LaLa herself, but, rather, insubordination. "What?" I said. He turned away. "Forget it. You're not going anywhere. You're the only one who can weed the flower beds without pulling up all the flowers." So I stayed.

But summer was coming to an end, and so is the story of Zeke. In the middle of August one of the women in the factory brought in a Ouija board, and during lunch break, she and the other women fiddled with it. I'd seen one a few times, was vaguely intrigued, but the ladies at lunch made sport of it, while entertaining some real fear or titillation that it might actually work. For a few days Zeke and I joined them in the cramped quarters, tucked in between threading machines and splicers, everyone taking turns sitting knee-to-knee, and moving (or did they?) the mysterious cursor across the board. It was all very silly, and the messages from beyond were inane and slightly risqué. We all laughed and laughed and laughed. One of the workers, an older woman named Lizzie who was a devout Presbyterian and notorious for getting speeding tickets on the way to church, was angry: she warned against trifling with the spirit world.

Zeke said nothing for a few days, standing there, arms folded, interested, but quiet. "You ever see one of these boards?" I asked him. He shook his head: no. "Wanna try?" one woman asked. He shook his head: no. "Come on," everyone said. Zeke sat down, touched knees with the woman who owned the nefarious board, and suddenly the atmosphere in the dark room changed. Everybody got very serious. It had to do with Zeke's demeanor. With rigid spine and red neck, with wide popping eyes, he obviously was taking this all very seriously. I tried to make a joke, but Zeke glared at me. Shut up. Just shut up. And so for maybe ten or so minutes until time to clock back in, Zeke's fingertips gently touched the cursor, which flew madly about the board. Someone standing over him read aloud: *The door in front of you is closed. Open it.* No one laughed. What followed was gobbledygook, hieroglyphics of nonsense, and then lunch was over. The woman who owned the board whispered to a friend that she hardly manipulated the cursor. She looked frightened. All afternoon Zeke was quiet, refusing to banter, ignoring my playful posturing and shoving. The next day at lunch he rushed to be the first with the board, but nothing happened. He monopolized the whole half hour, and the women drifted away. That afternoon the owner of the Ouija board took it home and didn't bring it back. Zeke asked her about it, but she said no: this was no longer fun.

Zeke was out of work for three or four days, the rest of the week, but on Monday he arrived a half hour late, driving the old battered station wagon with the simulated wood-grain panels and the bent antenna and dented fenders. I was brooming the parking lot when he pulled in. He stared straight ahead, ignoring my wave. And I noted that there was a book propped up on the steering wheel, open, with his fingers clutching both it and the wheel. A book? Zeke? A reader? When he went to clock in, incurring the frowns of the forewoman, I rushed to the car. Sitting on the dashboard was the Holy Bible. Holy shit! I thought. A Bible. He'd been reading the Bible. Opened to Leviticus, for some reason. Thus began Zeke's rapid-fire spiritual metamorphosis. All jollity ended, a deadly seriousness intruding on our long days. He'd get a faraway look in his eyes, and sometimes I thought he'd burst out crying. I knew he had some troubles at home, because he and his wife battled all the time. But something else was happening here. He scarcely said ten worlds to me in one long day.

One rainy afternoon we worked inside the factory, both of us at adjacent drill presses, punching holes into a one-inch square plates, one after the other—terrible, mindless work, not making a noticeable dent in the huge barrel of blanks nearby. Zeke had to drill one hole, slide the piece to me, and I added a different sized hole onto the template. Eli Whitney would have been proud of our rhythm. He's lucky I can't wring his neck. Exhausted, bored, I yawned, stretching my arms. Zeke stopped working, pulled out a pad and pen, and started scribbling. Suddenly he nudged my elbow and slid the small slip of paper over. I read: *"The winds of God are visions of justice."* I stared at him. "Zeke?" He resumed drilling. Minutes later, the same routine: *"God spelled backwards is dog."*

Later: *"Rivers belong in the night sky."* Or: *"Turn over the rock of the soul and there is the form of Jesus."*

I got scared. By four o'clock he'd stopped working entirely, and I covered for him, reaching over and drilling his piece, then mine, contorting my body to do so, fearing the forewoman would come in from another bungalow and discover him slacking off. "Zeke," I said. "Come on." He didn't answer. He clocked out early and drove away.

The next day he returned to work, Bible planted on the steering wheel—it was the talk of the place—and worked alongside me in the fields. At noon he clocked out, and went for a walk in the mountains behind the factory. At 12:30 he hadn't returned, and I stupidly clocked him back in. I clocked him out at 4:30, even though the forewoman was watching. She shook her head. What was going on? The next morning when we all arrived at work the station wagon was still in the parking lot, but it had been there all night long. Frantic, his wife called to say he hadn't come home the night before. The police were called but there seemed to be no wrongdoing. Zeke had wandered into the forest, and hadn't retuned.

Nearly a week went by. No Zeke.

Then, one morning, picking up a copy of *The New Haven Journal-Courier*, there was a small tidbit on a page buried deep inside. A motorist cruising the roads on the other side of the mountain, headed into North Guilford, had been stopped on a back road, confronted by a man dressed in what he said was burlap sack cloth, a man carrying a crude wooden staff, a man who announced that he was Elijah the Prophet. The driver had sped off and called the cops. I knew in my heart of hearts that this man was Zeke. We all did. And a few days later Zeke was spotted again, was cornered by the constable and quietly taken to a hospital. Virtually naked, incoherent, dressed in tattered clothing (not the sack cloth so described by the motorist), Zeke announced he was sent from God, that he had Jesus' work to do, that he was, indeed, Elijah the Prophet. Eventually he was sent for tests at the state mental hospital in Middletown.

After the initial buzzing during the factory coffee breaks, little was said. Perhaps we were all stunned. Perhaps we all blamed ourselves. His deterioration had come so rapidly, so unexpectedly. The only remark I heard after the buzzing died was said by LaLa, who'd been out of town at the funeral of her father (who'd lain in a vegetative state in a private nursing home for over years, "milking us bone dry," Mr. Leiderbacker said to me). LaLa cornered me and said, "I always knew he wasn't right in the head." I got pissed off. "And how did you know that?" I said, angry. "Why," she said, "you know he came from Maine." I started to ask what the hell that meant, but she just walked away.

That fall I worked weekends for Mr. Leiderbacker, and as I watched the trees turn glorious colors, cover the hills and mountains ringing the bungalows, I often thought of Zeke. To me, he was lumbering through that dense forest, staff in hand. Purposeful, delivering God's good meaning. That fall the warfare of Mrs. Leiderbacker and LaLa got more intense—the chilly weather exaggerated their cruelty to each other—and one day Mr. Leiderbacker, wanting exercise, was helping me rake leaves on the long driveway. It was Indian summer, a warm, luscious day with a bright, piercing sun and mellow air. I worked in a T-shirt. We'd built a huge pile of leaves, ready to bag them, when LaLa jumped into her Caddie, piled in the dogs, and stormed down the driveway. At the end of the summer she'd added a fourth poodle, named not for royalty but—for some reason—Marla, a hyper, totally insane, yelping dog that no one liked. The other poodles kept their distance. Even LaLa proclaimed the dog crazy and she planned on returning it to the breeder. So LaLa started down the driveway and, with a not-so-beatific smile on her poodle face, blithely sped through the pile of leaves Mr. Leiderbacker and I just raked. The convertible top was down on that unseasonably warm afternoon, and I saw her grinning. All our work came to naught. She sped down the hill and didn't look back. Watching, I saw five poodle heads looking straight ahead.

Mr. Leiderbacker went nuts, calling her every name he could think of. I'd never seen such a purple face, so frantic a man. "Come on," he said to me, "we don't have much time." I stood there. He motioned me to the side of the driveway, and I followed, thinking he was going to rake again and bag before her return from her drugstore errands. No: he started pushing one of the granite boulders he had lining the driveway. "Help me." "No," I said, not yet certain what he was up to. But it soon became abundantly clear. He managed to roll one of the round rocks a few feet. "Help me." I confess I did, loyal Nazi that I was. We maneuvered three rocks into the center of the driveway, three masses of stone, and I kept saying: "This is not a good idea, Mr. Leiderbacker." "I'm paying your salary," he said. I, the good guy, nodded. He covered the three boulders with leaves, creating a huge pile, just as LaLa churned up the driveway. I swear she drove at that pile with the widest grin I'd ever seen, a woman needing (and now able) to get back at her philandering husband.

She hit the boulders so hard that she pushed the whole front end of the car in, the radiator popped and fizzled, and the car ground to a halt. She sat there stunned, but Mr. Leiderbacker just laughed and laughed, walking in circles, his hands flying around like wild birds. LaLa Leiderbacker narrowed her eyes, and I knew this was the beginning of the final wars. At the moment of impact all of the dogs, hysterical and yipping in doggy falsetto, leapt from the convertible and tore off towards the house. All except little Marla, the black sheep, the new member of the family, who crawled out of the car, and then, to our horror, lay on her side and died.

Five years later: I am hiking through part of the Appalachian Trail that winds its way through the dense woods north of New Haven, up through Bethany and Woodbridge. My three friends and I are looking for a waterfall somewhere beyond the pine forest, but we've gotten lost, wandering in circles back to some landmark. It's a wonderful fall day, crisp and bright, and the sky is robin's egg blue. We don't care that we are lost. We are in the middle of nowhere, and we're laughing over our confused steps. We stop on a crest, trying to get our bearings. It will be dark in a couple of hours. "Should we look for berries?" I say. "We didn't pack food."

"Lord," one of my friends says, an edge in her voice.

We stare at the opposite ridge, and there is a solitary man standing there, watching us. I get chilled—it feels dangerous. But that man is just hiking the same trails, and we move on, headed toward each other. But I think we're all a little nervous. You don't see people out in the wilderness. You see squirrels and snakes and, if you're lucky, an owl perched on a white pine bough. When we get close, I think I'm seeing things. I believe it's Zeke, but I could be wrong. This man is really skinny, but he has the same frizzy black hair. I can't see the eyes yet. He's dressed in a red-flannel shirt, jeans, hiking boots—normal gear. And he's carrying a long, curved walking stick. He's walking fast, almost jauntily, and he seemed to be humming a song. Is it Zeke? It's been five or more years. Zeke? He looks too skinny.

We pass by each other, and he looks over. He stops for a second but doesn't really break his stride.

"Hi Ed," he says. And he smiles.

I see the eyes of the man.

"Hi Zeke," I say.

Gym Dandy

Like many self-defined and delusional high-school intellectuals, I hated gym. On principle. You couldn't read a book or parse a sentence or fashion an appropriate précis if you were sweating on first base or throwing up on the locker room floor.

I think of Larry Jacobson, an unremarkable boy in my high school gym class whose singular claim to fame and awful memory was the raging hard-on he produced while shimmying on a rope suspended from the gym ceiling. Now Larry—an otherwise pesky and rude boy, given to fits of testosteronic fury and blows to the back of the head of lesser mortals—was next in line to climb the rope, a feat I never really understood. What do you when you get there—to those regions of ether and thin air? It always struck me as a waste of a destination. Anyway, Larry's at bat—so to speak—and he grabs the rope, confident of his prowess, and begins to wriggle his frame upward. At that moment the gym teacher, fresh from Sadism Training School, spots Larry's boyish member, prominent against the tight gym shorts. It seems Larry has found his pubertic moment. It slips out. Mr. Simon, all aglee, approaches it, while Larry is suspended in air, helpless like a Viking maiden, and Mr. Simon announces to the class that Larry has an erection, and he actually brings his extended finger within inches of the red little adolescent trophy, so as to draw our attention to it. As Larry turns beet red, sort of like his mind-of-its-own penis, the rest of us stare, embarrassed, as though at a slithering snake, our own faces flushed, and Larry slips to the mat, a broken boy.

Nobody volunteered to follow that rope act.

Then there was Mr. Borelli, the following year. A hapless stupid man, directing us to run in circles while he sat on the bleachers sipping a soda, and—at least on a few occasions when I strolled past on my way to hide in the bathroom—talking to other teachers of how his mother was always yelling at him. A bulky, ungainly man with tuffs of uncombed hair and the perpetual smell of Witch Hazel and elbow grease, he was another tyrant. I was thin and famished looking, a nerd/slash/sissy to boot, and he didn't like such males. I didn't help matters by trying to skip class every chance I got. I'd walk in, tell him I was sick with a cold and could I please sit out this class, alone at the top of the bleachers with my James A. Michener novel while I listened to him relate his current skirmish with his mommy. He'd say no (mocking me: "You're *cough cough cough* sick?"), but I'd sneak away, tuck myself into the small group of disabled boys—the crippled, the spastic, the homos, the clumsy, the dead, the wretched refuse yearning to be gym-less—who were relieved from public disgrace for at least forty-five minutes a day. Sometimes he'd spot me and haul my ass back out center stage.

When we had wrestling exercises, he always pitted me against larger boys from the simian section of the gender. Early in the year he'd pitted me against a chubby, smelly boy named Harvey Whorms. I didn't want to touch—let alone wrestle—this product of some bad genetic coupling. As we assumed classic wrestling positions, I decided to go for the fall—much better than having the humongous lad topple on my fragile body, thus guaranteeing me a permanent spot on the disabled section of the bleachers. As Mr. Borelli blew his whistle, I misjudged. I toppled, helpless and defeated, to the mat, only vaguely realizing that the blubbering Harvey had not even touched me. While the class laughed at my attempt to lose and Harvey sputtered that it "ain't fair 'cuz I won't knock him dead," whatever the hell that meant, Mr. B. stepped up, pointed to me, and said I deserved the Oscar for best performance of the year. "Pathetic," he said. I longed for the bleachers and, at least, a minor disability.

That morning Mr. B. called me Gym Dandy, which, he explained to the uninformed, was his own creation for a sissy in his class. He even spelled the word: "g-y-m." "It's not j-i-m." I knew how to spell, too: j-e-r-k. Try that one on for size. Thinking back on it, I hazard a guess most of those lads had never heard of Jim Dandy, didn't know what the hell a "dandy" was. It didn't matter: Mr. B. guffawed and swayed back and forth, with spittle at the corners of his mouth. He'd created one joke in his sorry, mother-smothered life, and nobody got it.

He also had troubles with my last name—as, of course, most of the world did—and still does. The first day of class he called the roll: not If-ko-vic, three simple syllables, but some sort of reversal of the third and second syllables: "If-ic-kov." Something like that. I'd correct him. "Ifkovic—just like it sounds." No matter: he never said it correctly the whole year. I was "Ifickoff." I'd sigh, raise my hand. "Present," I say, adding "you idiot" in my head.

"How long have you been in America?" he once asked.

"I was born here."

"You don't have an American name?"

Puzzled: "What?"

"If-ic-koff ain't American."

And Borelli is?

My travails in high school gym class were made worse by Mr. Tucker, my American history teacher, whose class I had after gym and a study hall. During our swimming lesson—which I never mastered, being the only boy in class unable to dog paddle—Mr. Tucker would swim by himself in the pool. A odd, floating man, once a collegiate swimmer of note (supposedly), he'd hurl his massive, six-decade bulk into the pool, splash around, and then, refreshed, leave. But I was one of his favorite students, and one day he spotted me there and realized that I was unable to swim. My role those periods was to hang off the edge, kick my legs, look interested and waterlogged, and pray for the call to hit the showers. The shallow end was my shelter. "You can't swim?" he boomed. No, I said. In a class of perhaps fifty or more boys, I stood out. So Mr. Tucker, thinking he was helping me, got me out of the pool, took off the long green fins he'd been using, which made him look vaguely reptilian, and told me to put them on. I resisted. No, he insisted. So I put on the slimy appendages and he told me to walk around: I flopped around like some skinny prehistoric raptor, all clumsy and confused, until he told me to jump into the water. "Bring them to class when you come," he said, disappearing. Of course, everyone made tremendous fun of me, and I'm sure Mr. B. wet his pants (what will Mommy say?). When I got to American history, I handed over the fins. Everyone was watching. "Did they help?" he asked. I nodded, red faced.

Whenever I saw Mr. Tucker waddling into my gym class, I headed for the purgatory of the bleachers, even if it meant more abuse from Mr. B.

So—this is what I'm leading to all along—my entrance to college gym class was fraught with anxiety and despair. I could withstand the tedium of weight-lifting class, the brutality of touch football, or the stupor of track (shot put is a consonantal rhyme that nearly killed me), but I couldn't abide swimming class, always the curse that followed me. I was in a class of perhaps one hundred boys, and, yet again, was the only soul who could not swim. There might have been others, closety types who disguised their inability to do the Australian crawl, sheltering themselves in packs of moving swimmers, but I stood out. And there was only one problem. The college had a particularly dumb rule that every student had to swim the length of the Olympic-sized pool in order to graduate. Not just pass the one credit course, but to be awarded the bachelors degree itself. There was urban college legend of a long-gone student who *never* earned his BA because he couldn't do the simple butterfly stroke. I was destined to be one of them.

But I had a kind of curious luck. His name was Coach Brian Harkins, the varsity swimming coach himself, who was determined that no one "in my gym class can fail. No one. Not if I have any say in the matter." I became his pet project, despite my efforts to hide in the shadows of the shallow end. Here was a man determined to assume a doomed cause, clearly. On the first day, when my timidly raised hand informed the world that I could not swim, he singled me out for attention. I don't think he cared for me, but I was a mission he had to accomplish. I let him know I was not happy any place where the smell of chlorine dominated the landscape, and that his tutelage was not good news.

Now Coach, as we called him, was a robust young man, a star athlete at some university, affable and blond and blue eyed, someone who reeked of take-it-for-granted manliness. With his buzz-cut Marine haircut and his perpetual Southern-decaled windbreaker, he strutted around, barking orders, but he was certainly a kind guy, a real softie. He could be miserable to us, demanding *one more lap I said did you hear me*, but he could also joke. And, on analyzing the world of physical education as I'd come to know (and despise) it, he was neither a brute nor a sadist. But I wished he'd ignore me. Some people just don't take to water: please ignore me. I'm fine. Really.

No such luck, I'm afraid.

His theory of swimming education was simple—and thus staggeringly faulty. I was to do everything the class of competent swimmers did, and eventually I'd master it. So when, in successive lines, we all jumped into the pool, swimming from shallow end to deep, I leapt in with the other lemmings, but managed to swim only ten or so feet while the hordes were hurling themselves out the other end of the pool, dripping like wet dogs. He didn't care. "Better today," he'd yell at me, which was a bold-faced lie. I mastered only one thing each class: inertia.

But as the semester progressed, I expected disaster. We took up diving, which is basically something any nonswimmer had best avoid. Because, well, diving is done in the deep end of the pool, which was not my favorite province, much more content as

I was in the kiddie corner. Why was I the only person who understood this? We started on the low diving board, but what we were to execute was the back dive. A back dive! We lined up, each in turn walking to the edge of the board, turning our backs to the water, while Coach bellowed the orders. Lift your arms over your head, lean backwards until you see the water. Slip into the water like a sleek knife.

Lean backwards until you see the water? That's not a direction: that's a suicide note in the writing.

I prepared to die a watery death.

When it was my turn, I dawdled, taking forever to get out there, despite the giggling of the assembled masses. In my baggy institutional wet trunks (handed out before class by a boy who looked liked he'd overdosed on Kerouac novels), ill fitting on my bony body, and always in danger to sliding the floor, I stood with my back to the water. "Do it," Coach yelled.

Hours, it seemed, passed.

What the hell! I lifted my arms, arched my back, and suddenly, to my horror, heard the most ghastly sound echoing off the high-vaulted ceiling: a death wail, a gargled moaning that punctuated the air and made the silence in the pool eerie. What the hell was that? What wounded animal was caught in an air vent?

But as I toppled back into the water, I realized that that awful sound had come from my very own throat. I belly-flopped onto the water, sank, drifted back to the surface, and struggled the four feet to the side.

I was alive. Barely. As I drew myself out of the water, Coach (with the class) waited. "Now get up there and do it again," he said. "And this time keep your mouth closed. You sound like a pregnant cow stuck in a ravine." Did I mention that Coach was from Texas?

And then there was the ominous high-diving board. Death Camp Exercise 101. I protested to Coach that, as a nonswimmer, it was not a good idea to hurl oneself down twelve or so feet into vast depths. Of uncharted waters. It seemed, well, a pursuit for people who could *swim*. No, he said, it was simple—it wasn't even swimming. "It's just jumping." I didn't buy such a fine distinction because it still involved excessive gallons of water and me. "You're not diving, you're jumping," he said. Don't look down. Just jump. When you go under (I winced), push your hands down and your body will be drawn back to the surface. Then paddle four or five feet to the edge. "It's not swimming."

It sure looked like swimming to me: equal parts chlorine and water and unabashed terror.

I also had another problem: I had a friend taking the same gym class, a sort of buddy from Shakespeare class. Paul was from Iowa, a rarity on that commuting campus, but he was a star gymnast. And Southern had Abie Grossfeld, an erstwhile U.S. Olympic coach whose talent drew Olympic-gold hopefuls—like Paul—to Southern. Paul sat next to me in the dark cavernous lecture hall. It was unusual to see a non-English major in Shakespeare, let alone Paul who was definitely a campus heartthrob with the tight T-shirt pulled over a chiseled gymnast's body with a square-jawed Leyendecker model face. A friendly, outgoing student, he was lost amidst the Elizabethan verbiage and the un-air-conditioned darkness of the room. He turned to me—not to cheat, as one classmate alleged—but for simple tutelage. I helped out, the two of us sitting in the cafeteria or the lounge, or even late at night on the phone, with me reading lines, reviewing notes—his lecture notes looked like chicken scrawl—and I started enjoying it all. Shakespeare was becoming clear to me, and the lines sang. "Why are you in the class?" I asked once. "My mother," he said, simply. "I promised her I'd take Shakespeare. And here I am. The dummy." So be it. We must have looked like an odd couple as we strolled the campus, he all natural swagger and 1950s-style muscle magazine physique and me, well, the scarecrow in the wrinkled pants, lopsided crew cut, and Eisenhower pastiness.

What Paul couldn't understand was physical ineptitude, which I personified. His initial question in gym class was startling: "Why can't you just do it?" he asked, seeing me topple over. Everything came so effortlessly to him. I refused to let him tutor me in anything gym related, especially swimming. But he did offer.

Back to the high-diving board. I'm standing there, weak kneed, near tears, envisioning the memorial service attended by the students in the disabled section of the high-school bleachers—and I note Paul staring up at me. He's standing by himself, away from the other students, and he's shaking his head. My friend, the pitiful nerd.

I'm exhausted. The class has been doing exercises for most of the long period, laps and kicks and God knows what else. I've been dragging my sore body from one failure to the next, and now I'm standing on the high diving board. I have almost no energy left, so at that elevated height, staring out at the far reaches of the vast room, I am not only psychologically spent but have barely an ounce of physical strength left. It seems I stand there for hours because Coach is down there yelling at me: "We don't have all day," he says.

Well, I think, actually we do.

Behind me is a line of guys, ready to shine. Some are even poised on the ladder, anxious. I walk to the edge and figure—what the hell. I just jump. I hit the water with impact but, surprisingly, slide neatly into the cold. I remember to press my hands down and, as I near the bottom where I expect to smash my skull and turn the cruel waters some sad shade of crimson, I start to float to the top. My head bobs out of the water, and I feel some unusual exhilaration.

I'm alive and kicking. Well, actually not kicking. Floating there for a second, proud of myself, I attempt to lift my left arm out of the water to begin the half-assed paddle to the pool's edge. But something has happened. My arms have turned to lettuce. I have not a bit of strength left in my body. Every ounce of energy has disappeared, lost in the act of the awful dive. For a moment I float there, a mindless bobbin, stupefied driftwood, and then I realize I'm sinking. I go under, intake a quart of bitter water, rise again, and spit and scream. It happens again. And again. And again. Each time I stay under the water a little longer, lose a few more cherished brain cells, and rise to sputter and babble. Meantime Coach is nearby, imploring me to swim the scant five or six feet to the pool's edge. It does no good because I have become insensible, or, perhaps, fully brain dead. I remember Coach yelling at me: "Ifkovic, you are a rational human being"—he actually says that, no kidding—"so just put your mind to it." What he doesn't realize is that brain-dead souls lack mind power, so I go under again, turn in the water like a piece of chicken in a fryer, and then, in a flash, I have a photographic vision. I am five years old, being carried piggyback on my father's shoulders as he walks to our home from my grandparents' house on the hill. This image is so sharp, so unexpected, so new—that I scare myself. I've heard that people drowning have their lives flash before their eyes. Now up until that moment, with all that bobbing and weaving, I never believe I am in danger, just sinking for longer and longer periods of time. Now, with the snapshot etched on my frozen brain, I surface and scream out to the ceiling: "I'm drowning." And sink again.

When I surface again, now a shadow of my former brilliant self, I note Coach has jumped into the water. Swimming coaches don't like to get wet, in case you've never noticed, so this is a big move on his part. I'm flapping around like a punch-drunk cabbage head, battling for survival, my hands slapping the water ineffectively. Suddenly Coach is near and, quite frankly, he is a suitable landmass, an island in the sun, a rock-hard surface on which to drift ashore. As he nears, I find a sudden burst of energy and, like a maddened dolphin, leap out the water and onto his firm, broad back. He struggles with the ungainly weight but I'm not letting go. We go back and forth until, with all the power of his training and not a little anger, he flips me, slugs me on the side of the head, a little more powerfully than necessary perhaps, and, cradling my neck, he locks me at his side. Some of the boys haul me out, stretch me on the tile floor where I proceed to belch so loudly it registers in Detroit on the Richter scale, and then throw up loudly and unceremoniously on the floor. I close my eyes.

Somehow I am carried to the showers, deposited in a heap on the floor, with the showers turned on over me. Class comes to an end, and I lie there, the tepid water laving me. The guys leave, and a new class comes in. I lie there, swimming's final debris. I am looked at with curiosity, with pity, with humor. I lie there. A half hour later I struggle out to my car out back, assume the fetal position in the back seat, and sleep the afternoon away.

The next day, in Shakespeare, Paul said maybe three words to me.

But I had one more hurdle to face: the graduation requirement of swimming the length of the pool. That horrible day arrived, and dozens of swimmers made their way the length of the pool, thus qualifying for baccalaureate status and intellectual arrival. And then there was one more. I'd watched Paul swim the length in under two seconds—or so it seemed, his body barely getting wet, a flash of movement in the twink of an eye. I jumped in, with one proviso from Coach. "I don't care how long it takes you to get across, Ifkovic, just don't let your feet touch bottom. You hear me. Go." So I jumped. I swam the first part of the shallow end with no effort, buoyed by the idea that I might never have to jump into water ever again, but by the time I'd reached that ominous rope that signals perilous depths beyond, I faltered, and started to sink. "Float, damn it," Coach yelled. So I did for a few seconds, but even that became impossible. I started to sink. I knew I could not make it. Simple as that.

Then Coach's fury kicked in, the mild-mannered Clark Kent giving way to some red-faced, foul-mouthed tyrant. While the rest of the class watched, Coach walked alongside me, at the edge of the pool, goading, yelling, cursing, and pushing. A steam of inventive issued from his mouth. "You goddamn bastard, you fucking loser, this is how you come to end the semester, a loser, an A fucking student can't move his arms in the fucking water like a little baby, a little shit head—" On and on, more and more colorful. His voice—like my earlier death moan—echoed off the steel girders above.

I sank, I floated, I moved my arms. I was in deep water. And knew it. I was in deep shit. And knew it. I sank, I floated up. I flapped my arms like a squawking bird. I moved ahead. "You wanna get out of this fucking place, Ifkovic? So fucking move."

I did.

He cursed me across the pool, and it took fifteen to twenty minutes of floating, sinking, flapping, tumbling. I may actually have swum a few feet in the process. I almost reached the end, three feet from the edge, when I gave up. "Damn you," he yelled, and he kicked water into my face. With a burst of some reserve, I jerked myself to the edge, hung there like a barnacle on a ship, angry, and some guys lifted my lifeless body out of the water and onto the tile.

The whole gym burst into applause. I looked up through waterlogged eyes. Coach was grinning.

"You don't deserve it but I'm giving you a B. It's gonna break your straight A pussy-footing average, but that's all you're getting."

I spat up water in thanks.

Suddenly Paul was nearby, staring down at me. My eyesight was blurred, my head swam. Was this Banquo's ghost? But I could see that his face was drawn and frowning, and he turned to walk away. I watched him. But then he turned back, squinted his eyes, and I thought I saw a glimmer of a smile. Then he winked conspiratorially, and shaking his head, he walked away.

When we met the next afternoon for a review of *Titus Andronicus*, he brought me a brochure he'd picked up in the lobby of the student center. "Join the Navy," it said. "Here," he said, "now you can see the world."

Ghosts of North Carolina

By the end of October, I was dreaming of ghosts.

One reason: I was living in a haunted house deep in the woods of Chapel Hill, North Carolina, where I'd been studying at the university for an MA in American Literature. I hadn't planned on ghosts troubling my academic steps, but who does? That summer I'd visited Chapel Hill, hunting for a place to live, wanting one room in a private home. I'd located exactly what I wanted in a rambling old home, far out on Dixon Farm Road, a good half-hour walk from my classes. I would have no car. But it promised quiet, isolation, and, most importantly, atmosphere. When I'd strolled onto the lawn that summer, I walked beneath blooming wisteria, seemingly miles high, and the heady sweet aroma, coupled with overgrown bushes and towers of fir trees, suggested—to me at least—a Hollywood back lot of a Thomas Wolfe novel, the kind of place, I surmised, Wolfe himself would have inhabited when he was a student at the university. So, with a great deal of romanticism in my soul, I rented the tiny room (with bath), at the back of the old farmhouse that was sheltered under lofty pines. At night, with the coming of the autumn wind and winter cold, branches slapped the windows of the room, heat issued from the ducts near the floor, and I was sublimely happy, content with Bright's Old English Grammar in my lap.

Until the ghosts, that is. I was living in the home of a fairly affluent Chapel Hill family, the Myersons, attorneys if I remember correctly, whose daughter and son were at the University. Polished, kind people, they talked of books and food and friends. The mother was a gourmand and the only time I heard her raise her voice was when a casual friend asked for a particular recipe. "Every cook has to have one dish only *she* can make." I liked that.

I eavesdropped all the time. The family den shared a wall with my bedroom, and, bored with Old English Grammar and the histrionic Shakespearean instructor, I sat at the edge of my bathtub, a cup of instant coffee on hand, and enjoyed the late night conversations I heard. The family had a thick Southern accent, which amused me—I learned later that they smiled at my own New England speech. So one night, reviewing some class notes with half-closed eyes, I was jolted awake by this statement: "It made itself known two nights ago." What? I quietly said to myself. The mother was in the den talking to a friend. What? "The same routine?" the friend asked. "Yes." And then the mother outlined briefly—since, I assume, everyone was familiar with the patterns—the visitation: the sound of the front door closing (though it had not been opened), the swish of wind, the rush of steps up the stairs, the opening of a closet door, and then the rustle of wire hangers and boxes jostled inside. Then silence.

My spine tingled, and I'll tell you why. New to the home, I'd listened to all the comings and goings in an effort to learn about my new home. The family always entered by the back kitchen door. Only I used the front door. The night before I'd returned to a dark home, noticed no car in the driveway. In my room for about a half hour, I suddenly heard the front door slamming, a rush of wind, fast steps up to the second floor, a door opening, and then a flurry of noise. Then silence. But no human voice. An hour or so later, the whole family returned, talking loudly about something. I remember thinking: who had come into the house? What was I missing?

Now I knew. But it still didn't make any sense to me. Ghosts?

It turned out that the family had long ago accepted the presence of what they called its "friendly" presence in the old farmhouse. Slowly, eavesdropping, I constructed the story for myself. The ghost appeared every so often, did its little macabre dance, and then left. Sometimes, though, it was mischievous: a painting turned on the wall, an overturned teapot, a book opened and laid down on the floor, a flower plucked from the garden plot in a water glass on the kitchen table. One time, the daughter Tonya had lost her car keys in town and, a week later, they were resting at the center of the breakfast table. That struck me as bizarre—a ghost that accompanies you downtown? Now I learned all these anecdotes (and more) throughout that fall semester, as bits and pieces of the ghost story emerged. The family liked to talk of the ghost, especially to new friends of Tonya, although, not surprisingly, I was never told a word. They probably thought that I, a Yankee, was pragmatic and logical and brilliant, a naysayer. Or they simply thought I was a lily-livered coward who'd run screaming out the door, dragging my steamer trunk to the nearest taxi stand.

Now I'd always been intrigued by ghost's stories—what kid isn't? And the whole idea of fortune telling was a family obsession. I'd actually visited an old Ukrainian woman in her nineties who lived in a third floor walk up in a poor section of New Haven. She read tea leaves, and I remember sitting in her threadbare armchair while her arthritic fingers poured the water out of the teacup. She shivered. Which made me shiver. She *tsked*. I took a deep sigh. "Danger ahead," she said. That wasn't news to me—it was my life's resumé. "Pray to the Virgin Mary," she said. But I would emerge triumphant, she said, because there were spirits above me, hovering beneficial ghosts. At one point she said my tea leaves revealed one of the early Popes, as well as Joan of Arc, manifesting themselves in the wet leaves. But always at my side were two guardians: one a small child, who was always crying, a child who died a painful early death, but who stubbornly clung to my corporal being. More importantly, there was a man on horseback, in full military uniform, with saber drawn, a man with a black walrus moustache.

Eyes wide open, he watched out for me. I immediately imagined a soldier in the old Austro-Hungarian Empire, a soldier from the so-called Military Frontier, a boundary of territory between Europe and the Ottoman Empire, a territory some members of my family had long inhabited, the boys raised to fight the menacing Turks. There was a photograph of my grandfather standing at attention as a teenaged boy, dressed in some military garb.

My North Carolina ghost, however, seemed more inclined to have a good time with his presents (and his presence, I suppose) and his wanderings. But, in short order, I learned that he had a darker side. I'm assuming a male here, though this is unfair to female ghosts. But he had his moments during which he frightened visitors, because he seemed not to like intruders in the house. Visitors who slept in the den—business associates of the father and other guests— felt themselves threatened. Now this was not good news for me, the visitor who stayed a little too long. I remember discussing it with friends at the University, and one wag commented: "You know, he could really hate Yankees." Then he developed the theory that the house may have been built on a bloody Civil War battleground where a dead Confederate soldier, improperly buried, rose to extract revenge within the walls of the farm house. He liked the family—they had the same Southern accents, probably the same distant relative—but he still harbored a hatred for the Yankee bastard who did him in. Said facetiously, his words nevertheless had some possibility: what if this acreage had been a scorched and brutal battlefield? What if this unreconstituted rebel hovered over my quietly snoring body—filled as it was with Old English declensions and the aftertaste of grits and hush puppies— and wasn't happy that a Yankee was in the house?

"You like it here?" the father asked, one afternoon.

"Oh, yes," I said.

"Quiet enough for you?"

My big moment: "Yes." I smiled. "I even like the occasional noises the old house makes." How about that for a hint?

"Noises?"

"You know, wind against the old boards. Doors creaking." Rattling chains, Marley dead as a doornail.

Father looked at mother, mother looked at her nails. Nothing said.

But suddenly I got busy with my studies, the workload escalated, and my curiously declined. I spent long hours in the library, researching term papers. I had little time for the spirit world.

One night, headed home, I took a short cut past the hospital on the hill. I was depressed, bothered by one of my classes and the examination for my language requirement, and my mind wandered. As I walked I became aware of a dusky figure in the encroaching twilight, and there was something about the way he moved that caught my eye. Lost in shadows, then moving, he seemed to blend into the darkness. I assumed he was a patient, given the way he was dressed. But it was his erratic movements that caught my eye. Then, as I neared, he paused at the edge of the road, deliberated, while I turned away, headed in a different direction. But in the next second I heard the screech of tires as a car smashed into the figure. He'd paused there, and to this day I believe he'd been waiting for a car to approach. Within seconds there were people around, and I hurried home. The next morning, in American lit class, I learned that the great poet Randall Jarrell had died the day before, hit by a car, despondent over a cancer that was killing him. The instructor said it was a suicide, although years later published accounts of his life termed it an accident. I was there when it happened, and I walked home believing I'd just watched a suicide. Randall Jarrell, a poet I loved, had died on that lonely Carolina road. Depressed that night, I'd gone home to my own solitude and loneliness. I lay in bed thinking of that dead man. The next night, after learning who he was, I lay in bed and thought about him again. But now I had a name. I felt tightness in the room, the presence of spirits, but they were spirits I'd carried in with me.

I'd stroll to classes in the morning, and soon made the acquaintance of a guy named Johnny, who often gave me a lift to campus. "You want a ride?" he'd asked that first time, pulling the car alongside me. I nodded. So whenever he saw me, he stopped and I hopped in. Johnny was in his thirties, worked downtown, and was African American. Smart, articulate, funny, he was also a nonstop talker. I learned everything there was to know about his family tree. "You see," he said one morning, "I'm a distant cousin of the mayor of this here town." He paused. "He's white, of course." "Yeah?" I said. And Johnny went into the intricacies of black-and-white bloodlines in the small Southern town, which I found fascinating. This was as far from New England as I could imagine, this blending of racial bloods, these parallel universes of lineage. It seemed everybody knew what was what, who was related to whom, whose great uncle was this or that, but what I found curious were the quiet demarcations, the intricate boundaries. "Joe at the bank is a relative, but won't say a word to me, though we nod on the sidewalk or when we cross paths in front of the Friendly Book Store." He laughed: "But his sister Mattie hires my cousin Lucie to sweep her floors, and they chat over coffee about family, both Negro and white. She needs to know everything about all the relatives." So over time I learned something I'd never thought of: 1960s Southern life had its prickly thorns, predicated on the intricacies of important racial bloodlines, past and present. Johnny loved the notion of the mayor being distantly related, albeit the lines were charted back to slave days. "Most of us respect each other, even if we don't break bread together. But in the woodpile we all got the same great-great granddaddy."

This was, after all, the 1960s, a time of expanding civil rights agitation in North Carolina and in the Old South, and the specter of Martin Luther King's dream covered the land like a rising sun. I asked Johnny about King, although I was always nervous about bringing up civil rights topics with him. I'm not sure why. But Johnny had his own agendas. He had little to say about King and the movement: "Things happening," was all he said, but he looked at me quickly, a little nervously. Was it because I was white?

A liberal Northerner come down from Connecticut seeking the spirit of Thomas Wolfe and Paul Green at the oldest state university in America, I found myself hanging out with other

Northerners, mostly Jewish New Yorkers and an Irish Catholic guy from Boston. Eventually, in the spring, I would become close to a couple of Southern girls and one boy from Tennessee, all of them pro-civil rights. But I was constantly intrigued by Southern sensibility, a way of life different from my own. The young daughter of my house, a freshman at the University, was smart and accomplished, in a family of achievers, but she harbored some maddening Southern belle syndrome. She was dating her high-school sweetheart, a handsome young garage mechanic, dumb as unbuttered toast, and they would sit—that is, make out—in the family den. Bored and nosy, as I've said, I'd sit at the edge of the bathtub, especially when the two of them were going at it, pathetic voyeur that I was, and listen to his sophomoric, tepid erotic assaults on her willing body. But she played Southern belle, and that drove me crazy. He'd say the most insipid things and she'd praise him. Once, I swear, he said—I hope he was making a joke, but maybe not—that the "West" had been added to "Virginia" in order to let people know they were in another state. I almost slipped off the tub onto the tile floor. What Tonya said was: "Oh, my God, aren't you the most clever boy in the world? How do you come up with such things?" I imagined him preening, hands all over her body. Slurp, slurp. Feel, feel. At the University I had lunch with a young woman who praised my intelligence over and over, stunned and awed by my observations on Hemingway and Faulkner, while acknowledging that she could *never* come up with such meaningful insights. I later learned she was a National Merit Fellow, summa cum laude from Chicago, this and that. This and that. But she was from Georgia and was a Belle.

With my friends, I viewed the burgeoning civil rights movement from a safe distance. But not always. Sometimes we lived a little dangerously, or so we thought. These were violent, brutal times in some quarters. On Sundays we left the quiet of Chapel Hill for a small town nearby, known as a KKK stronghold, or so we were warned by professors. This thrilled us no end. We had a particular favorite restaurant, where they served scrumptious hush puppies in thick savory honey—and, as we waited for our order, the waitress provided each of us with a fresh copy of *The Fiery Cross* for our edification. I'm looking at one saved copy as I write. It has an attack on white Northerner Viola Liuzzo who went South in the cause and was found murdered. There's also a cartoon of a black man on the moon saying, first thing: *Take me to your welfare office.* In the restaurant, we read quietly, and a little frightened, but also titillated. An African-American friend from somewhere down South, a young woman named Grace, never came with us. Wisely, she stayed on campus. You saw so few black women on campus. She thought our behavior silly, but she also knew she could never enter that restaurant with us. In the window was a large, crude placard that read, emphatically: "Join the KKK. Help stamp out Catholics, Negroes, and Jews." Well, we were New York Jews and New England Catholics—and college students living on the edge. Even when we drove into the town we cruised under a welcome banner that announced the town as KKK territory. This, to us, was living. But we ate our hush puppies in thick honey in cowardly silence.

On Sunday afternoons, returning to campus and meeting Grace in the library, she'd shake her head and say, "One day you won't be coming back from there."

One time I told Johnny about our weekend trips. He never said a word. Perhaps he thought our behavior too insane for comment.

Returning by Greyhound from Connecticut to Chapel Hill in January, we encountered a ferocious snowstorm. Leaving Connecticut there was a dusting on the ground, but by the time we hit Baltimore and Washington D.C., it was a full-fledged blizzard. In Virginia the highways were virtually closed, the bus lumbering along, wind whipping snow against the windows. I was sitting next to a skinny young man, an African, who was dressed in a light spring jacket. His first time in America, he'd been given a scholarship to a small college in Raleigh, and was terrified of snow, which he'd never seen before. I asked him if he had a winter coat and he said no: he thought North Carolina was warm. The storm raged, we dragged along, and his anxiety increased.

Over and over he said the same thing to me: "I hope they like me." "I hope they like me there." "Why not?" I asked. Hesitantly: "I'm not white," he said. I assured him that times had changed, that universities were havens for tolerance, that he'd have no trouble there. "I hope they like me." I asked him why he chose to go South if he feared discrimination. But the answer was simple: the college was the only place that offered him money. We chatted and laughed, as he shivered against the cold outside the bus window. I had bag of chips, which we shared, and I gave him half a stale tuna sandwich I'd bought at bus stop depot. He relaxed a little.

He was getting off in Raleigh, he said, to be met by college officials. For some reason I thought it was our next stop. We both dozed—the bus barely crawled and time was endless—but I woke with a start. The bus had pulled into Raleigh, a few people got off, and was preparing to leave. I looked out through blinding snow. I woke up the young man, telling him we were in Raleigh. In a panic he grabbed his bag, shook my hand, and went flying down the aisle. I waved out the window as he pulled a suitcase from under the bus. I sat back. The bus driver put the bus into reverse and chugged through the snowdrift. I stared out at the young man, standing alone on the snowswept platform, watching for his greeters. He looked nervous, looking left and right. No one was around. My eyes drifted up, as the wind blew away gusts of snow, and I noticed that the sign said: Fayetteville.

Fayetteville? "Wait," I yelled to the driver.

I rushed up the aisle and told him I'd put off the African at the wrong (and, it turned out, unscheduled) stop. Grumpily, he pulled the bus back in, opened the door, and I scurried to the young man who looked more frightened than ever. I ushered him and his luggage back onto the bus. "I'm sorry," I said. "I thought it was Raleigh."

Back on the bus, shivering in his thin jacket, he asked the driver to tell him when we were in Raleigh. I went back to my seat and waited for him to join me. He looked back, caught my eye and, for me, it was an awful moment: his eyes were filled with fear and distrust. In that moment I seemed to have become that Southerner he had dreaded as he sat in his African home, preparing for his long journey to America. "I hope they like me." And the first American man he meets glibly betrays him. I waved his over, but he sat down in the empty seat behind the driver, his back stiff and his arms wrapped around his chest. Alone in my seat, I felt my face getting hot, embarrassed now, feeling guilty, as if I'd failed in some very elemental lesson in racial harmony.

I overtipped the black cabbie who carried me and my bags through the blizzard to my rooms.

That night, back in my Carolina bed, I woke to hear the snow and wind against my bedroom window, but then I heard something else: voices. I heard a small tinny voice, neither male nor female, cutting through the wind. "Let me in. Oh please, let me in. I beg you. Let me in." I sat up in bed, frightened. Was I dreaming? Was this the nightmare of the African on the bus? Had the ghost returned? Was it the wind? I got out of bed, felt the chill across the floor. Standing in the center of my bedroom, fully awake, I heard it again. Someone out in the wintry night playing a joke on me? "I beg you. Let me in."

I threw up the shades, peered into the pitch-black night, frost covering the panes, snow on the sills. Between blasts of shrill wind I heard the voice, drifting away now. I went back to bed, but I couldn't sleep. Not that night. I was scared. In the morning, groggy, I couldn't escape the thought of the African standing on that bus platform, the spring jacket no protection against the cold.

That spring semester moved quietly, and the ghost stayed away while I labored on a paper on D. H. Lawrence and one on French and Spanish translations of *Paradise Lost*. I hid for long hours in the library or bar-hopped Friday nights downtown, headed back home at three in the morning, moving through fraternity row where passed-out bodies littered the lawns. One evening, returning early to my room, I walked through the living room where six or seven women were gathered around a card table. They stopped when I walked in, not embarrassed but, rather, nervous about something that had nothing to do with me. Of course, behind my closed bedroom door, I dropped my books and pressed my ear to the wall. What I had interrupted, I learned, was an séance of sorts, with Tonya, her mother, an aunt, and other women huddled around a Ouija board. They resumed their meditations, at one point talking softly about the resident ghost, but that was not their present concern. They'd had a friend (not present) prepare a list of questions, twenty-five in number, and only the friend knew the answers. These women were testing the boundaries of the board, and I realized that they had been doing this for some time. So methodically, somberly, they quizzed Ouija and someone dutifully wrote down what the spirit world had to say. There was no humor, no raised voices—only a kind of reverential fear of the unknown. When the list was done, someone used the phone and compared results, while the mother served coffee and cake. Ouija was right seventeen of the twenty-five times. I heard whoops of congratulation, lots of laughter, but then, after a pause, Tonya and another woman returned to the board. The spirit world offered nothing new at first, but then Tonya brought up the subject of her good friend Gayle, who was leaving for Europe at the end of the semester. "Will Gayle meet the man of her dreams in Europe?" No. "Will she find love in Chapel Hill?" No. A pause. "When will she be married?" No answer. Through the walls I could sense the heaviness of the air, the quiet of the women. Then: "Will she get married?" No. Someone tittered. Another gasped. "Why not?" A pause. Accident. "Will she be in an accident?" Yes. "What accident?" No answer. "Will she be all right?" No. A pause. "Where will this accident happen?" A pause. In Europe.

Someone screamed. I heard the rustle of chairs, the movement of bodies. A sobbing.

Suddenly the room was empty, the women fleeing upstairs or out of the house.

I went to bed, myself addled. No homework that night, for sure. Restless, bothered, I fought with the image of Gayle in

Europe—I knew her by sight as a lithe, friendly girl, flirtatious and totally blonde, a young woman facing—what? —a fatal accident? I drifted into an awful sleep. For some reason I dreamed of John Milton, whose verse I'd been dealing with earlier that day in the library: *Ruling in hell . . . serving in heaven . . .*

In the deep of that night I woke with a start. I couldn't catch my breath and my skin was cold and clammy. I struggled to sit up but felt something smothering me, holding me to the mattress. I gasped. Was I dying? For Christ's sake, what was happening? Gasping aloud, choking, I managed to push myself up. There was little air in the room, a thick molasses-syrupy soup enveloping me, and I thought something had gone wrong with the gas jets. I had to move. I managed to swing my legs off the side of the bed, sat still, and there on the wall to the left I saw something horrible: a heavy, undulating, shifting fog, a grayish-white tapestry moving like a nightmare across the wall shared with the adjacent den. It had a life to it, a dull, plodding life to be sure, but I thought: yes, I am sleeping, I am dreaming. But I stood and it would not disappear. I was gasping for breath. I was going to die.

I fell back onto the mattress, powerless, but I thought of light. I needed light. I reached for the lamp on the nightstand and switched it on. Illumination flooded the room. The undulating film was gone now, the air began to clear, and I could breathe again. In frenzy, revitalized, I threw on the overhead light, the bathroom light, and the light by the radio. I created illumination that touched every corner of the room. Now I breathed freely, so I left the lights on all night long, and I sat there, wrapped in blankets, waiting for dawn. Sleep was impossible. In the morning I showered and walked to class, bone weary and feeling like I'd been on an all-night drunk. I told myself I had dreamed it all, but I knew that was not the case.

I told no one.

Two days later I met up with a bunch of my friends, heading to the auditorium to hear a lecture by Floyd McKissick, the new head of CORE, and, I believe, the first African-American graduate of the Chapel Hill Law School, a man who'd struggled to gain admission to the University years back. It was a monumental event. The outside world was coming to North Carolina. Earlier that semester we'd heard Marxist writer/activist Herbert Aptheker address the campus body from a sidewalk by Franklin Street as we—some thousand of us—congregated on campus. The revered North Carolina General Assembly had forbidden Marxists like Aptheker from speaking on public university property, an act opposed by the enlightened UNC faculty, and this was the compromise. Now the visit of McKissick was causing concern. The local KKK had threatened violence and destruction. All sorts of alerts had been issued.

Frankly, I couldn't wait to get there.

The area outside the auditorium was abuzz with throngs of students and townspeople, and ringing it all was a wall of state troopers. There were not hordes of white-sheeted KKK, no burning crosses, no bullhorn preaching white supremacy and the inferiority of the Negro. We lingered outside, waiting, I suppose, for the thrill of seeing actual KKK members close up. But all I saw were white liberals wearing pins that condemned the KKK and the Old South.

Inside the lecture went on without incident. But what I remember was the question-and-answer period. At one point the man sitting next to me started squirming, managed to get recognized, and stood up. Dressed in an ill-fitting suit, with a choppy haircut and a red, beaming face, he was perhaps forty-five or fifty, a tiny man, a kindly looking man, someone who reminded me of the older barber downtown who trimmed my hair, the same one who told me he disliked cutting the hair of boys from India or Pakistan because such hair seemed Negroid. He looked like someone's uncle, a dutiful husband. "My name," the man said in a surprisingly loud voice, "is the Rev. Mr. Jacob Thorne, pastor of the New Hope and Glory Baptist Church"—he mentioned some small town I'd never heard of— "and I am here as a proud member of the United Klan of these United States." I actually twitched, and then spun around to face him as he prattled on and on with some puerile racist crap about purity and justice and the American way. I was staring so intently into his rubbery face that I caught his attention. He threw a quick glance at me, but it was as though he were inspecting a fly on the wall.

When he sat down, my friend on my left whispered: "I thought you said your father was gonna sit this one out."

Outside, in the chill spring air, we huddled, the bunch of us, and laughed. "My luck," I said, "to be sitting next to that damn fool."

We were back at the edge of the lawn, near a line of thick hedges, and suddenly the friend I was facing got still, his eyes looking over my shoulder. I turned around and behind me were perhaps ten clansmen, in full white-robed regalia, a menacing line, shoulders touching, arms folded, planting themselves in a tight line. They appeared dim against the shadows of the Carolina night. I froze. My heart raced: this was a vision of pure evil. Later on I learned that the state troopers stood nearby, guarding, but at the time I saw only the redundant line of white robe, one after the other. I had just declared my dismissive line—"To be sitting next to that damn fool" At that moment, standing perhaps five feet from a clansman, I stared into the two dark vacant holes that were his eyes. We held eye contact. I was scared and couldn't move. What I remember after all these years is the unblinking, revolting look of absolute, unconditional hatred under those hoods, eyes so lit with fury that they seemed on fire. For a second we stood there, eyes locked, black dots of fury in the holes of white cotton, and I knew, as I had never known before in my life, the simple but awful equation of pure hatred.

The Summer Games

The vice-principal shifted gears when he turned corners. Corners of the hallway, that is, not the town roads. His hands punctuated the air as though he were dropping into second gear. He was a man in his fifties, a burlap bag of a man, with prominent jowls that trembled and swayed as he maneuvered the corners. Whenever I approached him, he shook his head, as though I were in need of admonishment for some grievous offense. "I don't like young teachers," he said once, "generally speaking." I waited. "They don't learn from their mistakes." "I plan to be different," I said. He shook his head. "You look like you're sixteen years old. The hooligans won't respect you."

So, on a sweltering early July morning, I entered the classroom to teach one section of summer school. I'd been hired right out of Chapel Hill, with my valued MA in hand, scheduled to teach junior English that fall at Cranfield High School. But then a frantic phone call begged me to teach summer school. The penciled-in teacher had had an emergency (a sudden whiff of sanity?), and could I please take over for six weeks? I felt I couldn't say no. So on the hot morning, I walked into a packed, un-air-conditioned room, and the entire back of the classroom burst into gales of uncontrolled laugher. This, I realized, was not going to be good.

I did look like a sixteen-year-old kid, skinny and gangly, with a tidy semi-Beatles haircut—grad school shagginess gone for the moment—but, worse, I wore a neatly pressed gray linen suit, accompanied by a poorly knotted tie and scuffed black tie shoes. One student, tears streaming down his cheeks, kept pointing and howling. I felt like Ichabod Crane with primer and indignation, suddenly come to life.

No one had warned me. It seemed the class consisted of those students—largely male—who'd flunked English the past year, and needed the credits. The vice-principal whispered to me the day before: "Just keep them in their seats. We don't expect you to teach them anything." A pause. "I think I know your family." I had no response to that. "They're losers," he said.

"My family?"

Perplexed: "What? The students you'll be teaching."

And, I suppose, they were. Half of the guys were football players, it turned out, a squad of beefy, ultimately cheerful boys who liked to bump against one another in the hallways and burp top-40 tunes. The other half was that new phenomenon: the longhaired hippie, the freaks, the counterculture souls soon to be so commonplace on the American landscape. Disaffected, unhappy, they were often extremely bright and clever, downright articulate on occasion. Needless to say, the hippies and the jocks did not get along, and the hippies sat bunched together on the side of the room. As well, there was a smattering of gum-clicking girls with tremendously high and dangerous hairdos, many of whom were girlfriends of the jocks, and one was proud to be the latest notch on their gang-bang belt. Of course, I didn't learn this that first morning, but within one week the chatty crowd couldn't keep their collective mouth shut.

So I'm standing there before them, the laughter subsiding only a bit, and I begin to call the roll: Adams, Belinski, Babin, and so forth. I stop. I hear something. It sounds like a duck. I continue. Carvelli, Corrigan, Davidson — Yes, a duck. Definitely a duck in distress. And it's coming from the back of the classroom. A low, insistent *quack, quack, quack.* I look up. The noise stops. Donatto, Dre — *Quack quack quack.* I spot where it is coming

Trespassing in the Garden of Eden

from: a massive kid I heard addressed by his buddies as Rich. Later I learn he's the star quarterback and all-around mover and shaker of the village teen scene. I look down. *Quack quack.* I look up. It stops. I am already sweating from the unbridled heat of the day and the dumb-ass tight suit jacket I'm strapped into.

Then the duck has company. The attendant ducklings begin to add their mellifluous chorus. Suddenly the whole back row is quacking in cacophonous splendor. I stop reading the names. I stare at them, and now they are emboldened and arrogant. I've lost them—well, actually, I've never even had them, the very first class. But I have six long, long weeks ahead of me. I just don't know what to do. "Please be quiet," I say, which leads to more uncontrolled laughter and quacking. "Come on, guys." An attempt at pity does nothing. Even the wide-eyed stoned hippies smile at that.

I decide to be clever, delivering some smart-alecky quip so stinging the ducks won't have any choice but to fall into line. I decide to say, in resounding, measured intonation: "I always flunk very duck in my class." I wait for a break in the quackery.

Loudly, clearly, enunciating syllable by syllable, but nervous as hell, I announce, "I always fuck every duck in my class."

A stunned silence covers the room. No one is more shocked than I am. Where the hell has that come from? Did I actually say *fuck?*

I feel my face getting flushed and I face the door, expecting the principal to be passing by. My first day of teaching, and ironically my last. Ever.

The ducks have not resumed their animal-farm symphony. Instead Rich is looking at me, eyes unblinking, mouth agape. And then, almost on cue, he and his boys start to giggle—not laugh, but *giggle.* Like prom queens tickled behind the school bleachers.

I don't know it then, but that class is mine for the taking. I've obviously passed some test with Rich, the leader of the pack, and, with his adolescent imprimatur, I am home free.

But I wait for the call from the principal, which luckily doesn't come.

But getting the guys to do work was not easy—or successful. I soon learned that any achievement needed to be measured in very small bits and pieces. And keeping them in their seats was a trial. I was often oblivious to the social dynamics before me. I might be at the board, working myself up into lather over noun-verb agreement, while disagreement of another sort was festering in the peanut gallery behind me. One day I was reading a poem to them (A poem!—this *was* my first teaching experience!). I read E. A. Robinson's "Richard Cory," hoping that the sheer melodrama of that final line ("and went home and put a bullet in his head") would shut them up. Suicide as opiate of the people. All of a sudden there was a battle in the room, as the jocks flew across the space to pummel the hippies. It seems one of the jocks, sitting purposely behind the hippie with especially long hair, had brought scissors to class and was just starting to snip away at the back of the unsuspecting lad. Chairs flying, desks overturned, punches hurled—there was a good five minutes of utter madness, with me rushing back and forth like (to use my mother's expression) a chicken with its head cut off. And then, like a flash flood, suddenly it ended, everyone back in his or her seats, everyone staring at me, still screaming like a banshee, as though I had suddenly lost my mind.

Rich became my good buddy, although he implied that he was somehow still the leader of the class, which included me. He said I was funny. He'd never had a "funny" teacher before, he said. One time a student named Tucker asked me for his grade. Trying to be "funny" I said: "I always spell Tucker with an F." I hadn't realized what I'd said until Rich informed the class. "He means Fucker. Fucker." No one believed my protestations to the contrary.

Late one period I had the students push their desks to the back walls of the room so that we could assemble in a circle and play some word games, with each student adding (or subtracting) from a passed-around sentence. I had pushed my own desk back against the blackboard. Sitting on the edge of my desk, I realized the flag was in the way, so I rolled it up and forgot about it. But the next day we

Trespassing in the Garden of Eden

were doing another such activity, the students in a circle and creating stories. In the middle of orchestrating the class, standing in the middle of the circle, I saw the door open and a pupil I'd never seen before—some skinny, wild-eyed boy—came rushing into the room, followed by a posse of similarly disheveled vigilantes. Momentarily confused, he headed to my desk, jumped on it, and proceeded to unroll the American flag. Members of the posse held onto his legs. With their motley clothing and fly-away hair, it reminded me for a moment of some hippie version of the famous Iwo Jima flag raising.

As he unraveled the flag he yelled at me: "Ifkovic, you Commie scumbag. You pinko. You—" He sputtered, and then jumped down and ran out of the room.

Giving chase, I caught up with him, grabbed his shoulder to stop him, and the two of us toppled to the floor. The vice principal suddenly arrived, shifting into third gear, yelling "Whoa" like Ward Bond on *Bonanza*, and the lad was led off to Siberia.

He was given three days' suspension. Within the hour, however, his mother called the school, protesting the punishment. His deed, she insisted, was an act of deliberate patriotism. Patriotism? He'd heard through the grapevine—as he huddled with cigarettes in the boy's room, where he spent most of his time—that I had rolled up the flag as a sign of disrespect for America and, in particular, a protest against the Vietnam War. I'd been very vocal in my protest against the War, often arguing with an old-time history teacher in the teacher's room. So I told the principal I'd rolled up the flag because, well, my head kept hitting it—this was no agitprop performance in some way-off Broadway theater, but Mommy insisted on a meeting.

A meeting with the parents! The one-act tragedy I would soon learn to dread! The next afternoon I met with Mommy and Daddy (who had taken time off from work and looked like he wanted to be anywhere else in the world but there), Junior, and the principal. Mr. Jamison, the aged principal had one principle: Appease the parents at any cost. I listened to Mr. Jamison supporting the decision to suspend with a curious diplomacy that largely *apologized* for *my* behavior.

"We have raised out kids to be proud and loyal Americans," Mommy said. "Jimmy was defending the flag."

"What?" From me.

"No need to get excited." From Mr. Jamison. Perhaps my voice was a little high. Many principals are former physical education teachers who hurt their knees and then entered academic administration.

"He heard you were against the war and you disrespected the flag."

"I rolled up the flag because my head hit it."

"My son was acting patriotic. He should be reinstated."

"He was suspended because he disrupted my class. If he had a question, he should have come in after class, and said, 'Are you a traitor?' Something like that."

"Don't make light of this." Mr. Jamison glared at me.

"He's that way in class, I hear," the mother said.

"I think—"

The mother frowned. "Could you answer me *one* question?"

"Sure."

"Are you or are you not a Communist?"

The question came out of nowhere. "What?"

Daddy spoke up for the first time. "A goddamned Commie. Jimmy says you're a Commie." I looked at Jimmy who seemed to be listening to some faraway dance music in his head. He noticed every eye on him, sat up, and yelled: "What?" Mommy tapped him on the knee. "Commie," she said, pointing at me. Jimmy grinned. He nodded: Yes. Thanks, Joseph McCarthy.

Mommy, back to me. "Are you a Commie?"

I waited for Mr. Jamison to say something but he seemed stunned with the recent knowledge that his faculty was infiltrated with the Red Menace—and no one informed him. Maybe he'd spent too much time in the gym, dreaming of lost glory.

"We're here to discuss your son's behavior," I said. "My politics are not an issue here."

Momma actually made sound like an *eeeeek*. She turned to Mr. Jamison. "There! I told you. He's a Commie."

Mr. Jamison stared, confused, probably remembering his days playing dodge ball with compliant adolescents. "I didn't hear him say—"

"A Commie. In your school."

Daddy said: "Here. Right here. Look." Everyone stared at me as though I had a hammer and sickle tattooed on my brow and was wearing a better-red-than-dead T-shirt.

So we went back and forth until, stupidly, all of us exhausted, we agreed to let Jimmy return to classes after he apologized to me and shook my hand. We all left in smiles. I'd later see Jimmy in the hallways and he'd give me a look that said something like—you look vaguely familiar. Haven't we met?

By the fourth week there were only five girls left in the class, and one was little Annie, who said not a word the whole time. She also did almost no work, which explained why she was in summer school. Tiny, pale, freckled, startlingly homely, she was ignored by the class who didn't deem her even worthy of abuse and mockery. She was also the only student who gave me no grief, hiding in the shadows of the room, hugging the back corner, her arms folded politely on her desktop. Most of the time I forgot Annie was there. Sometimes, when I scanned the class, I'd spot her staring at me, but I could never read her expression: an old mixture of utter blankness with a little unfocused curiosity. Maybe a little hostility.

One morning the class was rambunctious, and I was in no mood for it. I announced in a loud voice—my here-it-comes-you're-in-for-it voice—that the class had come to expect: "There's *one* student in *this* class that I can't stand. I mean, I really *dislike*. I'm not saying who it is, but there's *one* student who turns my stomach." All sorts of vaudeville emphasis and gesturing. It was a dumb thing to say but everyone burst out laughing, and calmed down. And Rich, beaming and thumping his chest, proudly said: "We know who that is." He pointed to himself. He stood and bowed. "No, no, not you," I said, grinning. And, with the class sitting up and behaving, we turned to the lesson of the day.

When I dismissed the class and was gathering my books, I looked up to see little Annie standing nearby. I had never spoken to her. "It's me, isn't it?" she asked.

"What?" I'd forgotten my line.

"It's me you hate." I was hearing her voice for the first time: timid, shaky, a baby-girl voice.

I was stupefied. "Annie, for God's sake. Why would I hate you? You're the only one who doesn't give me trouble."

"You hate me."

I stared at her, this pathetic lost child, all blemish and sadness, stooped over, self-loathing.

"Annie, no."

I protested over and over, and she looked ready to cry.

She started to turn away.

"Annie, wait." She turned back. "Believe me, you're one of the students I like. I like you, Annie. Believe me. I like you." She stared into my face, expectant. "Annie, you're no trouble. I like you. You I really *like*."

I like you, I like you, I like you like you like you like you like like like you like like like you

What she heard me say, of course, was: *Annie, I love you.*

I thought nothing about it until the next morning, driving to class, listening to a New Haven radio station, when I heard a call-in top-40 request: "For Eddie Ifkovic, the Teddy Bears," the DJ said, amused. "An oldie." And he sang the opening lines over the actual record: *To know know know him is to love love love him.*" I almost drove off the road. *Just to see him smile makes my life worthwhile.* "From Annie."

Before class, the vice-principal called me into his office. "What's the deal?"

I shrugged my shoulders. "I dunno."

"You got a thing for Annie?"

I shook my head.

Annie, it seems, had an infatuation as big as the moon. In class she simply sat there, staring without saying anything. But outside of class was a different matter: she was suddenly *everywhere*. I'm walking to my car and she's at the edge of the parking lot, watching. I'm at a faculty meeting in the vast cafeteria, and a small face is pasted against the small window. Staring. I kept reassuring the vice-principal that her infatuation—and that's all it was—would pass. You know, teenage girls. He didn't seem too happy. "People talk," he said. "Don't get caught with your pants down in education." I thought it would pass quickly. But I avoided her, uncomfortable. I was beating myself up: I thought I'd said *I like you I really like you* perhaps ten times too many.

That weekend I drove with some friends to the beach at Misquamicut in Rhode Island, where there are breathtaking waves. While friends surfed, I sat on the white sands and read an Erle Stanley Gardner mystery. Later that afternoon I drove home, into my parents' yard. I was living at home (my schoolteacher's salary was $5,000 that year!). I was barely out of the car when I saw my mother on the stoop, her lips pursed.

"Are you going out tonight?"

"No," I said. "Why?"

"The state police will be here in an hour to take your statement."

"What?" What?

She'd been waiting for my return, anxious that I not be late for my interrogation, and now she couldn't wait until I was in the house.

While I was away, it seemed, Annie had showed up at my parents' doorstep, hugging a small kitten to her chest, asking if anyone had lost a cat. When my mother said no, turning away, Annie tried to push by my mother, attempting to get into her beloved Eddie Ifkovic's sanctuary. *To know know know him . . .* My mother managed to get her out, but Annie soon had the neighbors in an uproar as she went from house to house, using her hapless kitten as an open-sesame. In no time at all, all the local housewives were gathered on front lawns, tongues wagging, arms gesturing, all circling around my mother—who wanted nothing more than to return to baking an apple pie in her kitchen. She had nothing more to add to the story. But world-of-mouth escalated the saga into an attempted breaking-and-entering scenario, with unknown intent—what would this little girl do when she got into my house? —inflaming imaginations and neighborly anger. Annie, meanwhile, doubtless frightened by the Cecil B. DeMille cast of thousands assembled on the lawn, fled the scene. After a while the housewives, venom and curiosity spent and no violator available for the stockade on the town green, returned to their kitchens, perhaps a little let down by the nonevent it turned out to be.

Except that someone—we never found out who—called the cops, not the local constable who was a notorious drunk and womanizer and was known to lock himself inside his car when teenaged punks made fun of him—but, rather, the Resident State Trooper, whom no one ever called for anything. We saved him for things like murder and the looting of the general store. A phone call to my mother, a curious silence on the other end of the phone as she recounted the afternoon's events, and thus the visit to my house by the trooper. By now my mother had gotten into the spirit of things, what with the savory apple-pie cooling on the rack and fresh coffee on the stove and the family supper dishes washed and put away. "Ma," I said, pleading, "the state trooper, for God's sake?" She started to say it was none of her doing when there was the knock on the door.

For a half hour we sat at the kitchen table, the three of us, and I was beginning to feel humiliation and embarrassment. No, the trooper said, he didn't want a piece of apple pie, though I saw him following the tantalizing smell to the counter, and, I swear, I noticed a slick bit of drool at the corners of his mouth. I wasn't happy. Here I was, still sandy from the Rhode Island beach, dressed in torn jeans, sandals, a rock 'n' roll T-shirt, my modified Beatles haircut in need of a trimming. One foot in the revolution, one foot tapping to Lawrence Welk on Saturday night. The trooper, a young guy perhaps twenty-five had close-cropped hair—fresh from Vietnam was he? —clean-cut Pat Boone Aryan looks, a posture that could snap a twig, and he looked so fresh-scrubbed and sterile and antiseptic in that squeaky clean and razor-sharp creased uniform that, for a moment, I thought I was talking to Switzerland. What made it worse, I realized, was that he was not taking any of this seriously. My mother, called upon to recount the remains of the day, rattled on and on, getting into the juice of it, relishing her role as town crier, amplifying the meager facts with asides that made the trooper cast sidelong glances at me. "All the girls are after him," she'd say, and the trooper— who probably knew that experience first hand—looked at the disheveled beach bum sitting there, all sunburn blotch and oily appeal. My mother was starting to sing *To know know know him is to love love love him*, when he interrupted. Thank God. Every so often he'd just jot something down in his notebook, but, craning though I did, I could make out nothing but scribbles. Perhaps he was sketching a resumé: after all, there had to be a better job than this. Finally, out of wind and anecdote, my mother stopped, sat back triumphantly, happy to have done her civic duty. She beamed: "Did I mention that it was a kitten and not a cat?"

"Yes, ma'am." Jack Webb. *Dragnet*.

A slight pause. He turned his mighty bulk towards me, and I swear I saw a sliver of a smile. He looked into my face. "All right, I'm ready for your statement"— pause—"Elvis."

Elvis!

It was downhill from there. I said little more, and he finally left, a smirk on his face. The school was contacted, and Annie was transferred out of my class. Nothing more was said. But a few days later I was turning the corner by the cafeteria, and I nearly collided with little Annie, hugging the walls, her arms cradled around some books. Nervous, I stopped, and I was ready to say something soft and kind to her, letting her know—what? That I had no hard feelings. That this too shall pass. That this was okay. But at that moment we made eye contact, and I saw in her eyes a love so raw and so deep that I nearly lost my breath. By the time I recovered, she had bustled by me, and I swear I smelled a noxious body odor that I would come to identify years later as raw fear.

The National Press Club

Todd and Sallye were holding their wedding reception at the National Press Club. I was immediately impressed. Not that I knew that much about that august club other than as a venue for public addresses by Washington politicos speaking before a cluttered bank of microphones. No fan of LBJ and the escalation of the war in Vietnam, I tended to turn off the TV when anything offended me—which seemed to be often those days. But I knew enough to be impressed by symbols, and the National Press Club was such a symbol.

It had been over a year since I'd got my MA at Chapel Hill, and Sallye and Todd had been part of my Chapel Hill world. Now a teacher at a public high school in Connecticut, I was surprised by the invitation to the wedding. I'd lost touch with that world. I never really expected the two to tie the old nuptial knot. Not really. We all considered their whirlwind courtship just a pleasant campus interlude. But now I wouldn't miss the wedding for anything. Todd was an inveterate scholar, a burn-the-midnight-oil student who could get all worked up over a diphthong. Handsome in a geeky, skinny way—hair askew above a bright face, eyeglasses always falling to the floor, fingernails bit to the nub—he had a boyish charm and a certain caustic Irish wit. People took to him before they questioned themselves why. He was just too erudite—some steep

Ivory Tower hermit. Sallye was his opposite, a girl more interested in a thong than diphthong—although I don't think such intimate apparel existed then, but you get my point. Bright herself, funny in her own quiet way, she was drop-dead gorgeous—willowy figure, a shock of brilliant auburn hair, a few well-placed freckles on an alabaster-white face. Sallye stopped conversation when she strolled into Faneuil Hall for a simple tuna on toast. Coming from money, Sallye had a wardrobe that never looked wrong, and she dressed to class as though she were going out to dance. She was getting an MA in literature, but, as she announced candidly, she was looking for a husband in law or medicine. She seemed to have had a charmed life living in some affluent Washington D.C. suburb, and, in fact, her claim to fame just before graduate school was being Miss Cherry Blossom the year before at the traditional D.C. celebration of that famous Japanese gift.

Both Todd and Sallye were part of our circle, but they never really liked each other, and so it was a surprise to everyone as we gathered one night in the cafeteria for dinner to see them stroll in together, walk by the rest of us at our usual corner, and then head to the opposite end of the cafeteria to grab an isolated table. There they sat, huddled, grinning, perhaps even giggling, while the rest of us, back at our own little table, glared, wondered, and even gossiped. No one had seen it coming—this impossible romance. But for the next three or four weeks Sallye and Todd occupied that table, and we ours. We talked of nothing else but them, and I surmise they scarcely mentioned us at all. But that's not true, because during the day, as we attended classes together, they were, indeed, our friends, and laughed and carried on with us. But no one mentioned the romance—truth to tell, we had no terms for what we were seeing. Up to that point, we'd just been boys and girls together, and no one dated within the circle. But three weeks later, early one evening, the two quietly rejoined our table, as though they had not missed a night, and they fit in seamlessly, naturally, and everything progressed as it always had. Except now they sometimes held hands and cooed at each other like lovesick puppies. Now, too, they no longer argued with each other on everything—she the knee-jerk Republican and he the fiery Democrat from Boston. They only had one story now.

Todd came from a comfortable middle-class background, with most of his family somehow connected with the Boston Public Library. But Sallye came from D.C. political royalty. I can't remember how high placed her father was, but Mommy, I recall, was some high muck-a-muck in the CIA, whose job was very hush hush. Sallye once—a little tipsy as we all strolled back from a downtown bar—confessed that her mother would disappear for a month at a time, and then one day Sallye would return home from school to discover her mother in the kitchen, baking a cake. Looking like Donna Reed in an apron. Once she actually discovered some papers her mother had inadvertently left under a file on a desk—Sallye admitted she snooped— and they were in Chinese. Sallye surmised that Mommy had been in Red China, and these were pre-Nixon Chinese diplomatic days. We all oohed and aahed over that. An American in China. Quotations from Chairman Mom. In her study Mommy would make late-night phone calls to various members of Congress.

Which explains exactly what we were all doing a year later at the National Press Club, celebrating the nuptials of this unlikely pair. Mommy had a lot of power. Probably cherry-blossom power.

I drove down from Connecticut and met two friends at the hotel near Alexandria, Virginia, where the wedding was taking place. I hadn't seen Fred and Joey since I left Chapel Hill in June of 1966. Fred was teaching English at a prep school in Vermont, but Joey had stayed in Chapel Hill, planning on getting Ph.D., though I learned he'd dropped out a semester later, disaffected.

The night before the wedding we hung out, the three of us, and I realized what a year could do to a lost soul.

Fred was the same—punctual, earnest, with a dark sense of humor. I always felt there was a veil of sorrow over him, even when he was laughing at something. Sometimes he'd shake his head and lapse into a deep reverie that lasted all night. I wasn't surprised when he killed himself fifteen years later.

But Joey, the academic imp, the passionate lover of Flannery O'Conner's short stories, had undergone a transformation. In the post-Beatles-in-America days Joey had embraced the nascent hippie movement, sporting messy (and messianic) long hair and writing lyrics to music no one would ever hear, defining himself as part of the new revolution, the campus freaks who were fusing civil rights and anti-war protest into some hypnotic vision of America's future. The clean-cut liberal had metamorphosed into the radical-as-unmade-bed.

"You look different, Joey," Fred said when we met in the lobby. And we all burst out laughing. Fred and I were still dressed like Eisenhower twins, although the crew cuts were long gone, but Joey had fully entered the new culture: uncombed hair, all wild and crazy, and a Bohemian assortment of Goodwill leftovers. Sandals on his feet, jeans with holes in the knees, and an unruly beard. "My outfit for the wedding," he said.

"The invitation didn't say come as you fell out of bed," Fred said.

Joey laughed.

Always the most political of the bunch, Joey launched into his artistic freedom tirade, the crippling of the individual soul, the death of individualism in a capitalist world. Fred and I looked at each other. Joey's father was a millionaire corporate lawyer with John Hancock in Boston. His mother was on the board of the Boston Museum of Fine Arts, and was an organizer of charity functions. The family owned something like four million homes, most of them on expensive water.

Then Joey dropped out of Chapel Hill.

In the hotel bar we munched on peanuts and draft beer.

"You've looking at the future of America," he said now, pointing to his chest.

"What?"

"My generation is gonna save this world." He was deadly serious. Keep in mind the boastful line had not yet become the clichéd response it shortly became in popular culture. "Everybody has fucked everything up. Now they gotta give into the young folks." "Young folks?" Fred echoed, grinning.

"You laugh." No humor. "We'll end this fucking war and made the black man free—"

Fred held up his hand. "Let's drink to Sallye and Todd."

Joey smiled. He raised his bottle of beer. "Even though," he added, "they'll be divorced in five years."

(He was only off a few years. It took seven years before Sallye left Todd, who then went on to get his Ph.D. in Linguistics and moved to Saudi Arabia. Sallye married a squirrelly lawyer who worked in the Nixon White House. You saw him in the crowd in the news footage that chronicled Nixon waving goodbye and getting on that final plane after resigning the Presidency.)

So the next day we celebrated Todd and Sallye's union, and followed a car caravan to the reception at the National Press Club, where we were in awe of the opulent splendor and the fact that most of the guests seemed over a hundred years old. Joey had pulled his hair into a ponytail—a capitalist gesture, I told him, to his chagrin—and wore a frayed tweedy sports jacket one size too big.

We all got drunk. There was nothing else to do. There were a few friends from Carolina, and some manic young people in business suits and prom dresses from Sallye and Todd's undergrad years at Rollins and Gettysburg, but they hid out with one another. The girls we knew at Carolina hadn't made the wedding, without explanation, so we were left alone. We got gloriously drunk, three isolatos on the town.

Later in the evening I sauntered up to the buffet, where I'd been picking my way through the mountain of glorious shrimp. There was a huge ice sculpture—I believe it was a swan but I remember it as a giant shrimp—covered as it was with succulent shrimp, skewered on toothpicks decorously embedded in the ice. To my dismay there was but one solitary shrimp left on the shiny ice, and I cheekily reached for it at the very moment some black-suited older gentleman made the same reach. Our hands collided, and we stared at each other a second before each reached again for the shrimp. I pushed his arm away, a mini struggle ensued, and I thought he was going to rip the shrimp from my trembling fingers. I won, enclosing my fingers around the morsel and leaving him with a naked toothpick. I dipped my shrimp into the cocktail sauce, and chomped on it happily. The man, shaking his head, walked away.

I licked my fingers and spotted Fred laughing. "I won," I smiled.

"So you won," he said. "Do you know who that is?"

I looked at the back of the distinguished man, now surrounded by other wedding guests. "No, not a clue."

"That's Senator Mark Hatfield of Oregon," he said. "You just took the last shrimp from Senator Hatfield."

"Well, I did get there first."

"I think he'd say he was there first."

"Politics is just differing perspectives on the same question," I said.

Later on we seemed to be the only ones left at the National Press Club except for the help, so we left. We had been waiting for the party that never happened. But the night was still young, and Joey suggested we hit a few D.C. strip clubs. This was 1967, the streets were alive, and there were staggering cultural changes afoot, mainly the advent of the legally topless girlie clubs. To see a woman dancing topless, well—unheard of. Fought in the courts, debated in the press, celebrated by degenerates everywhere, the issue had been resolved in favor of such necessary establishments. So places in D.C. suddenly had packed halls of half-naked women and totally drunk, slobbering men reinventing the red-light district. When Joey suggested we try to come to an understanding of this new cultural event, we unanimously agreed.

We walked into the first titty bar we stumbled upon—and I do mean stumbled upon. And it was packed, choked with acrid cigarette smoke, pulsating music, and fat-wallet corporate expense accounts. We were led to a tight table deep in the cavernous back, and Joey whispered: "This is the new America." "What?" From Fred. "Total freedom." "What?" I said. I could barely hear above the driving music. A stripper was dancing to The Stones' "Satisfaction."

Trespassing in the Garden of Eden

We ordered drinks from a topless waitress, but our eyes never left her breasts. At that moment we were thirteen-year-olds all over again, celebrating the triumph of puberty. I ordered a Scotch and soda, which I'd never tasted before. Previously the drink I always ordered was a rye-and-ginger, which was ironically my father's the favorite drink. But this was no time for paternal emulation. I took one sip and spit it out. "It's an acquitted taste," Fred said.

Joey was complaining. They'd situated us *behind* the stage, deep against the back wall. As the girls danced and frolicked on the stage, flirting with the fat cats, we had considerable views of their backs, with occasional side-angle shots. Mostly we saw the bobbing, bald heads of drunken men in front of us. The paying band of yahoos rocked back and forth in their seats like the Staten Island Ferry docking during a storm. I could have been watching TV I was so far back. Fred stopped a waitress and asked her to change our seats. She never even responded. I suppose we must have looked like young college kids on the town—penniless, horny, and low on the pecking order of testosteronic cash flow.

"Well, this sucks," Joey said. He hiccoughed, drunk as a skunk.

I sipped my Scotch, hated the taste of it—acquitted taste, my ass—and realized I was too drunk to take even one more sip of any drink. I'd throw up, and that I did not want to do that there. Almost immediately the waitress returned, asking if we were ready for another round. We'd had our drinks maybe three minutes. "No," I said. "We're not ready." She leaned in: "You have to order," she said. So we nodded. She returned with our drinks, we paid her the outrageous amount of money—this on top of the door charge—and I looked at my two Scotch-and-sodas on the table. Momentarily dizzy, I shifted and my hand hit one of the glasses, which toppled off the expensive plywood tabletop onto the floor, smashing into pieces. Within seconds, the waitress bustled near, swept up the debris. She leaned into me. Stupidly, I thought she was going to ask if the flying glass had cut me, half-naked Angel of Mercy that she was. What she actually said was: "That'll be fifteen dollars."

"For what?"

"For the glass. You broke our property."

Broken property? Had I damaged a table and chairs? Had I fallen into a plastic tree?

Now fifteen dollars was a huge sum of money in 1967 for a jelly glass, and so I said no. She walked away. I smiled: sometimes it was easy to win.

Within seconds two towering neckless bouncers were at my table, the waitress pointing at me with a sneer and a lacquered nail, and the talented steroid-induced wonders wanted to know if I happened to have fifteen dollars on me. Amazingly, I did, handing it over. Almost immediately both bozos came alongside, lifted me bodily from the seat, and started maneuvering me towards the door, half carrying me, half pushing. Fred and Joey, sheepish and no help at all, followed. I found myself unceremoniously tossed onto a D.C. sidewalk, a drunken lump of unhappy partier.

"And all I saw was their bony backs," I said to Fred and Joey.

So we strolled the packed neon streets, avoided the quick-talking hucksters who tried to seduce us into other titty bars. Joe started screaming out loud to anyone who passed by: "I wanna drop it in." We couldn't shut him up. "Oh yes, I wanna drop it in." Now Fred and I knew that Joey, the summer of love child, had been a virgin when last seen in Chapel Hill, and most likely still was, despite the love-the-one-you're-with sentiments of the day. So now we had to haul him back from approaching beautiful women—even from some less than beautiful hookers—all of whom were greeted with his happy, bubbly mantra: "I wanna drop it in."

Somehow we made it back to the hotel and Fred and I got Joey tucked into his room. His last words: "This is what the sixties are meant to be." As we closed the door, I heard him start to throw up.

I was planning to drive back to Connecticut the next day, but Joey, over a breakfast of coffee and more coffee, suggested we cruise down to Chapel Hill, stay at his apartment, spend a couple days there. I agreed.

Trespassing in the Garden of Eden

So our caravan of three cars drifted down to Chapel Hill, and we slept most of the afternoon and night away in his cramped apartment just off campus. I slept on the floor and Fred on the sofa.

At four the next morning, I woke with a start, bleary eyed and stomach sick, and stared through the faint morning light at a shadowy figure in the room. That's when I encountered John Lee, who was sitting on a hard-backed chair three feet from me, staring, just staring.

Joey hadn't mentioned a roommate. I guess he just forgot.

I could hear Joey snoring behind his closed bedroom door.

Four in the morning and the intense young man was inches away from me, staring through the dim early morning light. As I laid my head on a pillow, I realized he was not looking at me at all but at books on the shelf behind me. Silently he reached out, over me, withdrew a slim volume, leafed through it—so close it fanned my face—and then left, disappearing into his own bedroom.

Later that morning I learned that John Lee—a.k.a Hung Lee—a grad student on scholarship from Taiwan, was Joey's new roommate. Since Joey had dropped out of the university and his rich folks back home were teaching him a lesson, John Lee paid the bills. "He's here to make my life easy. He even cleans. He's like a machine. Very anal. He hates dust." Fred and I nodded. John Lee had not come out of his room all morning. "All he does is study, study, study. He thinks I'm a lazy bum."

"You are," I said.

"That's beside the point."

John Lee did sit with us at the supper table as we wolfed down a pizza with a six-pack. He munched gingerly on the crust of the slice and licked the rim of his beer bottle, looking as though he'd sipped arsenic (is that the smell of almonds in the air?) and then went back to study. A small, compact man, with a faint out-of-place moustache and a crew cut, he looked out at the world through owl-sized eyeglasses. Over dinner I'd mentioned taking my American literature classes at the University but he had no interest. "I'm getting a Ph.D.," he said in a thick almost comical accent, speaking over my sentence. "On John Steinbeck. My dissertation. *East of Eden.*"

"For what purpose?" Joey asked. I stared at Joey. It was as though he were talking to John Lee for the first time.

"To be a professor in Taiwan."

Out of the blue, Joey said: "You need to relax more."

Lee looked at him: "You relax too much."

Joey had been sitting at the table taking a hit off a joint and expelling the blue smoke into Lee's face. "Life means that you should relax."

Lee shook his head. "So this is the new America. Smoke that stuff and eat potato chips until you throw up."

Joey laughed. "Or be like you. Write papers on the split infinitive in *The Grapes of Wrath.*"

Lee shook his head again, looking from Fred to me. "Since I come here, I learn that in America the philosophy is good-enough."

"What?"

"You say to students—you can do better. They say to you—why? It's good enough."

"Turn it around," Joey said. "It's *enough* good."

Lee bit his lip. He rose from the table. "I need to study." He went over to the bookcase where he and I more or less met that morning, and he peered into the shelf.

Joey yelled over: "I may be the poster boy for taking life as it comes, and, and, and in believing in the ideals of a better society—" He stopped as though he'd forgotten where he was going. "But you're a hypocrite. Mr. Short Cut."

Lee walked back with a Monarch Guide, the precursor of today's yellow-back Cliff Notes, those revered abbreviated trots American students used in all their lit classes. Back then, we used the deep red-and-black Monarch Notes, and Lee had discovered their value. Now Joey chided him, "I see you making notes out of a Monarch guide."

Lee answered, "It's just a guide—and valuable."

"You're cheating," Joey said. He turned to us: "He owns the whole series."

"A gift," Lee said.

We looked at the bookcase, which had served as my headboard. It was filled with copies of Monarch Guides, hundreds and hundreds. It seemed Mr. Lee had discovered an error in one of the guides, probably some obscure Steinbeck novel, a misprint. Maybe they wrote *Of Mice and Mensch*. And he wrote a scathing letter to the publishers. He identified himself as a Taiwanese grad student in American literature, and, in short order, the company sent him—this I found hard to believe—every Monarch Guide. Every one. Lee spent his days lost in quick-fix summaries and pithy explanations, shadows on the cave of American literature. "Sometimes," Joey said, "when he actually picks up *The Grapes of Wrath*, he's surprised at the number of words."

Lee left the room.

It struck me as an unholy roommate alliance, this pairing of the increasingly disaffected Joey with the intense, feverishly dedicated Chinese student, but Joey concluded: "He's not so bad. Every so often a Chinese student here will commit suicide, but that won't happen to John. There's no Monarch Guide to, well, guide him."

"He sees you as the wasting away of America."

Joey laughed. "I am. But getting wasted in America is the future of America's success."

"What does that mean?"

"It's our secret plan of non-attack."

We stayed one more night. The next morning, adjusting my position on the hard floor, I rolled over, somehow managed to dislodge the flimsy shelf, and row after row of Monarch Guides toppled onto me. I woke yelling and drew the whole house to me. I was covered with *Leaves of Grass*, *Utopia*, *The Sound and the Fury*, Ben Franklin's *Autobiography*. Plato, Aristotle. All of Western Civilization blanketed me—in a condensed version, to be sure.

Lee came flying out of his room wearing nothing but voluminous boxer shorts with barber-pole stripes. He surveyed the carnage.

"Now look what you have done. I had everything in alphabetical order."

"I'm sorry."

"How can I put my hands on *Sister Carrie*? I am teaching it in freshman class this afternoon. It is very important that I—"

Joey stood in the shadowy doorway, a trace of a giggle in his words. "Maybe you can read the book."

Lee faced the darkness. "Of course, I've read it. But for freshman you only need to mention the main points." He started knocking guides off my inclined body, actually sending some onto my head, until he spotted the Theodore Dreiser guide. He smiled, clutched it to his breast. "This is the greatest American invention,." He tapped the guide. "This is better than the TV you Americans say you invented."

The Missionary Position

In the spring of 1969 I knew I'd be leaving the high school. I also knew the administration was guardedly happy, especially one of the vice principals, a serious man who took a dislike to me at the start of the year, and couldn't disguise it. Mr. Summers was a former English teacher, a supercilious pedant who claimed to be a Renaissance scholar. He'd done a textbook a century before on Elizabethan drama and spent much of one school day handing around a letter that accompanied a royalty check for $3.73. He was very proud of that check—"ten years after the book was published." He didn't show me the letter, however.

I'm not certain why he took a dislike to me, other than the obvious; my identification with 1960s counterculture was anathema, to be sure. But there were other young teachers who espoused student activism and radicalism in the classroom. A string of Yale wives—women whose husbands were finishing PhDs at the Ivy League school—were hired, mostly vocal peaceniks identified by their torn sweaters and disheveled hair and fiery eyes—but Mr. Summers seemed to love them. I was mild-mannered by comparison, a neat little freak in corduroy and loafers and tie. The real reason he disliked me, I was told a thousand times, was my being a male. He was more comfortable with women, any women. And he didn't like young men who challenged his authority. We were constantly butting heads.

He was convinced I was spouting "non-English curriculum" to my hapless charges. In one class—Creative Writing—my students wanted a "Love-In," to use the phrase of the day, and they built elaborate wooden platforms. Each student wrote a "love" poem—some to mothers, others to God, and one to a "goddess" who turned out to be a gum-clacking airhead who was nevertheless some boy's wonderful Muse. The students invited the class next door, lights were dimmed, and my students lighted candles in the dark and recited their poems. The effect was moving. I'd cleared it with the principal, of course, but Mr. Summers flew into my classroom at the end of the day. "You held a love-in?" he bellowed. "This the last straw."

We were constantly working that last straw.

Whenever I saw him lurking in the hallways, head bent and to the side, brow furrowed, spine curved, I thought immediately of Uriah Heap, Dickens' oily creation, without the sucking up. Mr. Summers never sucked up—he expected that servitude from the rest of us. I never did. Always dressed in faded black suits (I was convinced he bought them at some fire sale immediately after the Second World War), scuffed black tie shoes with socks that tended to bunch at the ankle, he strode through the hallways like an evil wind.

Another teacher told me that he deemed me an "unrepentant subversive," a phrase I came to cherish, largely because I had no idea where it came from and what, in truth, it actually meant. But one day, during a discussion in my late afternoon class, I sensed a presence in the hallway. Looking out, I saw Mr. Summers against the wall, near the door, listening. Or, rather, spying. He said nothing but rushed away. Another time, during homeroom as the class recited the Pledge of Allegiance, he suddenly darted in and told me that one of my students in the back of the room was bouncing a tennis ball on the floor. Of course, I should have noticed this transgression, but I'd been focusing on the shadow in the hallway. And another time, when one of my students was expounding a bizarre—and overtly sexual—interpretation of Jay Gatsby, met with laughter and cynicism from the other students—Mr. Summers, hidden in the shadows, could not contain himself. He strode into the classroom, palms together and shoulders slumped, and simply stood there, his body shaking and his eyes hard and steely. He just stared at me, probably not even actually aware that he was standing inside my room. "Can I help you, Mr. Summers?" Then, without a word, he left.

I suppose I made it worse by ignoring him. I was told by others to report him to the principal, but I didn't care. I suppose I also deliberately did I what wanted. I chaperoned school dances with other teachers, but Mr. Summers warned against dimming the lights. He knew for a fact that boys unzipped their pants and "rubbed" parts against virginal lasses during the slow dances. Our job was to patrol the gym, suppressing fornication. One time, headed to my car after the dance, I heard a noise and looked down a slight embankment. There was the cherubic face of one of the high school girls—an unlovely daughter of born-agains who wore her dresses below the knee—and on top of her was a rollicking lummox, a wisecracking bubblehead who was making a career of repeating his junior year. Neither had been at the dance. I guess they came just to use the facilities. I knew that the young girl, protected by her fundamentalist parents, wasn't allowed to dance or listen to music.

Perhaps Mr. Summers knew something I didn't.

After school I always had groups of students hanging out in the classroom, chatting, laughing, being comfortable. One afternoon I was next door talking to another teacher and one my the students told me I had an unexpected visitor, a "parent." I rushed back and shooed out the kids, and shook hands with Mr. Stacy, father of Sandra, a brilliant young woman in my Advanced English. Mr. Stacy was dressed in a dark suit and overcoat, with hat and gloves, a large imposing man, I was reminded of one of those turn-of-the-century titans, so graphically depicted by Theodore Dreiser. In fact, Mr. Stacy was a successful New York stockbroker who took the train out of New Haven into Grand

Central every weekday. "I took the afternoon off from the office," he began, without much preamble, "because this is important." My heart stopped.

"Mr. Summers," he said—and now my heart really stopped—"is an acquaintance from Rotary and he suggested we talk."

Mr. Stacy wasn't used to back talk, or, for that matter, any talk. I was a fresh scrubbed teacher who looked around nineteen at the time, and he had little patience with children. He was there to talk about Sandra, his beloved daughter, who, I realized, looked just like him—short, stocky, thick in the neck, without, to be sure, the suit and tie and overcoat (which he never removed). I managed to get in a few words of praise for Sandra because she was, indeed, a superior student. He barely listened, then interrupted. "She needs to get into Radcliffe," he said, for he'd gone to Harvard. "Well," I said, "I can't see a problem—"

"Then why did you give her a low grade?" Anger, force.

I tried to think. Sandra never got a low grade. Her essays, though mechanical and mostly uninspired, were flawless in execution. "What?"

"You gave her an A minus. A minus. She's never gotten a minus on anything."

What can you say to that? I guess my jaw must have dropped, and I sputtered something about Sandra doubtless getting a straight A for the entire term, but I suddenly became alarmed: Mr. Stacy was no longer looking at me, staring over my shoulder at the blackboard. What in God's name was there? I knew I'd erased the board at the end of the day. But Mr. Stacy, clearly flummoxed, muttered something conciliatory, reached over and shook my hand, and left the room abruptly.

I turned to the board behind me. One of my hanger-on students had scribbled in big block letters across the board: "A friend in need is a pain in the ass."

You can bet I heard about that from Mr. Summers.

When I was teaching some African-American poetry, I decided to invite some black students from New Haven to my class for a discussion, an attempt to make the literature more real for my largely coddled white suburban students. I cleared it with the principal, talked to some boy's club in New Haven, and one afternoon two young black men attended my classes and considered questions about their lives in New Haven, a life light years away from my students' world. Accompanied by a young white man who directed a program at the center (shabbily dressed, but a Yale grad, it turned out), the afternoon was wonderful. Other teachers brought in their classes. Lively, honest, energizing conversation. The only flap was when one of the older women teachers (who was the spitting and unfortunate image of George Washington) demanded: "Why can't you people pull yourselves up by your bootstraps?" But that, too, was handled diplomatically. Bootstraps?

Mr. Summers, not in attendance, was nevertheless unhappy. At lunchtime the next day he sat at my table and asked why it was necessary to bring those city kids into a literature class. He said it in a tone that sounded like: *Why are you deliberately trying to hurt me?* I babbled some response about making Nikki Giovanni and Baraka relevant but he interrupted me. "You're trying to—to foment trouble."

"No," I said, but he held up his hand. I yelled: "Maybe it's time somebody has to do it."

Then he said something bizarre: "If someone told you to jump off the Brooklyn Bridge, would you do it?"

I didn't answer.

"I thought so," he said, triumphant, standing and sliding away.

But I was told one morning to clear my schedule for a visit to my classroom for two local cops who were giving cautionary talks about the new menace of drugs in the small town. Both officers, in uniform, delivered reasonable warnings about drug addiction, albeit coated with some melodramatic caveats about playground seducers and the famous one-time-makes-you-an-addict lore. The students, a little wide eyed, viewed the discussion with quiet attention and (in some cases) slightly crooked smiles. No one asked questions, and the two cops seemed pleased to be finishing up. One held up a slender joint and said: "This is what a marijuana cigarette looks like." Smiles around the room. I'd already been told that the joint was a dummy—Marlboro tobacco rolled into E-Z Wider papers. There were chuckles in the room. When it was over, the cop placed the fake joint on the table, and the students filed out. We chatted a bit, and then, when they gathered their—um—paraphernalia, we noticed that two very real joints accompanied the fake joint, the surreptitious gift of a departing student. Both cops fumed, and one asked me how the two real joints (they sniffed them expertly) found their way onto the table, eyeing me suspiciously. I had no idea, but they bustled out, and within minutes the classroom intercom rang and Mr. Summers, some curious delight in his voice, informed me that drugs in the classroom were illegal and punishable by umpteen years in the Big House.

"They're not mine," I said, a little alarmed.

"Possession," he said, "is nine-tenths of the law."

"What does that mean?"

He hung up.

But during the Christmas assembly I wasn't the only teacher to incur his wrath. Students normally were rambunctious with the prospect of holiday and vacation, and the teachers were mandated to patrol the aisles, quelling skirmishes and stifling excess noise. But everyone was in a jovial mood, harmless and happy, until, that is, the announcement that one of the students had *invented* a new musical instrument. On the stage stood Johnny Merkowski, a hayseed of a student in the best of times, with his perennial flannel shirts and his huge ears and cowlicky blond hair (one student once described him as a taxi going down the street with both doors wide open). Why-oh-why he was allowed on the stage with this newfangled contraption I have no idea, but he stood there with a device that was part test tube, part garden hose, and part tinfoil. The foil caught the stage lights, and, from where I stood, it looked like he was packing weaponry. Johnny was going to play "Silent Night" on the as-yet-unnamed instrument.

Silence greeted the announcement.

Johnny began.

An awful sound emanated from the instrument, squeaky and shrill, but when he hit the lower notes—as in silent *night*, holy *night*—the sound the microphone magnified across the auditorium was remarkably like a calamitous and sloppy fart. There was no reaction during the first verses, but slowly I could hear the beginning of laughter rising in the assembly, low at first, but growing louder and louder. Up and down the aisles we teachers ran, shushing and hectoring, our fingers to our lips. I looked at one teacher and she seemed ready to burst, trying to keep composed. I was dying. All of a sudden, like unavoidable tidal wave, the dam broke, and shrieks of hysterical laughter rang out. Students were falling out of their seats. As Johnny hit a particularly egregious fart, I started to laugh so loudly, out of control, that I actually buckled over and slipped to the floor. When I looked up, I was staring into the puritanical visage—the only unsmiling face in the crowd—of the redoubtable Mr. Summers. For some reason that made me laugh all the harder, and at that point I didn't care. Johnny Merkowski was ending his musical career with a barrage of rat-a-tat farts that made some of the students scream out loud.

But nothing prepared me for the battle royal awaiting me that spring semester.

One afternoon I met my friend Lana for coffee at Friendly's but she was late, kept at a curriculum revision meeting, or whatever it was called. Lana taught sophomore English, and Mr. Summers chaired a mandated curriculum revision. Deadly, stultifying labor at best, such work was often made more onerous by Mr. Summers who would bring in stacks of reviews to shoot down any radical shift in textbook selection. (When I wanted to teach James Kirkland's *There Must Be a Pony* to slow readers, he quoted a *New York Times* review to say my selection was inappropriate. Some students had been selecting it for book reports, so I knew virtual nonreaders found the book enjoyable.) So I laughed with Lana's stories, and that night, at home, I spent some time sorting through a big carton of old books I'd bought as a box lot at an auction. At the bottom of the box I found a thick book written in what I assumed were Chinese characters. I was about to discard it when I noticed some Christian symbols speckled throughout—particularly simple crosses. I realized this was probably a missionary tract of some sort, if not, in fact, a Chinese Bible. I left it on my nightstand.

The next morning, hurrying for class, I spotted the volume and remembered Lana's account of her curriculum committee work. Hastily I scribbled a note to her. To the best of my memory it said: "Dear Lana, Please consider the accompanying book as a possible addition to the sophomore English curriculum." I smiled, knowing she'd grin. But then, to continue the humor, I foolishly signed it, "Harold Summers." I slipped the note in the book and, in the school mailroom, placed it in Lana's mailbox. I headed to my homeroom, fully expecting to hear Lana's infectious laughter on my classroom phone.

No such luck.

This is what happened.

Lana arrived at school, arriving late, found the book, and was just reading the note when Mr. Summers walked in. Giving him more credit than he deserved, she spontaneously laughed: "Harold, what a delightful joke." As she told me later, she realized her mistake at that instant, for his face fell. He grabbed the note and book, read it, made a death-knell sound from the back of his throat, and yelled: "I'll get to the bottom of this!"

So began the long, long day. Within seconds Lana realized my part in the failed joke, called me—I did detect barely surprised laughter in her quick warning—and I fully expected Mr. Summers to be barging into my homeroom, Chinese Bible in one hand, note in the other, spouting the fires of educational damnation. But Mr. Summers clearly became a man possessed, and went about his investigations methodically, if insanely. He suspended all his appointments, I soon learned, and was sitting in the vault that contained student records and faculty and staff applications. Why? He was matching the signature on the note with the penmanship on the various school records, trying to locate the forger of his revered name. That being unsuccessful, he began interviewing staff at the front desk, asking whether anyone noticed suspicious activity around the mailboxes that morning. Of course, everyone went there first thing in the morning, so no one could provide info for him. Undaunted, he specifically wanted to know if anyone had seen anyone carrying a Chinese Bible.

By lunch period the school was in an uproar. I went about my business, not understanding why Mr. Summers hadn't approached me. For one, I was Lana's closest friend. For another, he blamed me for everything anyway. It was almost as though he were enjoying this a little too much, sensing that this was the Big One—my ultimate and lethal mistake. This was his slow process of getting to me, Chinese water torture, if you will. Of course, the faculty was hysterical with delight, and over lunch some teachers could talk of nothing else. One compared it to Captain Queeg and the strawberries. "He's wandering the hallways, asking everyone to give evidence." Then one teacher turned to me: "Why don't you just confess?"

"What?"

"The whole school knows it was you."

"How?"

"Come on."

One of the teachers laughed: "You know what the faculty is calling it?"

"What?"

"The missionary position."

And later that afternoon, I found a piece of paper on my desk. "What do you know about the missionary position?" It wasn't signed.

At three o'clock, the school day over, I sat in my homeroom finishing some paperwork. A little nervous, I waited for the phone call, which finally came.

His first words, I swear: "Do you know anything about recent recommendations to the sophomore curriculum?"

I paused. "Mr. Summers, if you mean the Chinese Bible, well, yes. I meant that as a joke for Lana and—"

He cut me off. "Forgery is no joke."

"It was meant—"

"We will meet tomorrow at three in my office." He hung up.

Leaving school that afternoon, someone in a passing car yelled, "Bless you." I waved.

Two teachers passed by me. One said, "Dominus vobiscum. Et cum spiritu tu tuo."

The other: "With Jesus you get egg roll."

The first: "Baptism column A, confession column B. White rice."

The second: "Jesus number one son."

I waved goodbye.

The next afternoon I sat across from Mr. Summers, who stared at me from beneath his hooded cobra brows. "Well—" he began, then waited.

"Mr. Summers, I was playing a joke on Lana—"

He held up his hand: Stop. For the next half hour he lectured me, berating me for forgery—which he would forgive this time—and childish, unprofessional behavior. There was no humor in his voice, no softness, and only now and then did he dare any direct eye contact, used only as punctuation for a particular deadly assault on my crime and misdemeanor. "You don't realize how serious this is. The selection of curriculum for the sophomore class is vitally important because the education of the youth of the town is our responsibility. What if a parents learned about this?"

"They might think it was a joke."

"No, they wouldn't. They would assume you are making a comment about the worth of our textbook selection. By reading a Bible in Chinese—which would make little sense to our students, who are not Chinese, you may have noticed—you are, in effect, saying that the given current curriculum is as incomprehensible as a Chinese Bible. The books we use daily in our classrooms thus have no value."

"No one," I interrupted, "could possibly make such a conclusion—"

"I did," he said.

After a half hour of stern reprimand, he suddenly abandoned bad cop for good. His voice softened. "But I'm going to let this pass, Ed. I will chalk this up to your youth, your naiveté, and your inexperience. You are hardly a seasoned teacher. You made a mistake. Maybe you will learn from this. In later life you'll thank me"—a sliver of a smile on the craggy face—"for teaching you about responsibility. Someone else would have had you, well, arrested. I understand your—your greenness." He extended his hand across the table, I shook it, and he stood. "This will not happen again."

"Of course not," I said.

He reached behind him and located the Chinese Bible. I was wondering where it was. "This, I believe, is yours." I took it. "I'll keep the note. After all, it has my signature on it." I nodded.

And then what he said to my departing back surprised me and made me realize he had heard the scuttlebutt in the school hallways.

"I'm surprised someone like you has even heard of the missionary position."

I looked back at him. There was an odd, quizzical look on his face, and I swear he seemed on the verge of smiling, something he would never allow himself to do.

I walked out of the office but I found myself thinking: I might actually find myself liking this man if I stayed at the high school. But on the way home I started writing my letter of resignation.

Where Did Our Love Go?

When I think of the 1960s, I'm hanging out in a record store. Or I am listening to music. Most of the time, as the decade throbbed with student riots, the war in Vietnam, civil rights marches, and my own intoxication with running the streets—most of the time in the background was the pulsating, rhythmic force of sweet Motown, Berry Gordy's hypnotic symphony out of the raw, untutored streets of Detroit. The Temptations, The Four Tips, Marvin Gaye, Smokey Robinson, The Marvelettes, Martha and The Vandelas, but especially the super-duper Supremes with Diana Ross—these singers punctuated my days and nights like a dream you never wanted to end. As an undergrad I'd started buying the 45s of Smokey Robinson and then The Marvelettes, and then I heard "Where Did Our Love Go?" with Diana's little kewpie-doll voice, backed by the floor stomping beat no one had really ever heard before. This was, I believed, the very life force of the student uprisings, the civil rights, and the change-is-in-the-air 1960s. And the song, to me, had a symbolic meaning, as well. Released on June 17, 1964, the song appeared one day after my twenty-first birthday: June 16, I was an adult now, officially, in my majority as they say, and I could play with the grownups, whoever they were. From that day forward I reveled in the music of my new generation. If I didn't know where the love had gone, I thought I knew now where I'd be able to find it.

My particular attraction to The Supremes was abetted by their repeated appearances on *The Ed Sullivan Show*, where Diana Ross, learning to be the consummate entertainer, caught the loving eye of the TV camera, as she dipped and winked and swooped, with that cavernous mouth, with the exaggerated splendor of teeth, a face dominated by the midnight eyes she popped and blinked like she had a speck of sand in them. Black people on TV, Oprah Winfrey recalled, as she telephoned friends. Black people on TV. The Supremes represented arrival, destiny, crossover—and I, the liberal small-town white boy, was overjoyed. America, indeed, was changing. In a barbershop, leafing through a *Look* magazine, I read an article on "things good to look at" in America: Diana Ross of The Supremes was listed. I shook my head in agreement. I'll say.

This soundtrack hit home in November 1965 when I bought a ticket to see The Supremes in the auditorium at Chapel Hill, North Carolina. A chilly Sunday afternoon, I drifted into the hall, and watched, mesmerized, as Diana, Mary and Flo went through their charming paces. When it was all over, I was in love. Yes, this was the new America. I wandered downtown where I attempted to buy the LP *Where Did Our Love Go?* but it was sold out. Instead, I bought the rare LP *Meet the Supremes*, with their odd doo-wop renditions and faltering attempts to find a style and voice. The No-Hit Supremes, they were back then. But now it was Sups On. That Christmas, back in Connecticut, I played and replayed that LP until it was scratched and jumpy. I didn't care: I'd located my own heartbeat.

This is not to say that I didn't relish the other revolutionary music going on. Throughout the 1960s, to be sure, through the pivotal year 1969, I followed The Supremes and the other Motown groups on TV variety shows and in person—I saw Stevie Wonder, The Temptations, and The Supremes over and over again (at Yale Bowl, in New York City, in New Jersey, in Hartford). But I also enjoyed The Beatles, savoring each new LP like a precious gift, The

Rolling Stones (seeing them at Madison Square Garden, a ticket won by lottery), and even crashing a Janis Joplin and Big Brother concert in New Haven. The Doors, Lovin' Spoonful, Simon and Garfunkel. Flash-in-the-pan rockers like Rhinoceros made me dizzy with happiness.

But it was Motown and The Supremes that said something particular to me, and I suppose it had something to do with its being indigenous, black music. When I was in junior high, I accompanied my mother on the bus to New Haven to buy groceries at the small markets on State Street, one of them a butcher shop with sawdust on the floor and the stink of dried blood everywhere. While she shopped, I wandered into a nearby black music store were the owner, doubtless wide-eyed at the milk-fed white boy leafing through piles of five-cent 78 rpm records, took an interest. Week after week I strolled in, and eventually he directed me to the greatest music: Mickey and Sylvia's "Love is Strange," Fats Domino's "Blueberry Hill," "Let the Good Times Roll," and Little Richard's manic "Tutti Fruiti." "The Book of Love," "Love Potion Number 9." So many others. My education on the edge of New Haven. And then he introduced me to New Haven's own Five Satins. And I bought "In the Still of the Night" on 78, a record that used to make me get all choked up. At home I'd play those fragile records over and over on the console hi-fi that my parents bought at Shartenberg's until they were scratched and inevitably broken. So by the time I entered high school I didn't know any black people, but I hungered for their music. I respected, venerated, and was absolutely enthralled by—their records. Rock 'n' roll was being born, and I even had tickets to The Alan Freed Show at the New Haven Arena, a show that was cancelled by Mayor Richard C. Lee who, like many misguided elders, thought the rock 'n' roll was the brainchild of the devil. They didn't know, as I (and others did) that rock 'n' roll was here to say, and would never die. It was meant to be that way, though I don't know why. Or so said the song lyrics. To me rock 'n' roll was escape, delirium, passion, joy, anguish, despair, and anger. It had the words to say things I was only just beginning to feel. Dance music. I danced on *Connecticut Bandstand,* hosted by Jim Gallant, a local variation on Dick Clark's *American Bandstand,* a show that disappeared after the payola scandal, and I even asked for the collective autograph of a girl group called The Paris Sisters, who sang "I Love How You Love Me." Those were wonderful days.

And they got better. This was the music of the streets. Dancing in the streets. I'm driving down Dixwell Avenue in New Haven, largely an African-American avenue, and, stopped at a light, I hear music wafting out from speakers situated in a window five floors up: "Stop! In the Name of Love." My car seemed to shake with the beat because the song is also on my car radio. In the middle of winter I'm in a taxi, headed up an ice-slicked street to Wagner College on Staten Island, and the Middle-Eastern cabbie has the radio on low. I hear "I'm Gonna Make You Love Me," Diana Ross and The Supremes with The Temptations. "Turn that louder," I say. He smiles. "She's a skinny little thing," he answers, "but there ain't nothing like her in the world." There is a Diana Ross doll from Ideal on the market that Christmas, and all the grownups buy them. We have parties the night the TV special *T.C.B., Takin' Care of Business* is on, a spectacular pioneering program for prime time American TV. Black people on TV. The next day at the high school, people talk of nothing else, especially Diana Ross' "Afro-Centric" dance. I take students to see a modern version of Shakespeare's *Love's Labors Lost* at the Stratford Theatre, and the gaudy spectacle, with motorcycles and futuristic costume, includes a brief tableau of three black women in shimmering gowns and mushroom Afros, doing a sudden wah-do-wah movement. And then, of course, there was the much ballyhooed moment in *Hair* where three black singers in one tight red sheath mimic The Supremes' legendary choreography, singing *White boys are delicious.* Well, we certainly were.

I lent two friends Tom and Cindy my double *Supremes Greatest Hits,* and they played the discs throughout Christmas break, over and over, Cindy told me, until the grooves skipped. Tom taught at Yale and he analyzed Supremes songs as being "circular," like the eternal feminine, the songs revolving around themselves, unlike men's songs, which were straight-ahead bullets. Even Carol Burnett, with Eydie Gorme and (I think) Joan Rivers did a mock interview a la Diana Ross and the Supremes, and I think Diana was called Deena Rose. As a black friend said to me, "It's good white America is suddenly comfortable satirizing black stars, with delicious humor and without malice afterthought." Yes, indeed. But by the end of the decade some called them sell-outs, "too white" for the new Black Power movement. They seemed, well, anemic. Aretha took over. The Supremes had become too Las Vegas show time. *The Village Voice*, I remember, laughed at "Reflections" with its electronic beeping, as a "feeble attempt to blow the mind." So be it.

We thought the party would never end. I know that sounds naïve now, but the heady rush of popular images on TV and concert halls seemed to suspend time: were The Beatles and The Supremes only around for five or six years? It seemed they'd been in our line of vision forever. Well, let the band play on, Casey dancing with the strawberry blonde. As the streets erupted with protest against the war in Vietnam and for civil rights legislation, it did seem as if the revolution would go on and on. We were, indeed, creating a new world order, a better one, a fertile one that nullified the moribund stupidity of our nowhere parents. We were dancing in that new street. I marched in civil rights demonstrations through New Haven. I wanted to end the war in Vietnam. I went to the Bobby Seale rally on the New Haven Green I sent *The New Yorker* a story, "Viet Cong Mon Amour," and it came back with a printed rejection slip, but someone had scribbled "Sorry" with a big black marker. That "Sorry" made my day. I wrote a novel called *O My America My New Found Land*—the title from John Donne—a hip narrative about a guy named Bruce Baby, his half-white half-black friend, and their village chicks—and Grove Press actually held it for over a year, maybe more, with teasing notes along the way. Then they couldn't find the manuscript—it had been misplaced. Then they said no. I didn't care. Someone else, I felt, would publish my hymn to dancing in the streets.

Life at high tide: emotions loud and fiery: the future could only be brilliant. For all of us. And then something happened. Suddenly it seemed like the wind was being let out of the pretty balloon. The happening was starting to end. There was something ominous in the air, and we tried to ignore it, to skirt around it. Within the coming years the Pied Pipers would start to die: Jim Morrison of the Doors, Jimi Hendrix, Janis Joplin. There were rumors of the breakup of The Beatles. Impossible. There were rumors of the breakup of The Supremes. Impossible. Back in 1967 Flo Ballard had disappeared from the lineup, which stopped me for a moment, replaced in the lineup by look-alike Cindy Birdsong. And the band played on—anemically, with their dependable stable of writers Holland Dozier Holland leaving Motown. The group was now Diana Ross and The Supremes. Ross was no longer a Supreme, it seemed.

The one night, listening to WDRC I heard the announcement: "In your wildest dreams, would you believe—Diana Ross and her Supremes . . . in Hartford." They were coming to town. And I heard through the sparse media grapevine that they were splitting up. Diana Ross would become a solo artist. Rumors were surfacing about tension, jealousy, anger—all counter to Berry Gordy's PR machine that always depicted The Supremes as "America's Sweethearts," three little ex-ghetto girls whose wealth and sophistication had not diminished their love for one another—and actually liking bowling and fried chicken. I had believed every bit of it, not yet as cynical as we'd all become about media hype in ensuing years. After all, Nixon and his cohorts hadn't blackened our souls yet. Their song "Someday We'll Be Together" was all over the radio, their last number one, an ironic lyric, of course, and we knew, in our heart of hearts, that love is the answer, that my world is empty without you baby, it was like an itching in your heart, come see about me, when the lovelight starts shining through your eyes, and, well, how can Mary tell me what to do when she's lost her love so true, and Flo she don't know cuz the boy she loves is a Romeo. Back in my arms again. Flo didn't know. Well, Flo was gone, and in a few years she'd die, overweight and on welfare, defeated, back in the hardscrabble life she'd left once in Detroit. Diana went first to Hollywood, stepping lively and constantly on the way to superstardom, a siren to a whole generation of lovers, while Mary dreamed of writing her best-selling tell-all memoirs and started accepting invitations to sing at the back lot stage at the Big E cow parade in Springfield, Massachusetts, while NASCAR fans chopped on candied apples.

But not yet.

Excited, my friend Lana and I bought our tickets, even though the concert would not be until October 5. The two shows, as I expected, sold out early. This was an event. A happening. What I didn't know was that this show at the storied Bushnell Theater in Hartford was to be their very last concert on tour—the end of the line. Five years and twelve number one hits since it all began, with The Supremes' aficionados now understanding that the sad end was near. *The Hartford Courant* talked of "rumblings" of a split. Jealously, the paper reported, in a kind of tabloid reportage, was dividing the singers.

But that night in October, it didn't matter, as the sold-out audience—with Standing Room Only—rocked the infectious soul. I marveled once again at the visual aesthetic of three beautiful women, moving and swaying in perfect harmony, an iconic triptych that dominated the showbiz landscape. From their first few words—*Stop whatever you're doing*—the opening from the TV special—to the lachrymose finale—"Someday We'll Be Together"—it was a stand-on-your feet orgiastic moment, the audience whipped up and delirious. I'm not exaggerating. I never do.

But it was also a bittersweet moment for me. When Diana sat alone at the edge of the stage to sing "My Man," I knew an era was ending. The press hinted that Hartford was the last concert booked. Others labeled it "the farewell tour." And the title proved apt all too soon. After Hartford, there would be just two more performances: a coveted spot on *The Ed Sullivan Show*, where they'd walk into the background and shadows holding hands, and the famous January farewell night in Las Vegas, with hoopla and celebration and a recorded two-disc box set. No wonder fans flocked to the Hartford show: all these white people in love. This was intoxicating.

I wish now I'd bought a ticket for the second show, but I never thought to do so. Driving back to the Connecticut coast, I regretted it. Throngs were then dancing in the aisles when I turned down I-91, elated but depressed. I learned later on that another friend, also a big fan, had actually followed The Supremes' limo to Bradley Airport, and trailed them inside. That was a smart move. They waited for their plane. He talked with them briefly. They were three young women without make-up or guile, without the obligatory wigs and eyelashes, without the sequins and costume jewelry, sitting at a cafeteria counter munching on cheeseburgers and fries and Cokes. They seemed happy to have the attention.

I remember other such stories. When they first hit big in 1964, a friend of mine, a white boy living in Detroit, made a pilgrimage to the Brewster Projects, where Diana Ross —Diane—lived. Her mother let him in, gave him something to drink, and said that Diane was at the market picking up groceries. A number one hit and she's out buying Wonder Bread and milk! And still living in the projects. He waited until she returned home in order to get her autograph. But he forgot to bring a pen, and, oddly, at the moment no one could locate pen or pencil in the apartment. So he thanked everyone and caught the bus back home. I always liked that story.

I also like my friend Ted's story. As a small boy in Tennessee, he was awakened one night by his father because The Supremes were bowling in an alley nearby in the neighborhood. Hurriedly dressed, he accompanied his father—and, it turned out, a good part of the neighborhood—to watch Diana, Mary and Flo hurl balls down lanes. Somehow, in that black neighborhood, the three girls symbolized some amazing arrival. It's a moment he never forgot, and it convinced me that the Motown Press Machine was, indeed, truthful about some things. The Supremes, after all, did love to bowl.

Trespassing in the Garden of Eden

I'd always remember that beautiful night in Hartford. October 1969. That final concert. For me, it was one of the defining moments that ended the 1960s. Whenever I see black-and-white footage of the decade, with its tie-dyed hippie protests in the streets, with the awful newsreels of carnage in Vietnam, with the assassination of the Kennedys, of Martin Luther King Jr., of Malcolm X—whenever I see that pivotal decade, I begin to hear the music in my head. In 1969 I quit my job teaching high school English and headed back to grad school, working on a Ph.D. I watched as the world underwent a sea change with the bittersweet end of the Vietnam War and the start of the Nixon debacle. Sex, drugs and rock 'n' roll—that banner cry was soon to be replaced by a vacuous decade of apology and apathy. The world we had hoped to bring about did not happen. Somebody else had all the power, and they used it to sap our energy, our verve. Instead we found cynicism and scandal, conservatism and conceit. Hardly a decent legacy. Even Motown ended, Berry Gordy moving the operations to Los Angeles and thereby cutting off the roots that made his music what it was. So Motown, too, would die, like so many of our dreams.

Years later I spoke to Diana Ross in her dressing room in Detroit: "I was at your last Supremes concert in Hartford." I don't know what I expected her to say, but I was really saying it for myself: I was identifying a touchstone of memory. She just smiled. What could she say? I was really talking to myself. But she did hug me when I said that the 1960s, to me, were The Supremes. She remembered, too.

But, as I moved to Massachusetts that fall of 1969, going back to grad school, I brought my music with me. I smile to think of the drugged-out student, sitting alone at a table in the student center, pounding the table and humming loudly to the long version of Diana's "Ain't No Mountain High Enough." But the 1960s were over, and yet Motown had kept us light-hearted though some grim, despairing days. But now it was over.

But those were not my thoughts a year before on that October 5. That night, I was dancing in the aisles with the rest of the happy crowd. I still believed I'd dance forever. To this day, whenever I listen to "I Hear a Symphony" or "Love Child," I am taken back to a time when I was more driven, more carefree, more dedicated, more idealistic, more enthusiastic, more—and maybe this is the word I'm looking for—*young*.

The End

Made in the USA
Las Vegas, NV
24 March 2025